THE LOST CHILD COMPLEX IN AUSTRALIAN FILM

The mythologising of lost and abandoned children significantly influences Australian storytelling. In *The Lost Child Complex in Australian Film*, Terrie Waddell looks at the concept of the 'lost child' from a psychological and cultural perspective. Taking an interdisciplinary Jungian approach, she re-evaluates this cyclic storytelling motif in history, literature and the creative arts as the nucleus of a cultural complex – a group obsession that as Jung argued of all complexes, *has us*.

Waddell explores 'the lost child' in its many manifestations, as an element of the individual and collective psyche, historically related to the trauma of colonisation and war, and as a key theme in Australian cinema from the industry's formative years to the present day. The films discussed in textual depth transcend literal *lost in the bush* mythologies, or actual cases of displaced children, to focus on vulnerable children rendered lost through government and institutional practices and adult/parental characters developmentally arrested by comforting or traumatic childhood memories. The victory/winning fixation governing the USA – diametrically opposed to the lost child motif – is also discussed as a comparative example of the mesmerising nature of the cultural complex. Examining iconic characters and events, including the Gallipoli Campaign and Trump's presidency, and the films *Lion*, *The Babadook* and *Predestination*, this book scrutinises the way that a culture talks to itself, about itself. This analysis looks beyond the melancholy traditionally ascribed to the lost child, by arguing that the repetitive and prolific imagery that this theme stimulates can be positive and inspiring.

The Lost Child Complex in Australian Film is a unique and compelling work – highly relevant for academics and students of Jungian and post-Jungian ideas, cultural studies, screen and media studies. It will also appeal to Jungian psychotherapists and analytical psychologists as well as readers with a broader interest in Australian history and politics.

Terrie Waddell, PhD, is Associate Professor of Screen Studies at La Trobe University, Australia. The author of Routledge's *Mis/takes: Archetype, Myth and Identity in Screen Fiction* and *Wild/lives: Trickster, Place and Liminality on Screen*, and a contributor to *The International Handbook of Jungian Film Studies*, she researches and publishes in the areas of screen media, myth, literature, gender, popular culture and Jungian-based psychology.

"This book is the beautiful lost child of film theory. It rescues and rehabilitates familiar Oedipal themes and reclothes them in a rich Jungian guise. In a compelling manner, it brings together social and cultural history, with discerning interpretations of important films. *The Lost Child Complex* reveals how cinema painfully illuminates the deepest structures in ourselves and our societies. While Australian in focus, its themes of loss, discovery and tragedy sound a timely warning that rings out across the continents. As film scholars and cultural critics alike we didn't know what we'd lost, until now. This important book brings it resoundingly to our attention – the body politic and the psychological body, perfectly combined into the image of the lost child."

– **Dr Luke Hockley, Professor of Media Analysis at University of Bedfordshire, UK; SFHEA, UKCP, MBACP, FRSA, President of the Jungian Society for Scholarly Studies; co-author of *Jungian Film Studies: The Essential Guide* and editor of the Routledge *International Handbook of Jungian Film Studies***

"In a marvelously insightful exploration of the post-Jungian cultural complex in psyche, history and cinema, Terrie Waddell's *The Lost Child Complex* digs deep into the pernicious wounds of colonialism and racism while providing new and liberatory ways to study psychology and film. It is Jungian studies as engaged, socially transformative and necessary. Waddell demonstrates that the lost child is an archetypal presence in Australian life that shapes its art. Also, by reading the lost child complex against the American victory complex, this book shows that pathology can be read creatively for a more positive future."

– **Susan Rowland, PhD, Core Faculty at Pacifica Graduate Institute, California, USA. Her recent books include *The Ecocritical Psyche* (2012); *Remembering Dionysus* (2017) and *Jungian Literary Criticism: The Essential Guide* (2019), all Routledge**

"Terrie Waddell's *The Lost Child Complex* offers a fascinating and erudite study of this dominant archetype in Australian settler history, screen culture and the arts. Focussing on the cinema, Waddell explores the powerful attraction of this child motif from narratives of actual lost children to the tragedy of the 'Stolen Generations', refugee children and more abstract concepts of displaced childhood. Drawing on Jungian theory, she explores with insight and intelligence the strange uncanny appeal of this complex myth and its place in the Australian imaginary and its relevance to contemporary social justice issues. *The Lost Child* is a challenging and highly original study of cinematic representations of the child and childhood, and the role of the spectator in creating meaning from these complex concepts. It is a must for anyone interested in the workings of memory, the significance of archetypes and the relevance of the lost child complex for the way we understand our past and how we might live in the present and future with ourselves and with others. A compelling and important book."

– **Barbara Creed, Redmond Barry Distinguished Honorary Professor, Screen Studies, The University of Melbourne, Australia**

THE LOST CHILD COMPLEX IN AUSTRALIAN FILM

Jung, Story and Playing Beneath the Past

Terrie Waddell

LONDON AND NEW YORK

First published 2019
by Routledge
2 Park Square, Milton Park, Abingdon, Oxon OX14 4RN

and by Routledge
52 Vanderbilt Avenue, New York, NY 10017

Routledge is an imprint of the Taylor & Francis Group, an informa business

© 2019 Terrie Waddell

The right of Terrie Waddell to be identified as author of this work has been asserted by her in accordance with sections 77 and 78 of the Copyright, Designs and Patents Act 1988.

All rights reserved. No part of this book may be reprinted or reproduced or utilised in any form or by any electronic, mechanical, or other means, now known or hereafter invented, including photocopying and recording, or in any information storage or retrieval system, without permission in writing from the publishers.

Trademark notice: Product or corporate names may be trademarks or registered trademarks, and are used only for identification and explanation without intent to infringe.

British Library Cataloguing-in-Publication Data
A catalogue record for this book is available from the British Library

Library of Congress Cataloging-in-Publication Data
A catalog record for this book has been requested

ISBN: 978-1-138-93968-4 (hbk)
ISBN: 978-1-138-93969-1 (pbk)
ISBN: 978-1-315-67478-0 (ebk)

Typeset in Bembo
by Apex CoVantage, LLC

CONTENTS

Acknowledgements	*vii*
Introduction	1

PART ONE
The lost child complex – a cultural and screen history   **7**

1   Beginnings: complex, settlement, cultural memory   9

2   Literally lost: searchers, the searched for and grail metaphors   26

3   Celebrating defeat: the blooded child of war and sport   43

PART TWO
Double wounding   **61**

4   Double wounding: imposing lostness   63

5   Inner and outer twinning: parent as lost child/lost child as parent   85

PART THREE
Inner children and the victory complex   **101**

6   Stuck in the past: lost child as earworm   103

7   The victory complex: nostalgia for the American dream and the art of the win   119

Concluding remarks   138

References   *141*
Screen references   *152*
Index   *156*

ACKNOWLEDGEMENTS

I appreciate the thoughtfulness of a number of colleagues for their valued suggestions, most particularly staff in the Screen Studies discipline, department of Creative Arts and English at La Trobe University. Special thanks go to my colleagues Felicity Collins, Hester Joyce and Glenda Hambly for their generosity, guidance and assistance. The committed work of my research assistant Amalya Ashman is also deeply appreciated. Amalya compiled an exhaustive list of lost child-related Australian film and television programmes in the early stages of the research. It wasn't possible of course to include everything that was captured in this series of intricate spreadsheets, but the overall perspective she provided was invaluable. During this formative period, I spent a great deal of time at The Australian Centre for the Moving Image viewing archival films borrowed from The National Film and Sound Archive of Australia. The support of both organisations in their efficient and considered assistance with this project is gratefully acknowledged.

Without the financial support of La Trobe University's School of Humanities and Social Sciences, this book would not have been possible. The School granted me six months research leave in the Outside Study Programme to work on this book, and financed the various international conferences and forums where I discussed the lost child in cinema as indicative of a cultural complex. Pacifica Graduate Institute generously allowed me the use of their OPUS Archives and Research Center. I am indebted to Pacifica's Susan Rowland and her graduate students for their valuable feedback after presenting the seeds of this work at a seminar in 2015. Susannah Frearson and Heather Evans of Routledge's Mental Health portfolio have been extremely encouraging and always supportive. I thank them for such commitment to this project and the area of Jungian Studies. I would also like to acknowledge the support of the PAMII group (Psychology and the Moving Image International).

I worked with Timothy Jones, a colleague from La Trobe's History discipline, on a journal article, 'The spoken and unspoken nature of child abuse in the mini-series *Devil's Playground*: The Royal Commission into Institutional Responses to Child Sexual Abuse, the Catholic Church and television drama in Australia' (*Media International Australia*, 2016) – I thank Tim for his permission to include a small reference to this research in Chapter 4. I also gratefully acknowledge image permission from Long Way Home Holdings Pty. Ltd. and photographer Mark Rogers, for the use of the cover shot of Sunny Pawar as 'Saroo Brierley' in the 2016 film *Lion*.

Finally, thanks, as always, to Sally and Arkie Waddell for their advice and support.

INTRODUCTION

When I was child I nearly drowned. It was summer. We were a group of under ten-year-olds on the beach with a teenager looking after us, and even though swimming was compulsory at school, Australia wasn't as vigilant about beach safety as it is now. Mum took the kids in our family for extra lessons once a week and that's what saved me. While the girl in charge sunbaked, we played in the surf – I wandered out a bit too far, preoccupied by a surfer in the distance. I don't really know how it happened but I went from floating, to being gently pulled out to sea. The beach seemed to move further and further away – I was passing the surfer. There was no panic, just a sense of trying to figure out how to get back. Free-styling straight ahead didn't seem to be getting me anywhere, so I backstroked because it was easier and my teacher said I had a knack for it. There was no stopping till my fingers touched the sand under the water. I didn't know about rips, that I'd been caught in one, or that you had to swim across, not through, them – I saved myself because I couldn't see where I was going and I was good at backstroke. The sunbaking girl was still stretched out on her stomach soaking up the heat when I eventually got back, so my big survival went unnoticed till mum found out . . . let's just say the atmosphere became 'tense' for those running the holiday camp.

I could very well have been a lost child – swept into history, one among the many little girls of English, Irish and Scottish ancestry who seemed to be inexplicably and silently taken by this country. 'Drowning' writes Kim Torney, 'was the most common cause of accidental child mortality, and children drowned in all manner of places – in dams, creeks and rivers, water tanks, the ocean, mud pools, quarries, washtubs, sludge holes, reservoirs, and even the City Baths' (2005, p. 13). As an island isolated by water it seems reasonable to assume that Australians would have a testing relationship with the sea, but the interior looms larger. *Lost in the bush* is a common Australian trope. Since colonisation, the lost child as an idea, an emotion and an 'anxiety' as Peter Pierce writes (1999), is still one of the most culturally embedded stories we tell ourselves, about ourselves. Not only is childhood abandonment to the environment reinvented and re-mourned, but *lostness* was also imposed on indigenous children for whom both the bush and the sea was/is their first home. These histories, dominant ghosts in our culture, are revived and recreated through literature, art and cinema. As amplifiers of dominant cultural preoccupations, the arts help us to challenge and accept obsessions that hold us in thrall, seemingly beyond our will – psychological stumbling blocks that *have us*.

One way of approaching *our* lost child 'block' is through the theory of *complexes*. The Oedipus complex, in its broadest sense, is a fairly entrenched phrase in pop culture, diluted from Freud's original theory, to include sexual obsessions with all things *mother* (Freud, 1899/1991). Jung though, took the idea of complexes further, seeing them as unconscious structures interconnected with, and centring on, specific unconscious patterns, or *archetypes*. He argued that in their possession of us, complexes give the impression of behaving autonomously. 'Everyone knows . . . that people "have complexes"' he wrote, 'What is not so well known . . . is that complexes *have us*' (1960/1969: § 200). Thinking back to Pierce's description of the lost child as a cultural anxiety, post-Jungian scholar James Hillman reminds us that, 'anxiety reveals the deepest shadow' (1975/1991, p. 23). In Jung's formative work, the *shadow* was theorised as an unconscious archetypal pattern in opposition to, or uncomfortable with, all that the ego finds acceptable. It can operate on a group and individual level. This is the closest Jung came to discussing how a society could be overtaken by unconscious material. Thomas Singer and Samuel Kimbles' theory of the *cultural complex* was an adaptation of the collectively shared shadow.

The title of this book makes my focus fairly transparent. I argue that the lost child in its capacity to capture the imagination of a culture on the level of history, politics and the arts, can be understood as the archetypal core of a cultural complex. Having written about screen culture through classical and post-Jungian psychology, I am a strong advocate of cinema's capacity to amplify not only the conscious, but also the unconscious preoccupations of a culture. Grappling with how the lost child has been identified and imagined in Australian cinema, is also about grappling with the cultural complex: trying to unpick what, in its persistence, it wants us to address. In other words, what we are saying to ourselves about ourselves. Jung was optimistic about the potential of the unconscious to work *for*, not *against*, us – if we listened. As sobering as the concept of the vulnerable, fearful or unanchored lost child might seem, I understand it as a much more positive and potentially energising quality.

The theory of archetypes is still contentious. As psychologically configured patterns of the unconscious, we know them through outward projection in the form of images, obsessions and behaviours. Corresponding to instincts, but quite different in their function, archetypes were thought to be intangible components of the psyche that *kicked-in* to support, not our physical welfare as do instincts, but our psychological well-being (Shelburne, 1988). In Singer and Kimbles' formulation, the cultural complex is couched around an archetypal core and has the capacity to substantially influence communities as well as individuals within those groups. If a culture is a collection of qualities with multiple and overlapping points of identification, it is unrealistic to talk about *an* Australian identity. It is equally naive to talk about just one national obsession – one cultural complex. The lost child, a dominant theme of 'our' settler history and the arts, is nestled among a network of fixations. It has become so conspicuous though, that it falls into cliché. Despite its familiarity, there are always more layers to peel back.

I was grateful to Long Way Holdings and photographer Mark Rogers for allowing me to use the image from *Lion* (dir. Davis, 2016) on the cover. The character of little Saroo (Sunny Pawar) in this shot – joyful, open, in anticipation of something waiting to happen – encapsulates the sense of confidence in the lost child that guides this book. While trauma sets in motion the complex and the stories of lost children, the mythical/fantasy child *as a concept* rather than *a case study*, according to Jung, 'means something evolving toward independence. This it cannot do without detaching itself from its origins: abandonment is therefore a necessary condition' (1959/1968: § 287). The lost child, as he and Hillman would agree, is both a *source* of insight and the *possibility* of insight – 'knowledge going beyond our present day consciousness, is equivalent to being *all alone in the world*' (Jung, 1959/1969: § 288).

Lostness as a point of recognition

The large 1913 domed auditorium, the La Trobe Reading Room, is the central feature of the State Library of Victoria (Melbourne) where I'm writing this introduction. The three gallery levels house significant tourist and educational attractions, including a permanent exhibition of the bushranger Ned Kelly's letters and armour. The current hero status afforded Kelly, hanged in the Old Melbourne Gaol (1880), two blocks from the library, is still perplexing. An egalitarian symbol of class injustice, Kelly was also a ruthless bushranger who throughout his short poverty-stricken twenty-five-year life, robbed banks, murdered police, stole livestock and held multiple hostages at gunpoint (Gaunson, 2013). Film depictions of his last stand, a shootout between the Kelly gang, with Kelly sheathed in homemade tin armour, and the Victorian police in the country town of Glenrowan, construct him as an embattled hero – a victim and champion of victims. He epitomises a particular brand of Australian heroism marked by lostness and defeat.

Charles Tait's *The Story of the Kelly Gang* (1906), the world's first narrative-length film, was shot in the formative years of the Australian film industry. Despite early 1912 attempts (in New South Wales) to ban the morally questionable bushranger genre from cinema, he remains an against-the-odds touchstone (Reynaud, 2007). Kelly is not an obvious lost child, but there is a sense of displaced childhood, *lost in the bush* and lost to the *romanticism of the bush* attached to the legend. With sixteen Australian films retelling his story, the last, *Ned Kelly* (dir. Jordan, 2003) with Heath Ledger in the title role, he remains ubiquitous in both cinema and the wider mythmaking of tourism industries. The very concept of lostness is enshrined in this figure who grew up in poverty with a string of offences and convictions as an adolescent. He was mythologised as a champion for the rights of impoverished Irish settlers under British rule.

In Australia, this idea of the lost and vulnerable and/or the lost and defeated colonial, is the stuff of memorialisation, discussed the first and third chapter. Like the concept of the abandoned child, distinct from the actual child who provides a projective *hook*, Kelly in his elevation to folk-hero could be argued to signify a sense of futurity, liberation and the now growing republican sentiment of emancipation from parental/British governance. I raise the spectre of Kelly, not because his story is a traditionally identifiable lost in the bush cliché, but because of his immortalisation in the world's first feature film, his ongoing attraction and his connection to the lost child complex.

Lost on screen

Perhaps the irony of this book and its title is that I am not actually talking about children. Even the concept of the child and the notion of childhood was for Hillman a set of assumptions made by adults that spoke more to their biases and inner child-related needs. Characters, images and cases of lost children will be discussed in terms of their role as signifiers for the archetypal child at the heart of the complex. Adult-driven narratives and characters that reveal the psychological ghosts of the child motif are also addressed, often drawing on imagery from children, or figures/adults who adopt qualities ascribed to children: projections of internal processes. These narratives are still consistently reimagined in literature, but the lost child on screen is a vibrant form of storytelling. While television also continues to produce these kinds of fictional, documentary and reality format stories, the main focus here is cinema.

Discussions of specific films are approached intertexually – informed by popular culture, politics and history. As Janice Hocker Rushing and Thomas Frentz make clear in their work on cinema and Jungian-based psychology (1995), cinema like dreams should not be interpreted in isolation: 'If films are to a large extent public dreams, then our roles as critics is similar to that of the depth analyst: to interpret how the film as a collective dream provides a picture of the cultural unconscious' (p. 47). We might think of cinema as the amplification of collective preoccupations, obsessions and the more confronting shadow material that we as a culture find challenging. The films discussed generally and in textual depth, explore the obvious and insidious ways that the lost child complex expresses itself.

Parts one, two and three

The first of three sections, 'The lost child complex – a cultural and screen history', establishes key arguments and provides a background of the histories and literary/screen contributions to the developing lost child theme. The first chapter looks at the concept of the complex and the lost child as an archetypal focus for the cultural (also referred to as 'group' and 'collective') complex. To explore the circumstances that most obviously stimulated this psychological condition, it is important to trace the traumatic beginnings of British transportation, colonisation and migration to this remote and unfamiliar country. Early stories and reportage of childhood lostness, coupled with the burrowing of these narratives into the cultural memory over generations, will be briefly traced to periods of emerging nationhood, and discussed as hooks/projections for the complex.

Having established the underlying tensions and potential of the lost child, Chapter 2 turns to film that epitomises and reinforces the complex. The range of examples, from formative to the most current cinema, demonstrates the tenacious grip that the complex still has over the structure and content of Australian storytelling. Previously theorised as a combination of hero-quest and trauma-driven narratives, the possibility that lost child films can be read through traditional grail mythology is also introduced (Dermody, 1980; Collins and Davis, 2004; Cooper, 2011). Chapter 3 examines screen texts and related mythmaking celebrations that draw on a form of heroism defined by youth, sorrow and servitude. The zealously defended and repeatedly memorialised Australian and New Zealand Army Corps (ANZAC) defeat at Gaba Tepe (Anzac Cove) in the first world war, suggests that Australia's sense of nationhood has been disproportionately built on a legend of overwhelming loss (Lake et al., 2010). This particularly Australian inflected idea of heroism that attempts to foster a sense of unification is also linked to sport through not-so-subtle marketing and political strategies.

The second section, 'Double wounding', focuses on how trauma can be felt inwardly and projected externally. Chapter 4 explores a concept that I have called *double wounding* – the rendering of vulnerable child *others* lost through an outward projection of the complex – by taking an interdisciplinary approach that combines history, politics, current affairs and screen representations of past harms done to the 'Stolen Generations' of indigenous children, children abused in religious institutions and children rendered lost through punitive refugee policies. A number of national enquiries and commissions have attempted to atone for past injustices against children – individual acts of aggression and institutional/governmental failures to act, which in some instances have been understood as complicity. Gestures toward compensation have been fraught with inequality and backpedalling, which all play into the more shadowy aspects of the complex, as if an intricate dance (in a collective sense) is taking place between acknowledging the pain of lostness/displacement and never quite being able to move beyond it. There might be royal commissions, reports, enquiries and attempted reforms, but it is debatable whether the lost children at the heart of these gestures will ever be fully recovered. The following chapter deals with the same basic principle of double wounding, through biopics and fictional narratives, but adds the concept of *parentification* – endowing children with adult/parental roles. The four films chosen for textual analysis deal with parents for whom the combination of the archetypal child and a traumatic sense of lostness and grief is overwhelming.

Their children, although resilient and compassionate in their willingness to care for their troubled parents, in these cases mothers, are nevertheless also rendered lost to varying degrees by the isolation and displacement imposed upon them.

The third and final part of the book, 'Inner children and the victory complex' tackles two quite different subjects: childhood memories that haunt adult characters and the cultural complex of the USA, identified as a *victory complex*. Unshakable memories of childhood selves that continue to influence and dominate a sense of identity are discussed in Chapter 6. As a way of feeding the dramatic action, many of these characters are unable to move beyond the restricting limits that the complex places on their reflections, perceptions and behaviours. The stories of those who manage to move forward in their lives, despite restrictions imposed during childhood, are useful devices for acknowledging the complex, understanding its influence and potentially easing/limiting its reach. One of the most significant films to emerge in the last decade, *Predestination* (The Spierig brothers, 2014) will be discussed for its ability to draw all the previous elements of the chapter together. In each of the screen texts dealing with the reflections and consequences of the lost child, no central character remains unscathed. They may emerge more knowing, but they never escape. This is a dilemma that the Spierig brothers capture in this noir, American accented, yet intrinsically Australian themed thriller.

To bring some international perspective to the idea of complexes and the uniqueness of the lost child complex, the final chapter looks to North America's deeply embedded emphasis on winning, a complex sustained by the ideology of *The American Dream*. Australia's obsession with lost child thinking and feeling could not be more opposed to the obsession with success as an automatic right, and loss as shameful defeat. Our cinema narratives do not automatically assume victory – our heroes are very differently defined, and loss is of course not a source of disgrace, but an opportunity for rediscovery.

By returning to our lost children on screen, I revisit a significant aspect of the collective self. This return, as form of education, acknowledgement and confrontation, is a very positive and humbling aspect of Australian culture. I don't believe that our cinema, generally speaking and certainly in terms of the lost child, is driven by the need to emerge triumphant. If our endings are made more optimistic through a sense of achievement – having strived for and reached a goal – they are also tempered by an underlying acceptance that while this state is only temporary, the lost child is forever. As Hillman says of psychotherapy, and we might also say of our lost child cinema:

> Here is a haven, to creep out of hiding; here one may show one's unwanted, unlovable, ugly concealments, and one's huge hopes . . . that always these childish pathological conditions contain futurity. The very way forward through the condition so unwanted, ugly and preposterously expectant lies just in the conditions themselves. The pathology is also the futurity.
>
> *(1975/1991, p. 19)*

PART ONE

The lost child complex – a cultural and screen history

1
BEGINNINGS
Complex, settlement, cultural memory

Much of this chapter, like the introduction, was written in the historic State Library of Victoria where Ned Kelly's armour is kept. On each visit I passed a bronze statue of doomed nineteenth-century explorers, Burke and Wills, marking the corner of busy Collins and Swanston Street in Melbourne's central business district. In the last few years of monument controversy, particularly with confederate statues toppling in the United States, it seemed *of the times* that the couple were removed. This came about not because Robert Burke and William Wills were inappropriate icons – white, male, ill-prepared, British and Irish explorers who failed to accept advice and assistance from local indigenous people on their mission to cross Australia vertically from Melbourne to the Gulf of Carpentaria, consequently dying of starvation *en route* back to Melbourne in 1861 – but because the statute needed to be relocated to make way for a new metro-rail project (Hancock, 2017). That the folly of these men – lostness itself – should be immortalised in the heart of the city always struck me as misdirected. But the monument had its logic when considering the odes and marketed tours dedicated to lost children in regional centres, and the ever evolving *lost in the bush* narratives of novels and cinema. With seventy deaths reported from 1860 to 1869, the lost child popularised in colonial literature and poetry is now reimagined on the screen as a fusion of literal child, inner child and disavowed child (Torney, 2005). It is a theme, or perhaps a pulse, that keeps audiences engaged. More than a cultural memory of vulnerability in a country colonised through violence, empire building and the misery of Britain's convict 'orphans', it is a psychological obsession – a cultural complex that can't be shaken.

The complex and the child

Hillman asks, 'What is this "child" – that is surely the first question. Whatever we say about children and childhood is not altogether about children and childhood . . . some realm of the psyche called "childhood" is being personified by the child and carried by the child for the adult' (1975/1991, p. 8). The idea of the child and childhood as a liminal experience between birth and adolescence (itself a twentieth-century concept) has been a debated topic for both sociology and the various schools and offshoots of psychoanalysis (see Jenks, 1996; Main, 2008). Joyce Mercer (2003) discusses Freud and Jung's abstract rather than lived approach to childhood, generally presenting male development as normative in their theoretical models. Psychoanalysis challenged the nineteenth-century association of childhood with sexual innocence, in its insistence that early sexuality was central to psychological development; for Freud, the child was *polymorphously perverse*, capable of undifferentiated sexual arousal beyond bodily erogenous zones (Freud, 1905/1953). Although Jung didn't place great weight on Oedipally focussed concepts of development, like Freud, he distanced himself from the real-world lives of children, elevating *the child* to an archetypal symbol of futurity, eternity and divinity: a figure signifying the promise of conscious and unconscious union (Jung, 1959/1968).

Archetypes as unconscious motifs or patterns that influence emotional behaviour, in Jung's thinking were only realised only through personal and cultural projection: 'The archetype is essentially an unconscious content that is altered by becoming conscious and by being perceived' (1959/1968: § 6). By couching the archetype as element of the unconscious, either dormant or seeking conscious recognition, Jung was clear that these structures are perceived and driven by both culture and the individual's experiences; in this way they 'change their shape continually' but their essence is unchanging (1959/1968: § 301). In his formulation of archetypal psychology in the 1970s, Hillman approached the concept of the archetype a little differently by arguing that the image *is the archetype* and the key to self-understanding involves engaging with this energy/image on its own terms – as it appears and behaves, without imposing rational meanings or definitions. He described archetypes as 'the deepest patterns of psychic functioning, the roots of the soul governing the perspectives we have of ourselves and the world . . . axiomatic, self-evident images to which psychic life and our theories about it ever return' (1989, p. 23).

While Mercer focuses on Jung's lack of empirical and sociological research, claiming that his abstractions, 'while upholding a basically hopeful and positive view of the child, risks distortions in over-idealized spiritualities of childhood' (p. 115), the value of conflating the actual child, the internal child and child-as-archetypal symbol is a useful stratagem for exploring the lost child as a cultural complex. It might seem convoluted, but while this book will discuss the plight of actual children, particularly in Chapter 4, these generalised cases are argued to provide projective hooks for the inner/archetypal child at the core of the complex. Jung more figuratively drew on divine child imagery, its psychological significance and its sinuous connection to more culturally generated ideas of the child. With the same reasoning, images, events, fantasies, constructions and histories of the lost child are presented here as signifiers for unconsciously embedded and recurring archetypal matter. Mythological and romanticised lost children in the arts, often inspired from, but not facsimiles of, flesh and blood subjects, tell us more about various aspects of our (creators and audiences) individual and collective psyches. Simply put, they can be thought of as persistent internal voices/images that seek attention. Jungian and archetypal psychology encourages us to listen to, learn from and develop relationships with these presences.

Complexes as the common and inevitable consequence of an archetypally configured psyche were argued to be entangled with lived experience, psychological motifs and autonomous emotions that stem from unconscious rather than ego activity, or *affects* in Jung's thinking (Jung, 1960/1969; Perry, 1970). While Freud pathologised the complex, largely in relation to a matrix of Oedipal-related conflicts, Jung expanded on the concept and was less invested in understanding its hold on the personality in entirely negative terms (Freud, 1899/1991). As knotted clusters of lived and unconscious material framed around an archetypal core, ostensibly problematic to the subject and considered to be activated by trauma, complexes – also called 'splinter psyches' – were thought to aid individuation, or psychological growth (Jung, 1960/1969: § 204). Traditionally complexes were seen to operate on a personal rather than collective level, but Singer and Kimbles reframed the idea of the complex to include its potential influence on cultures and nations, enfolding individuals and collectives simultaneously: 'Much of what tears us apart can be understood as the manifestations of autonomous processes in the collective and individual psyche that organize themselves as cultural complexes' (2004, p. 1). They characterise the group complex as a cyclic reimagining of a particular archetypally themed fixation, capable of erupting on a personal and collective level:

> cultural complexes are based on repetitive, historical group experiences which have taken root in the cultural unconscious of the group. At any ripe time, these slumbering cultural complexes can be activated in the cultural unconscious and take hold of the collective psyche of the group and the individual/collective psyche of individual members of the group. The inner sociology of the cultural complexes can seize the imagination, the behaviour and the emotions of the collective psyche and unleash tremendously irrational forces in the name of their 'logic'.
> *(Singer and Kimbles, 2004, p. 7)*

Referencing Donald Kalsched (1996) in particular, they focus on trauma as a trigger for the complex – 'wound[s] that cry out', as Cathy Caruth refers to this form of suffering (1996, p. 4). She echoes the nature of the complex in its cultural aspect when talking of the Freudian repetition or resurfacing of trauma related *affects*, not consciously 'initiated by the individual's own acts but rather appear as the possession of some people by a sort of fate, a series of painful events to which they are subjected, and which seem to be entirely outside their wish or control' (Caruth, 1996, p. 2).

This has resonance with Jung's formulation of the complex in its capacity to disrupt conscious will and illicit compulsive thoughts and physical responses that as 'have us'. Caruth credits Freud's great insight in *Moses and Monotheism* to be 'that history, like trauma, is never simply one's own, that history is precisely the way we are implicated in each other's trauma's' (1996, p. 24). To refine this idea further, the cultural complex not only entangles individuals in each other's disparate traumas, but as previously mentioned, is capable of simultaneously enfolding individuals and groups into a commonly themed and repetitive trauma. Anne Kaplan in 'Traumatic Contact Zones and Embodied Translators: with reference to select Australian texts', recognises the cultural symptoms of complex-like eruptions that involve trauma and repetition:

> When catastrophe affects a group of people, as in the case of holocaust, slavery or colonization . . . one can perhaps talk of 'collective' or 'shared' trauma. If the events are overwhelming, groups may 'forget' horrendous actions from the past, and simply split them off from daily consciousness. Yet, although not 'remembered' . . . the impact of such actions may evidence itself in cultural symptoms of various kinds.
>
> *(Kaplan, 2004, p. 46)*

Such symptoms can present as cyclical images and/or narratives. In the Australian context, one of many of these collective obsessions is the lost child. The breadth of scenarios and concepts that revisit and reconfigure the trauma of a combined sense/memory/fantasy of childhood and displacement is testament to the depth of the complex and its intransigent hold. Thinking in this way, the notion of the complex acting autonomously, against our will, corresponds in a similar way to the sexual connotation of the term 'having us' – drawing us into a state of intoxication, neutralising the will to disengage and seemingly depleting our agency.

Australian cinema's relationship with the complex is variously expressed. It can simply revolve around a sense of nostalgia and mourning for lost children as projections of an inner child, stifled perhaps in the process of colonisation – an *affect* of forgotten ancestral trauma still rooted in the collective unconscious – and can also present in its shadow/disavowed aspect. When the complex manifests in this way, lostness can also be *displaced onto others* as a means of exorcism or avoiding the challenge of confrontation and acceptance. In terms of postcolonialism, Kaplan argues, that trauma disrupts not only settler cultures but also subjugated indigenous communities: 'both colonizing culture and that of the colonized are mutually impacted and changed. Mingling inevitably takes place, and racial purity is a myth' (p. 53). Related to social 'mingling' is the idea that the complex has the potential to become a shared, and arguably, inflicted, psychological condition. As will be explored in Chapter 4, the lost child complex, possibly stirred by European separation and abandonment, was through successive generations, projected onto indigenous, vulnerable, war-torn and refugee *others*. Undocumented children trying to enter Australia have been the most recent group to epitomise the lost, displaced and neglected.

If we consider the arts as an amplifier of cultural obsessions, neurosis and inadequacies, then proliferation of lost child narratives on screen suggests a complex at work. While it is more comfortable, yet still confronting, to accept our own responses to the lost child, it is also incumbent upon us to also explore the possibility and damage of our projections. Jung argued that trying to rid oneself of complexes was as counterproductive as trying to rid oneself of the *shadow* – aspects of the personality unacceptable to the ego. The notion of the collective shadow was the closest Jung came to hypothesising a cultural/collective complex, but in both structures, the key to understanding the complex lays in developing a connection to it – exploring what its presence might be telling us about ourselves.

It is critical to understand the archetypal energy at the heart of the complex if any kind of relationship is to be formed. If for instance, we think of more stereotypically structured films, consciously utilising a cultural obsession (or complex) for narrative intrigue, it is easy to pinpoint where the pivotal archetypal pattern is projected – usually onto an object that is ultimately ungraspable. We might look at the Oedipal developmental stage (to some a fiction in itself, but nevertheless a good story) where, usually from a Freudian hetero-male perspective, the child bonds with the mother and so competes with the father/lover to assume his position in the world. When morphing into a more intractable complex, the child develops an obsession for the mother and women/objects signifying this familial role (Freud, 1899/1991). The energy or concept of *mother* can then be identified as the archetypal core, usually triggered by an actual mother or mother figure. This *idea of mother* then, can never be obtained and yet remains the focus of the subject's life, obsessions, projections and ambitions. Like desire, the archetypal mother is only ever imagined and searched for. The same logic applies to the lost child – as an inner element of the psyche, it can never be materially possessed – and it can never be found.

Singer argues that cultural complexes can be entangled 'not only with our personal history and complexes but with other cultural complexes as well' (Singer and Kimbles, 2004, p. 32). This generational *feeding on* and being *fed by* multiple psychological fixations according to Singer, creates 'exotic permutations and combinations within ourselves and between us and others, creating what I have come to think of as "recombinant visionary mythologies"' (Singer and Kimbles, 2004, p. 32). As discussed further in the chapter, these genetic-like 'visionary mythologies' become obvious in Australian literature's diverse lost child incarnations since colonisation, and the early stages of our film industry in 1906 with the release of *The Story of the Kelly Gang*. But before exploring tangible expressions of the lost child in Australian cinema, it is important to grapple with the concept of the child itself and the various, often fanciful, signifiers attached to this stage of life.

The child as divine, a concept of soul, and lost

Mercer's identification of Jung's disproportionate focus on the child not as an empirical being, but a symbol and archetypal image of the divine in mythology, is for her a point of frustration in his work: 'it is a wonder-child, a divine child, begotten, born and brought up in quite extraordinary circumstances, and not – this is the point – a human child' (Jung, 1959/1968: § 21). In terms of the *transcendent function* – a process of self-understanding arrived at by a union of unconscious material and consciousness, a birth of sorts that gives rise to a new realisation/assessment – the divine child is the product of a joining of these opposites, a third emergent force, a symbol of futurity, wholeness and the unifying factor itself (Jung, 1959/1969; Miller, 2005; Kalsched, 2013). Wholeness and the capacity to unify are qualities that Jung also attributes to the *Self*, variously defined as a symbol of unification and the primary regulator of the psyche (Jung, 1959/1969, 1963/1970). Jung's mythological child took many forms – largely human, but also divinely endowed animals and objects:

> Often the child is formed after the Christian model; more often, though, it develops from earlier, altogether non-Christian levels-that is to say, out of chthonic animals such as crocodiles, dragons, serpents, or monkeys. Sometimes the child appears in the cup of a flower, or out of a golden egg, or as the center of a mandala. In dreams it often appears as the dreamer's son or daughter or as a boy, youth, or young girl . . . appearing more cosmically, surrounded by stars or with a starry coronet; or as the king's son or the witch's child with daemonic attributes. Seen as a special instance of 'the treasure hard to attain' motif, the child motif is extremely variable and assumes all manner of shapes, such as the jewel, the pearl, the flower, the chalice, the golden egg, the quaternity, the golden ball, and so on. It can be interchanged with these and similar images almost without limit.
>
> *(Jung, 1959/1968: § 270)*

The numinous elevation of the child to divine-like energy is a metaphor for the function of the internal child in Jung's configuration of the psyche; particularly in the context of individuation. During this process of self-discovery, that in classical Jungian thought lead to a sense of unity, the child emerges as a dominant and significant psychological motif, guiding the subject's inner development and potential. Jung uses the concept of the divine child as bourgeoning saviour to suggest its capacity to pave 'the way for a future change of personality' a product of the integration of conscious and unconscious material (Jung, 1959/1968: § 278).

In addition to divinity, the child has also been equated to *soul* – the core or essence of being. For Kalsched, Jung is trying to protect and preserve an 'innocent true self' against the harsh realities of inner and outer worlds (2013, p. 16). This becomes significant to Kalsched's formulation of what he calls *the self-care system* – a pathological function adopted by the psyche when a trauma-induced split occurs to disrupt the individuation process. He argues that protective (terrorising) aspects of the psyche perversely enforce a holding pattern for the wounded (victim) aspect, by terrorising her/him into inaction when triggers appear, often in the form of objects relating to, or holding some resonance with, the original trauma. The damaged childlike element is therefore misguidedly 'protected' from contact with the perceived threat. Kalsched (1996) refers to patients who repeatedly experienced the self-care system through nightmares and fantasies that played out as scenarios more violent than the original trauma, re-traumatising them over again. Despite the *affect* produced by this split psyche dynamic, Kalsched argues that, 'the survival of the soul is the main purpose of the self-care system' (2013, p. 29). The concept of soul is entwined with the wounded and fragile child aspect of the psyche in need of protection and, as seen below, appears collapsed into Jung's sense of divine: 'The divine child or human/divine soul within us is not an artefact of the defensive process, but everything the defensive process is protecting. And it is protecting it because it is sacred – the very core of our aliveness' (Kalsched, 2013, p. 242).

Kalsched emphasises that Jung's child also straddles conscious and unconscious content – negotiating these domains as does the soul, and holding the tension and possibility that each offers the other: 'this idea of the soul as a relationship between two worlds is why the image of the part-human, part-divine "child" which seemed to represent the soul in Jung's dreams was so powerful for him' (2013, p. 264). He further likens this liminal quality to paediatrician Donald Winnicott's *transitional space* – a psychological transfer in infancy from omnipotence to grounded subjectivity, where the infant begins to separate and distinguish itself from the mother/primary carer, signified through the breast, by attaching itself to a series of replacement objects such as soft toys, blankets etc. that will be eventually discarded and acknowledged as distinct things in themselves (Winnicott, 1971). Kalsched refocuses this stage in a Jungian frame when he suggests that: 'There is also an inner process – a transitional space between ego and its deep ground in what Jung called the Self. This is apparently the "space" where angels and other hybrid *daimonic* beings have their hybrid existence' (2013, p. 30).

Related to the idea of the soul's purity and the unconscious need to protect it, render it divine and shelter it from corruption, is the concept of innocence. The depth of feeling often attached to lost child fictions and reportage in Australian popular culture and media is often determined by the level of innocence attached to the subject, with age used as a gauge. For Kalsched, 'that elusive essence at the very core of our aliveness' is directly associated with '"innocence" . . . the guileless simplicity and wide-eyed trust of young children' (2013, p. 214). Freud's early interventions into entrenched Victorian notions of childhood innocence with his description of children as polymorphously perverse, were supported by child psychoanalyst Melanie Klein's formulation of death instinct driven hostilities against mother that challenged any idea of an essential innocence: 'For Klein one did not start with innocence but with guilt – a kind of psychoanalytic original sin – and worked toward the possibility of goodness and gratitude while moving from the paranoid persecutory to the depressive position' (Kalsched, 2013, p. 214). But Kalsched adds that, 'recent developments in attachment theory, infant observation, relational theory, and the self-psychology initiated by Heinz Kohut . . . all support a more sympathetic view of primal innocence in the child's infancy' (2013, p. 214).

From the sociological perspective, childhood and popular concepts of the child are socially constructed projections by adults, influenced by Enlightenment values (Jenks, 1996). For Annette Appell in her study of legal discriminations and the rights of children, this view renders children 'without wisdom, knowledge, or political, moral, or legal competence, thus excluding them from governance and self-determination' (Appell, 2013, p. 722). She argues that the (North American) legal position on children is more closely aligned with disability or human rights models than the less sympathetically regarded categories of *otherness* like gender, race or sexuality. Despite the gap between Freud's theories of childhood sexuality and the current legal systems of many countries, the law understands children to be both non-actively sexual by nature and 'vulnerable to harm arising out of sexual acts and sexual representation well into their teenage years' (Appell, 2013, p. 770). The Australian Institute of Family Studies takes a holistic approach, balancing age of consent laws 'between protecting children and young people from exploitation and other harms, and preserving their right to privacy and healthy sexual development' (AIFS, 2018). This brings us back to the question of innocence and the imperative of adults (and the unconscious) to adopt a protective role. There is obvious religious resonance here with 'the fall' and the consequent state of 'original sin', if innocence is considered to be the condition prior to knowingness. The child then suggests the Judeo-Christian concept of Eden – purity, vulnerability, eternal happiness and protection but under the eye of an omnipotent and punishing god.

While American screen culture is a discussion for the final chapter, at this point it would seem remiss to not raise, the Hulu streaming company's *The Handmaids' Tale* (2017–) based on Margaret Atwood's futuristic novel of the same name. In the fictional Republic of Gilead, annexed over much of the United States – oppressive to women, violently religious and fanatically preoccupied with infertility, pregnancy, birth and motherhood – the character of fifteen-year-old Eden (Sydney Sweeny) is the hoped for catalyst to the theocracy's fall. Accused of being corrupted by her love for a man, innocence, piety, youth and obedience do not redeem her from a state-sanctioned public drowning with her lover (season 2, episode 12 'Postpartum'). This ground-breaking series will be touched on in the conclusion, but this turning point in the programme's second season alludes to Eden as the embodiment of the divine child – abandoned, projected upon, a symbol of futurity and an agent of change. It seems likely at this stage in the drama that Eden's death will set in motion the transcendent function.

To render the child (Eden) lost in this religious/televisual context is to position it halfway between paradise and expulsion, for the celestial child holds the tension of psychological opposites and inhabits the half-world of the demigod with its mortal and immortal parentage. This liminality can also be seen in Winnicott's developmental transitional space between the breast/mother and subjectivity. While embodying potential, futurity and overcoming, Jung's divine child, as Mercer reminds us, must also be associated with abandonment and loss: it must relinquish ties to fulfil its potential, remembering that the child in this magical context is symbolic of new insight and knowledge (Jung, 1959/1968).

It seems that the child, as guide to development, in the state of becoming lost, is stuck – the process of forward movement is caught between a *desire*, or gesture, to move forward (signified by the child in an archetypal sense) and the *act of moving* forward, if we consider Jung's positioning of the divine child as representative of 'the strongest, the most ineluctable urge in every human being, namely the urge to realize itself' (Jung, 1959/1968, p. 170). It superficially appears then as if the culture remains in a potential state of *becoming* rather than actively embracing and exploring the sense of futurity that the child is theorised to facilitate, but, 'The negative features of the child archetype – abandonment, helplessness – were for Jung necessary features. He called for negativity to be lived with and transformed rather than repressed' (Mercer, 2003, p. 127).

The divine child is spared from the real-world pathologies/*affects* of abandonment argues Jung, so that parental separation is merely a test from which it emerges victorious into consciousness. Tied into this symbolism is the uncomfortable certainty that estrangement and loss are prerequisites for independence and progress: 'it is only separation, detachment, and agonizing confrontation through opposition that produce consciousness and insight' (Jung, 1959/1968: § 289). The persistence of the lost child complex, in its focus on lostness and/or abandonment, suggests that *we* imagine *ourselves* as being held in kind of limbo. But bearing in mind Jung's writing on the divine child, this lack of anchorage does not necessarily suggest, as Pierce writes, that to 'be "lost" is to be in stasis' (1999, p. 51). Within this seeming helpless and exposed state, there can be a sense of forward movement: an opportunity to go beyond the known, into the unknown, and acquire new knowledge.

In the archetypal lost child's return again and again through film, it is as if we are trying to understand what this perennial child means to us. In the process, we are building a relationship with it – one that I argue is not as much about stasis, as the possibility of change and discovery. Jolande Jacobi, an early psychologist and colleague of Jung's, sums up the potential of complexes that 'often act invisibly', as if 'preparing the way for some transformation' (1959, p. 10). Hillman argues that the child must remain lost so that it can be repeatedly sourced, similar to the process of returning to the child and attempting to recover repressed material in depth therapies.

Archetypes themselves do not change. It is our interpretation of the lost child, our evolving relationship to it that allows for access to a richer sense of self-awareness. The divine child of mythology Jung theorised as an archetypal motif, is eternal and timeless. Similarly the lost child appearing in Australian culture can also be interpreted as a symbol that cannot be confined by temporal and spatial concepts. It is however, possible to hypothesise when it began to emerge as a source of unease. Before European settlement, the First Australians as custodians of the land, were not lost. Lostness was foisted upon these indigenous communities. This wave of displacement began with colonisation, which could well have set the conditions for the complex to surface and generationally work its way, through the arts, into the cultural memory.

Cultural memory, collective identity and generational remembering

Singer and Kimbles argue that the need to forge a sense of collective identity can become confused with, and impact on, existing cultural complexes, 'which have accrued historical experience and memory over centuries of trauma and lie slumbering in the cultural unconscious, waiting to be awakened by the trigger of new trauma' (2004, p. 5). This suggests that through the trauma of British convict transportation, colonisation and migration to a remote and unfamiliar country, the archetypal lost child was not created, but energised.

Between 1787 and 1868 the British parliament identified Australia as a site of convict transportation, given North America's War of Independence (1775–1783). In the history of transportation, this was the furthest a penal colony had been established from its country of origin (Hughes, 1986). From May 13, 1787 to January 26, 1788 (250 days) Captain Arthur Phillips' eleven-strong first fleet travelled from Portsmouth in England to Australia's Sydney Cove, Port Jackson (now Sydney Harbour), or *the fatal shore* as it was known in convict ballads (Hughes, 1986). The 1,487 travellers comprised: '*Marines*: 252 men, wives and children. *Crew*: 210 (navy), 233 (merchant). *Convicts*: 568 male, 191 female, 13 children. *Officials*: 20' (Currey, 2006, p. 12). The six convict ships – the *Alexander, Charlotte, Friendship, Lady Penrhyn, Prince of Wales* and *Scarborough* – were accompanied by two King's ships, HMS *Sirius* and *Supply* and three store ships, the *Borrowdale, Fishburn* and *Golden Grove* (Currey, 2006). The arrival marked the colonisation of Australia and the steady fragmentation of indigenous communities that at the time of settlement were thought to constitute 250 separate language groups. Today less than twenty languages are spoken with any degree of fluidity by all Aboriginal generations (Australian Bureau of Statistics, 2015). Surviving personal letters and journals of high-ranking crew and early settlers in the eighteenth and nineteenth century detail the hardships of transport and colonisation, these included: hanging and punishment (commonly flogging) for criminal misdemeanours and convict desertion, convict hard labour, famine in the colony, attacks on convicts and scouting parties by indigenous Australians, drunkenness and illness (Currey, 2006; Clendinnen, 2003; Irvine, 1988).

The difference between Australia and other Great British colonies was its sheer distance from England and its foundation through convict transportation, unlike North America which was settled by the Pilgrim Fathers in 1620 at Plymouth, ninety-seven years before the Great Britain legislated the Transportation Act of 1717 (4 Geo.1 c.11). Historian Kim Torney in *Babes in the Bush: The making of an Australian image* (2005), claims that the overshadowing cultural anxiety around children lost in the outback is particular to Australia: 'No other comparable settler society – not America, Canada or New Zealand – explicitly displayed this fear, even though the likelihood of such an occurrence was just the same' (p. 47). It is easy to see how the trauma of transportation and colonisation for settlers and indigenous communities has become embedded in cultural memory. January the twenty-sixth is celebrated every year as 'Australia Day', or alternatively, 'Invasion Day', complete with celebrations for the winner of Australian of the Year and the announcement of honour awards to Australians. The notion of lostness is repeatedly embedded into this nationalistic attempt to reinforce both the 'birthing' of white Australia and its continuing ties to Britain – an abandoned child perhaps basking in its 'becoming'.

Those forcibly relocated to Australia and the free settlers seeking opportunities for a new life found themselves in a hostile and at times unforgiving environment. From this initial trauma further waves of immigrants likely added to the initial wounds of separation while also allowing people to establish new and more prosperous lives: the migration of Chinese and Irish in the gold rush period, the 1950s movement of 'ten-pound Poms' from Britian and southern European migrants, and United Kingdom orphans sent to Australia after the second world war, many of whom were later abused in religious and state-run care organisations. Germaine Greer characterised the feeling of displacement as 'the pain of unbelonging' (Collingwood-Whittick, 2007, p. 119).

This sense of lostness from 1788 was passed onto the indigenous population, rendered lost through the decimation of their territories and culture by European settlers and the policies of British authorities (see AIATSIS, 2018; Edwards and Read, 1989). As in Pierce's central thesis, the lost child acts as a conduit or symbol for the unresolved psychological struggles of initial and succeeding generations of white colonisers (1999, p. xii). Stories and reportage of childhood lostness during this period of early nineteenth-century settlement in particular serve as metaphors for the sense of abandon and identity struggles that took place during key periods of emerging nationhood. But even more significantly, these struggles, appear to have been intensified by a cultural complex operating as if autonomously.

Lost child mythologies – early reportage and storytelling

Having discussed the psychological nature of the lost child through a Jungian-based framework, it is important to briefly look at diverse projections of the complex in its formative years – the external images, figures and case studies that served as triggers or *hooks* for the surfacing archetype. Elspeth Tilley (2012), Pierce and most particularly Torney's work on the historical and literary lost child in Australian culture are significant contributions to understanding the momentum, fears, anxieties and fascination of *literally* lost children. Their historical and sociological research also explores how the concept of *lost in the bush* became a classical narrative for the arts, particularly early literature, and in Pierce's analysis of seven twentieth-century films, Australian cinema.

Torney details the lost colonial child from transportation, where under British law in 1847 children 'between seven and fourteen years were subject to the full range of penalties – corporal and capital punishment, imprisonment and transportation' (2005, p. 55). Childhood for convicts was considered to have ended at the age of twelve, but younger children entered the labour force carrying out gender specific duties – domestic related tasks for girls and agricultural or construction labour for boys (Torney, 2005).

> The presence of eighteen child convicts in the First Fleet, plus the fact that records show some convicts were as young as eight or nine years, and that about fifteen per cent (25,000) of all convicts transported to Australia were aged eighteen years or under confirm that eighteenth-century Britain attributed legal responsibility to children in a way that modern society does not.
>
> *(Torney, 2005, p. 54)*

Point Peur, the male convict facility for juveniles located on a promontory in Opossum Bay (Port Arthur, Tasmania) (1834–1849), trained boys for employment in the new colonies. In charting the experiences of the institution's first intake (1834) of sixty-eight child convicts, Peter Macfie and Nigel Hargraves argue that the boys' moral and practical skills training had mixed results in equipping them for life in the colonies. Punished, poorly fed and subject to military-style discipline, this 'first stolen generation' of children were the leftovers of convict children not immediately assigned to work for the government or private settlers (1999, p. 129). The romanticised stories of suicide pacts among the boys, described in Marcus Clarke's 1874 novelisation of convict life, *For The Term Of His Natural Life* (1874/1897), 'have become part of the marketing of the convict site for tourism' writes Pierce of this 'wholly fictional' incident (1999, p. 45). The brutality of the institution and the adult Port Arthur prison nearby, have an uncanny relevance to Australian and, ever increasingly, North American culture. As touched on in Chapter 6, Port Arthur, now a historic tourist precinct, was the site of a gun massacre in 1996 that targeted children and their families. It immediately set in motion Australian gun law reforms, still rigorously enforced and inspiring in light of the overwhelming number of mass shootings and lax gun regulations in the USA (Phillips, Park and Lorimer, 2007).

Nineteenth-century children reported missing in the bush were either found alive or their bodies recovered by search parties, many were the lost 'children of poor settlers – shepherds, small selectors, miners and timber-cutters' (Torney, 2004, p. 53). Their stories became part of the bush mythology, particularly the saga of the lost and found Duff siblings in 1864: Isaac Cooper nine years old, Jane

Cooper seven years old and Frank Duff, three years old. Jane, who nurtured her brothers on their nine-day ordeal in the Wimmera (Horsham, Victoria), died in 1932. A memorial stone funded by schoolchildren was erected in 1935. The story became a state and national celebration of heroism that inspired literature and the film *Lost in the Bush* (dir. Dodds, 1973).

> The story of the Duff children was also the basis for *A Little Australian Girl*, or *The Babes in the Bush*, by children's writer Robert Richardson, which was published in the late 1870s. This seems the first incidence of the use of the word 'bush' (to replace 'forest' or 'wood') with the 'babies' imagery, thus creating a distinctly Australian folklore image.
> *(Torney, 2005, pp. 30–31)*

Cemetery tours are still conducted to Jane's grave and a request by one of the guides to have Dodds' film updated to DVD 'snowballed into a nine-day, 150th anniversary festival' of the event (Webb, 2014). Along with the Dodds children, the small, now tourist spa country town of Daylesford in Victoria, memorialises its lost child history with literature, a memorial to three missing boys whose bodies were found in 1867, its Three Lost Children Reserve and a walking trail (Menadue, 1975). The country's many memorials to lost children, along with *lost in the bush* storytelling though the arts writes Torney, keeps the cultural memory alive, but more particularly these physical monuments, 'like graves, served to bind settlers emotionally to the land, to create the links and stories by which to understand and interpret their experiences' (2005, pp. 225–227).

From Australian impressionist Frederick McCubbin's famous painting *Lost* (1886) with the figure of a child surrounded by bushland, the poetry of early bush authors, Henry Lawson's *The Babes in the Bush* (1899) and Banjo Patterson's *Lost* (1887), the colonial literature outlined by Tilly, Pierce and Torney, to a childhood favourite of mine, the television series *Seven little Australians* (dir. Way, 1974) adapted from Ethel Turner's 1894 novel – the lost child is now most prolifically reimagined in Australian film and television. Because the cultural storytelling of literature, art, music, theatre and screen has long been acknowledged as a way of influencing identity and grappling with the past, it is not surprising that early *lost in the bush* stories foreshadowed contemporary narratives of lostness that focus on literal, remembered and metaphorical childhoods.

Collective belonging and memories

Through early storytelling it becomes clear just how much the maintenance, repetition and massaging of lost child narratives contributes to a sense of national belonging. They hold a reverential place in the construction of our cultural memory. Because they are so tenaciously sustained through the generations and readapted for contemporary audiences, it is understandable to ask how this image or state serves us – what is it saying and why has it become a point of collective identification? These questions will be looked at in later chapters, but for the moment it's important to address the practices of lost child nurture and preservation.

Duncan Bell (2003) differentiates memory from mythology in his discussion of national identity. To more clearly demonstrate how these terms can borrow from each other he employs the concept of *mythscape*: 'the temporally and spatially extended discursive realm in which the myths of the nation are forged, transmitted, negotiated, and reconstructed constantly' (p. 63). The films and related screen texts discussed in this book might be said to provide such a mythscape, a 'perpetually mutating repository for the representation of the past for the purposes of the present' (Bell, 2003, p. 66). The lost child films under discussion have been influential in the development of the Australian film industry and an ever evolving and diverse sense of collective identities: one might even say that they have contributed to galvanising a sense of identity and belonging. The following brief examples carry and rework the theme as an historical event, tempered with fictional reimaging and mythologising: *The Story of the Kelly Gang* (dir. Tait, 1906), *Picnic at Hanging Rock* (dir. Weir, 1975), *Gallipoli* (dir. Weir, 1981), *Rabbit Proof Fence* (dir. Noyce, 2002), *Romulus My Father* (dir. Roxburgh, 2007), *Lion* (dir. Davis, 2016).

Bell stresses the importance of fusing the personal and the collective in the 'rhetoric' of nationalism (p. 64), much as Singer and Kimbles' rationale that the cultural complex is formed through a synthesis of the individual and the group. The particular nature and proliferation of the lost child in Australia is quite particular to this country. Other current and former British colonies that influence Australian culture (North America in particular) incorporate 'the child' literally and symbolically, but in a very different manner. It is not that the lost child is unique to this country, but its very dominance and generational reinvention through the arts, arguably sets us apart. This cultural memory and complex therefore potentially offers a sense of cohesion, and to some degree distinctiveness. As will be discussed in Chapter 4, one often pathologically and destructively projected outward as a means of rendering *others* lost.

Bell acknowledges that 'binding memories' can be generationally and temporally circulated in a very intentional and manipulative manner – as with the rhetoric and ideology of nationalism – but they can also function as collectively unconscious matter seeking acknowledgement through projection and *affects*: 'They [memories] can (allegedly) be invented, acquired, and embellished, although more often than not they assume a life-force of their own, escaping the clutches of any individual or group and becoming embedded in the very fabric, material and psychologically, of the nation' (2003, p. 70). Bell also argues that the notion of generational memories is misleading. Memory is not transferable 'to those who have not experienced the events that an individual recalls, which means that it cannot be passed down from generation to generation, let alone "cultivated" or constructed in the minds of those who live often hundreds of years after an event (real or imagined)' (Bell, 2003, p. 73). Of course it is not the actual memory of a child lost that *has us* beyond a sense of rationality, it is the mythscape we are drawn into. Each generation adds their own experiences and by doing this, the phenomenon gains momentum. The complex can mature in a similar fashion. While Bell holds that myths transmitted through the arts are socially and ideologically constructed, Jung believes that mythologies are the expression of collectively unconscious archetypal energies (Jung, 1959/1969). What *is* culturally mediated, is the interpretation, projection and organisation of these interconnected motifs.

The concept of collective cultural memory introduced in the 1930s by sociologist Maurice Haleachs and art historian Abby Warburg departs from Jung's biologically, archetypally configured collective unconscious (Assmann and Czaplicka, 1995). Haleachs and Warburg distinguished 'cultural memory' from 'communicative/everyday memory' with the later not dependent on culture, but relying on oral interactions between individuals. In this way they theorised that memories are passed on within a specific familial or social network to facilitate a sense of identity and group cohesion. Cultural memory on the other hand is defined as 'a collective concept for all knowledge that directs behaviour and experience in the interactive framework of a society and one that obtains through generations in repeated societal practice and initiation' (Assmann and Czaplicka, 1995, p. 126). If individual memory is sustained through repetition, cultural memory is punctuated with 'fixed points' or 'figures of memory' that are preserved by ritual and reimaged through the arts, memorials, media, maintenance and the exhibition of various historical documents and recordings etc. (Assmann and Czaplicka, 1995, p. 129). In their analysis of Haleachs' and Warburg's research, Assman and Czaplicka theorise cultural memory to be a link between 'memory (the contemporized past), culture, and the group (society) to each other' (p. 129).

> The concept of cultural memory comprises that body of reusable texts, images, and rituals specific to each society in each epoch, whose 'cultivation' serves to stabilize and convey that society's self-image. Upon such collective knowledge, for the most part (but not exclusively) of the past, each group bases its awareness of unity and particularity.
>
> The content of such knowledge varies from culture to culture as well as from epoch to epoch. The manner of its organization, its media, and its institutions, are also highly variable. The binding and reflexive character of a heritage can display varying intensities and appear in various aggregations.
>
> *(Assmann and Czaplicka, 1995, pp. 132–133)*

A psychologically driven unconscious cultural complex and a sociologically driven collective memory are not mutually exclusive. For the purposes of this analysis, both perspectives – a biological predisposition to collective archetypal phenomena and a generationally preserved memory of culturally nurtured and reimagined key events – adds to our understanding of the prolific nature of the lost child as a cultural artefact, a consciously maintained memory and a deeply psychological pattern forming the core of a cultural complex. Astrid Erll draws on John Locke's linkage of memory and identity to suggest that the fluid and shifting nature of memory contributes to an evolving sense of identity, and in this process the 'past Self' is identified largely in relation to 'the present Self' (Erll, 2008a, p. 6).

The interdisciplinary nature of memory studies has been an emerging area of scholarship since the 1980s attracting a divergent range of disciplines and approaches to the nature of cultural and individual pasts. For Erll, the reimagining of key historical events in novels and cinema are guided by cultural tastes. Rather than focusing on historical accuracy, she argues that such texts 'cater to the public with what is variously termed "authenticity" or "truthfulness". They create images of the past which resonate with cultural memory' (Erll, 2008b, p. 389). It is not particular media forms and narratives alone that shape cultural memory, but for Erll, how the 'phenomena within, between, and around those media' are instrumental in these kinds of collective manipulations (Erll, 2008b, p. 390). This returns us to the cultural complex of the lost child, for this kind of focused cinema can not only take us back to culturally tainted fictions and reportage of lost children, but can also tap into personal and collective psychological associations of childhood, lostness, divinity and soul.

> On an individual level, media representations provide those schemata and scripts which allow us to create in our minds certain images of the past and which may even shape our own experience and autobiographical memories. . . . The 'cultural mind' is in many ways a 'medial mind': It is the patterns derived from the media cultures we live in, especially (albeit often unintentionally) from fictions, that shape our idea of reality and our memories. This insight calls for interdisciplinary collaboration between what may seem to be disciplines situated farthest apart on the spectrum of memory studies: literary and media studies on the one hand and psychology and the neurosciences on the other.
>
> *(Erll, 2008b, p. 397)*

A fusion of screen culture, cultural memory, the collective unconscious and, according to Singer and Kimbles, trauma, allows us to interpret repeated lost child 'memories', phenomenon or *affects*, as all interconnected to a culturally dominant complex. For Stef Craps, memories in their ability to become mobile, transcending nationalities through mass media, make it 'increasingly possible for people to take on memories of events not "their own", events that they did not live through themselves and to which they have no familial, ethnic, or national tie' (2013, p. 74).

Martin Zierold (2008) concentrates on the media's capacity to affect cultural memory, but rather than limiting this to screen and literary cultures, he sees the development of all forms of media, from screen to print and radio, as connected to the fluctuating forms of cultural memory. He suggests that social memory shifts with technological advances and newly developed media platforms: 'no single aspect of the integrative connection of a complex concept of media can be regarded independently of the others. The effects of technologies always depend on the specific applications in the production and use of media offers, which are always contingent and culturally variable' (Zierold, 2008, p. 404). Further analysis of the complex and cultural memory in relation to social media and the increasing and damaging phenomena of online child and adolescent bullying for instance, in yet another manifestation of the lost child, is beyond the scope of this study, but deserves further consideration.

Many of the film narratives explored in the following chapters have been reworked from novels, memoirs, histories and theatre – even the films themselves have inspired further adaptation into television miniseries and plays, ensuring that the lost child is made relevant for the next generation and reminding us perhaps, that the cultural complex still, as Jung would say, *has us*. Psychotherapist and academic Luke Hockley argues for the *somatic* nature of cinema; its ability to stir us on a bodily/sensory level, so that 'the act of being-in-the cinema is related via all the senses' (2014, p. 31). By projecting aspects of ourselves, the inner archetypal child for instance, onto screen material that provides either an obvious trigger or a more covert *hook*, Hockley believes that 'we find ourselves in films' (p. 107). We can also find ourselves in complexes, driven by an archetypal and cultural fusion of persistent psychological material that holds us in thrall. Hockley sees film as a confronting medium that allows for what he calls a 'third image' where the 'intersubjective space between the viewer and the screen' make self-reflection and change possible (p. 7). Going back to the child again and again, as we do in depth psychologies and cinema, to revisit and reassess the repressed, can lead to new discoveries. Film can then allow us to meet the lost child, and rather than disavow, understand it – form a relationship with it in all its guises and by doing this glimpse a third possibility/image. This third is also for Jung, that which springs from a meeting of consciousness and the unconscious *and* that which unifies these polarities – both symbolised in the divine child:

> literature, film, music, an 'epiphany' of beauty in the natural world, or an experience of a numinous vision or dream may evoke our truer deeper selves, liberating us momentarily from the deforming images we have acquired and allowing us to see through into a deeper truth about ourselves and our potential life. . . . Some of our best therapy comes from these private inner resources
>
> *(Kalsched, 2013, p. 160)*

2
LITERALLY LOST
Searchers, the searched for and grail metaphors

While the previous chapter aimed to contextualise ideas of the child and lostness from an Australian perspective by considering the historical, cultural and psychological dynamics that play into the lost child complex, here I'm going to look at screen representations of the archetypal motif as economically, and yet as representatively, as possible. In gathering material on more literal lost child narratives in film – children who are physically lost, missing and so the object of extensive searches – it became obvious that there was a clear division, and a lesser third category, into which these stories could be divided. The first are structured from the perspectives of the lost child/children – typically culminating in rescue or escape. The second, and most prolific, where the lost are often not found, focuses on the experiences of the searchers. And the third, more contemporary category centres on rare stories of the lost child as both searcher and object of the quest; Garth Davis' *Lion* (2016), detailed further in this chapter, and the Spierig brothers' *Predestination* (2014) explored in Chapter 6, are two significant examples of this merging. While films carrying a *lost in the bush* ethos have been described as romantic quests by Susan Dermody (1980), and stolen generation films like *Rabbit Proof Fence* as 'trauma cinema in which spectators are addressed as witnesses' by Collins and Davis (2004, p. 145), it is worth extending these descriptors by thinking about this themed material as particularly Australian inflected versions of the grail myth. This kind of interpretation is not however, modelled on the Christopher Vogler (1998/2007) inspired generic hero-cycle/archetypal scriptwriting technique that tends to saturate American *victory* driven quests (discussed in the final chapter), but draws on specific mythology that helps us to understand the lost child as embodying both the *ideal of the grail* and the figure of Perceval, the mythic young knight *questing for the grail*. In an Australian context, it becomes increasingly apparent that the grail is never ultimately located, but remains an intangible source of aspiration and inspiration in the cyclic hunt for an evolving, yet never fully becoming, sense of individual and collective identity.

In *The Lost Child in Literature and Culture*, Mark Froud tackles the theme from a global perspective and understands the prolific imagery of lost children to embody, 'the supernatural or ghostly . . . a site without borders . . . victim to the rampant imaginings of adult readers and viewers' (2017, p. 18). Melbourne photographer Polixeni Papapetrou's 2006 'Haunted Country' collection is inspired by culturally recognisable images of children isolated in Australian landscapes (mimicking the stories of screen, literature and art). They are intimately connected to the more mythic forms of settler outback disorientation and the kind of nation birthing trauma discussed in the previous chapter, rather than lostness arising from abandonment, mistreatment, psychological isolation/confusion, illegitimacy and racism that tends to shape these figures in contemporary screen narratives and imagery. Allusions to haunting and being haunted are significant in lost child stories from the perspective of history and memory, to a sense of the figure as an intangible aspect of the personality; an archetypal eruption, capable of psychologically imposing its power up on us, as will be explored in Chapters 5 and 6 when the lost child is discussed as a liminal presence for adult characters. This idea of haunting can also be applied to the Australian film industry's impact on audiences. With its history of independent, government funded and internationally supported material, no matter how eclectic, film always appears to return to themes of the lost child, resolutely entertaining us with ever incarnating projections of this motif. Those who have created, directed and portrayed characters embodying the lost child have been our most lionised artists – their awards, critical acceptance and relevance to screen scholarship have sutured them into the cultural imaginary along with the ghosts they conjure.

From of directors Ken Hall and Raymond Longford, working in the foundational years of the Australian film industry, the lost child of earlier art and literature became a familiar cinema theme: *The Woman Suffers* (dir. Longford, 1918), *Strike Me Lucky* (dir. Hall, 1934) and *Orphan of the Wilderness* (dir. Hall, 1936). After the second world war, with lost child films such as *The Back of Beyond* (dir. Heyer, 1954) and *Jedda* (dir. Chauvel, 1955), the development of government film financing bodies and taxation concessions, fuelled the 'New Wave' or 'film revival' of the 1970s to mid-1980s, and the lost child gathered momentum with pivotal films such as *Walkabout* (dir. Roeg, 1971), *Picnic at Hanging Rock* and *Careful He Might Hear You* (dir. Schultz, 1983). During the 'Post New Wave', beginning in 1990, variations of the lost child continued as stable plot devices and since 2000, particularly in the last few years of this decade, there has been a surge in lost child themed film and television. While one might have imagined that the complex was fading at the turn of the twenty-first century, current screen offerings suggest that this energy still underlies multiple and often conflicting challenges to a collectively evolving sense of self-understanding.

Overlapping more literal *lost in the bush* films and the numerous screen texts discussed throughout the book that adopt and abstract the lost child theme, is the concept of illegitimacy or uncertain parentage. This source of confusion and displacement for actual child characters or the inner lost child of adults, takes us back to the possible traumatic origins of the complex. Given the historical and mythically embellished record of colonisation as a both a form of abduction (convict resettlement) and a wrenching from a distant and absent mother/fatherland for free settlers, it is unsurprising that this loss of 'parental' anchorage, translated into stories where illegitimacy – with its connotations of illegality and religious defiance – and/or ambiguous origin, became a defining theme. Films focusing on a sense of displacement and uncertainty for the actual and inner child include: *The Woman Suffers, A Girl of the Bush* (dir. Barrett, 1921), *Know Thy Child* (dir. Barrett, 1921), *Jedda, Walkabout, Fran* (dir. Hambly, 1985), *Somersault* (dir. Shortland, 2004), *Irresistible* (dir. Turner, 2006), *Australia* (dir. Luhrmann, 2008), *Oranges and Sunshine* (dir. Loach, 2010), *Predestination, The Daughter* (dir. Stone, 2015) and *Lion*. The notion of forced or voluntary parental abandonment can also be factored into *The Shiralee* (dir. Norman, 1957), *Careful He Might Hear You, High Tide* (dir. Armstrong, 1987), *Evil Angels* (dir: Schepisi, 1988), *The Sound of One Hand Clapping* (dir. Flanagan, 1997), *Erskinville Kings* (dir. White, 1999), *Romulus, My Father, The Home Song Stories* (dir. Ayres, 2007), *Polly and Me* (dir. Darling, 2010), *Here I Am* (dir. Cole, 2011) and *Lore* (dir. Shortland, 2012) . . . and of course, the list goes on.

The films discussed below, representative of what might loosely be called a *genre*, focus on a variety of characters imagined as lost children. The age range embraces infants to bourgeoning adults in mid-adolescence, but all become enfolded as lost children in the cultural imagination. Even if not technically 'children', they all carry the archetypal symbolism of the child at the core of the complex. As Froud argues, 'The child is the object not the subject' (Froud, 2017, p. 18). The actual protagonist or seeming subject of the quest, nearly always becomes a referent through which we understand the grief, desperation and emotional disorientation of those who search, and even more profoundly, other, even more lost children. In this sense the character one imagines to epitomise the idea of the lost child becomes an indexical figure that brings awareness to more complex webs of actual, metaphorical or potential loss.

Whether the object of a search, an actual child seeking *home* in the form of a place or person, or the combination of both positions, the lost child is central to the quest and the complex, enfolding all peripheral characters who impact on or are impacted by this figure. Understanding, and living with complexes in general, involves examining what the pivotal motif might symbolise and attempting to psychologically integrate that element. For Froud, 'the deeper the child figure is as an aspect of our self, the more we need to position it outside of ourselves so we can look at it' (p. 2). Added to this way of more objectively appreciating this potent aspect of our collective selves, he adds that the omnipresence of this image, 'would suggest that the internal child is the part of ourselves that we mourn, or that we are afraid of, or that we despise, and because of this we must eject it from our mind and body, like a contagion' (p. 2). Although the idea of projection and disavowal is discussed in Chapter 4, more classically lost child films can be read as searches for that ideal part of ourselves we re-quest for, attempt to find succour from, but never capture: it is not necessarily fear or the need for distance that the figure elicits, but a desire for closeness. As Hillman argues, the child has traditionally constituted that element of our lives that in psychoanalysis and depth psychology is thought to be central to our character and because of this, plays a healing role (1975/1991). Searching for the child is therefore closely related to the individuation process that shapes the *self* (our personal identity) and is modulated in Jungian thought by the concept of the *Self* (the organising core of the psyche, the totality of the psyche, a unifier of psychic material and a concept of wholeness) (Jung, 1959/1968, 1959/1969, 1963/1970). This kind of psychological unfolding is a life-long process of individual and collective exploration.

While *the search* in relation to the lost child genre is often embedded in trauma, as Collins and Davis so cogently outline, I am less convinced by the efficacy of the generalised 'quest-romance' angle proposed by Dermody almost forty years ago to encompass Australian lost child films. But as Collins and Davies demonstrate in their analysis of the stolen indigenous generations film *Rabbit Proof Fence*, it can be usefully applied to particular texts: 'we have shown how *Rabbit-Proof Fence* grafts the political-historical drama genre onto the romance-quest to create a compelling story that invokes and at the same time reworks many of the themes, conventions and melodramatic aspects of the Australian cultural tradition of the lost child in the bush narratives' (Collins and Davis, 2004, p. 144). In Vogler hero-myth fashion, Dermody sees lost child plots as action-adventures driven by an idealist hero who is tested against 'difficult or harsh terrain' (1980, p. 79). Rather than a generic or clichéd *romance* quest, that Dermody doesn't historically locate or specify, Australian lost child stories are also driven by one of the most celebrated romance cycles – a modified grail quest – where the notion of the hero is contestable, the quest has varying degrees of climactic or enigmatic endpoints, and the idea of the grail is transfigured into the figure or memory of a child. Before looking at specific Australian films, it is worth outlining the basic formula of the labyrinth-like grail legends and how they might be usefully employed to interpret the psychological value of lost child cinema.

The lost child as multiple elements of the grail myth

In their overview of the grail legend, Emma Jung and Marie-Louise Von Franz (1960/1998) trace the meandering origins of the Christian story from the grail's mythic passage from Jerusalem to Britain by the *Grail* or *Templar* knights after Christ's death, its evolution into Arthurian mythology with Perceval as its key protagonist, and the grail stories, with their various character permutations, as allegories of psychological significance. Imagined in a Christian context by Robert de Boron's *Joseph d'Arimathie* (thirteenth century) to have been Christ's drinking bowl from at the last supper, later used by Joseph of Arimathea to catch the dripping blood of Christ's lanced wound during crucifixion, the grail was romanticised into a mediaeval alchemical vessel with the capacity to replenish, heal and offer salvation. In splintered literary versions of the myth, the grail is entrusted to a line of grail kings after its transportation to Britain, including the Fisher King.

The Arthurian story of Perceval and the Fisher King is perhaps the most well-known aspect of the grail legend, somewhat eclipsing the feats and struggles of the mediaeval Knights Templar despite their presence in literature, art and cinema. The initial stories of Perceval, incorporated in the French Vulgate cycle written between 1180 and 1230 by Chretien de Troyes and later Gerbert de Montreuil, predate the inclusion of Christianity. Wager's opera *Parsifal* (1882) was inspired by Wolfram von Eschenbach's 1210 version of the story, *Parzival*, and subsequent Christian variations of the myth culminated in Sir Thomas Malory's classic fifteenth-century Celtic adaptation 'The Nobel Tale of the Sankgreal' in *Le Morte d'Arthur* (1485) (Birch, 2009; Loomis, 1963; Lupack, 2007). The search for the grail (in a variety of forms) and versions of Perceval on screen have been satirised in *Monty Python and the Holy Grail* (dirs. Gilliam and Jones, 1975) and adapted in Terry Gilliam's *The Fisher King* (1991), *Indiana Jones and the Last Crusade* (dir. Spielberg, 1989), *The Da Vinci Code* (dir. Howard, 2006) and the miniseries *Knightfall* (exec. prods. Handfield and Raynor, 2017).

The most basic current outline of the narrative centres on the guardian of the grail, a wounded king – alternatively referred to as the Fisher King or the Fisher King's father – disabled by a sword laceration to the thigh, who remains confined to his mysterious and fantastically opulent castle set in a fertile valley, but doomed to become a wasteland if the king is not healed. His restoration and the prosperity of his land lie in the hands of a knight who is able to enter this mysterious kingdom and ask him two specifically meaningful questions. King Arthur's youngest knight, Perceval, happens across the Fisher King, son of the wounded king, who shelters him in his castle. During supper, when the life preserving grail is presented, Perceval fails to ask his host the appropriate questions – *what afflicts you?* and *who does the grail serve*? When he wakes in the morning the castle and its occupants have disappeared. 'Do you know what will happen if the King does not hold his lands and is not healed of his wounds?' a damsel (Eschenbach's 'Cundrie', an envoy for the grail) asks Perceval. 'Ladies will lose their husbands, lands will be laid waste, maidens, helpless, will remain orphans, and many knights will die. All these calamities will befall because of you' (quoted from Chrétien de Troyes *Der Percevalroman* in Loomis, 1963, p. 40). In Wofram's *Parzival*, Perceval revisits the palace and poses the correct questions to the wounded king. The lands are assured of their fertility with the king's recovery and Perceval becomes Lord of the Grail (Loomis, 1963).

The quest and questions that drive Perceval appear to be more important than the answers. For John-Raphael Staude, Jung's early life taught him the implication of the answer to the question of who the grail serves – the grail serves the Grail King: 'He came to realize that the Grail King is the Self, that centre of our interior castle, that circle whose centre is everywhere and whose circumference is nowhere' (Staude, 1981, p. 38). In a Jungian interpretation, the quest is internalised and the grail can be understood as a uniting element, or transcendent function, that allows for 'a psychic synthesizes of consciousness and the unconscious through which it becomes possible for the psychic totality, the Self, to come into consciousness' (Jung and Von Franz, 1960/1998, p. 156). From this perspective, the grail becomes a metaphor for that which sustains life; that which energises the libido, a term in analytical psychology that refers to *life-force*, which when considering the Freudian use of the word, may include, but is not limited to sexuality (Freud, 1905/1953; Jung, 1956/1967). Emma Jung and Von Franz endow the grail with archetypal qualities and argue that when stripped 'of the personal and viewed as an object, the vessel does not explicitly represent a human reality but rather an idea, a primordial image' (1998, p. 113). Although they rather reductively equate the notion of the 'vessel' with ideas of an archetypal 'feminine', or 'anima', in describing the grail as having a 'numinous character', this sense of the primordial can be applied to the archetypal motif that governs the lost child complex (Jung and Von Franz, 1960/1998, p. 113). We might therefore interpret the symbolism of the grail and the lost child as synonymous – unconscious resources, related to a sense of life-force and repeatedly returned to for sustenance – hence their necessary mystery and association with loss.

> That the vessel is so frequently considered to be life-giving or life-maintaining is readily understandable when we realize how extremely important it must have been . . . to possess a receptacle in which, for instance, water, the stuff of life par excellence, could be transported or stored. According to Jung's definition, the archetype represents innate predispositions to human behavior in certain life situations and the ability to grasp their meaning. The image of the vessel could therefore correspond to such a 'pattern,' to a possibility inherent in the psyche of finding or producing a vessel and of discovering its uses.
>
> *(Jung and Von Franz, 1960/1998, p. 114)*

If the grail directs us to the Self, as an agent of healing, unity and individuation, then, to extend the metaphor, the king in the legend would appear to symbolise a wounded Self in need of healing. Both the grail and the king can therefore be interpreted as elements of the psyche, and the wound might be read as a block to psychological development or an unattended cleavage of oppositions yet to be consciously reconciled or productively transformed into future possibilities. For Linda Cooper, in 'Cormac McCarthy's "The Road" as Apocalyptic Grail Narrative' (2011), 'The salient theme of these contemporary versions of the grail . . . is that of a contest between fertility and sterility, the fertility symbolized by the grail, the object without which the Fisher King will die and the world along with him' (p. 220).

Cooper provides an eloquent framework for understanding the lost child in Australian cinema as a combination of grail, grail-bearer, and in more contemporary narratives, quester of the grail. In working through the grail myth as the root of Cormac McCarty's apocalyptical novel *The Road* (2006), she argues that the young son, struggling for survival with his father, after a non-specific global event – a nuclear or possibly meteor strike that has laid waste much of North America – symbolises both the grail and Perceval. After the boy's mother commits suicide, father and son journey though the American wasteland in search of food and shelter, vigilantly protecting themselves against the threat of cannibalism. The father eventually dies, leaving the young boy to attach himself to other lost children; 'Because early drafts of this novel were titled The Grail, it is clear that McCarthy positioned the novel as a type of grail narrative from the book's genesis. However, while the boy is the symbolic grail of the early draft's title, narrative patterns suggest that he is a Perceval figure as well' (Cooper, 2011, p. 222). In terms of North American victory-driven film narratives, *The Road*, in both its literary and screen version (2009), directed perhaps unsurprisingly by Australian John Hillcoat, suggests some hope for the lost children, but never assures us of their survival. In charting Cooper's argument as it applies to the Australian lost child complex, it is also important to keep in mind that in the Australian storytelling context, victory in the form of conquering loss or reclaiming the lost is not a common outcome. It is more appropriate perhaps to argue that the grail quest is internally and outwardly cyclic – a uroboric questing that is discussed in more depth with the analysis of *Predestination* (Chapter 6).

Cooper equates the boy with Perceval, referring to the emphasis of traditional grail stories 'on the purity of the grail bearer as an essential component of the grail's ability return to humankind' (p. 223). In reading the boy as Perceval she also argues for McCarthy writing into him the qualities of the grail itself, 'while the boy is described as a vessel for divinity many times throughout the novel, those descriptions emphasize the more ephemeral qualities of divinity. In addition to being filled with light, the boy is also the very "word of God" and, elsewhere, the "breath of God"' (p. 225). In situating the child as 'both grail and grail-bearer, vessel and antidote to the world's toxicity' Cooper positions the father as 'the elder Fisher King, wounded and infected by that which is destroying the land' (p. 226).

In terms of the lost child, particularly in narratives focusing on *lost in the bush* themes, we might see the unfamiliar, usually interior, landscapes into which, particularly non-indigenous, children disappear, not as wastelands but as both *fecund and treacherous* environments. The visual backdrop in films such as *Walkabout*, *Picnic at Hanging Rock*, *Evil Angels*, *One Night the Moon* (dir. Rachel Perkins, 2001), *Mystery Road* (dir. Sen, 2013) or *Strangerland* (dir. Farrant, 2015) is often incorporated into the visual narrative as one of, if not the, central character that emerges as both unforgiving and exquisitely beautiful: a source/site of vulnerability and death. Like Chretien de Troyes' version of the grail myth, the wounded king's fertile land and kingdom is in danger of becoming barren should he not recover. While these Australian stories often have either no, or obscurely redemptive conclusions, Cooper reads *The Road's* central child as the grail and the grail seeker/keeper – one who embodies relationship, goodness and futurity;

> Ultimately, the grail is not an object capable of healing the human race of its wickedness; instead, the grail is pictured as a small child walking down a road. The novel thus expresses a deep pessimism regarding humanity's self-destructiveness, but it concurrently proffers an affirmation of the individual's ability to experience a transcendent, and perhaps ultimately redemptive, empathic connection with others.
> *(Cooper, 2011, p. 234)*

In the end, Cooper sees the lost child, endowed by McCarthy with the breath of god, as driven to pursue connection and survival in the midst of destruction, destructiveness and uncertainty. In viewing this inner need for community and human relationship at the ambivalent conclusion of *The Road*, Cooper concludes her analysis by summing up McCarthy's grail journey in a brief closing sentence: 'In a world poisoned by greed, dissociation, and despair, longing may itself be a form of redemption' (p. 234).

Unlike the boy in *The Road*, our lost children carry a less literal but nevertheless tangible sense of the grail and Perceval. McCarthy's lost boy appears to embody the right questions – who does the grail serve? and what ails you? As the grail himself, the boy serves the wounded King (his father) and the wounded world in which he walks, by offering the hope of connection and a sense of unity – the Jungian Self. The Australian twist to our grail quests carry a different kind of redemptive longing. While the lost child, as grail and central focus of the cultural complex, is the subject of intense and passionate searching – with the child as a metaphor for the inner child to whom we return for guidance – our longing for *it*, 'may itself be a form of redemption'. It is possible to argue that we do not ask, or have not articulated, the correct question – whom does the grail/child serve? This book is invested in re-evaluating the lost child as a signifier for the archetypal core of the cultural complex. The child therefore serves us, by compelling us to look inward. Like Perceval, having missed the opportunity to pose the correct question, we can return – as we do again and again – to the king/grail embraced in our lost child stories, reframe the conversation and ask the appropriate questions. In the most recent evolution of lost child cinema, where the child is envisaged as a combination of the searched for object (grail), the searcher (Perceval) and the wounded King – *Oranges and Sunshine*, *Lion* and *Predestination* – it would appear that the narrative is shifting and heading in a more uroboric direction with the child encompassing evermore aspects of cyclic return and discovery.

By concurrently maintaining its mystery, preserving its redemptive qualities, understanding it as central to our identities and now finally recognising its curative potential, the lost child serves both the individual and the culture captured/wounded by the complex. In relation to the grail myth and the many instances of the boy's compassionate nature in *The Road*, drawing on Joseph Campbell (1990) Cooper argues that recognising the right question and directing it toward the appropriate subject, 'indicates a heart that is pure and noble and suggests a spontaneity of affection only possible where there is genuine compassion' (p. 230). She elaborates on the curative potential of the grail/boy, that 'the right questions are those that lead not to the correct answers but to "correct" actions – to behavior consistent with an internalized ethics' (p. 231). It can be argued that the evolving permutations of the lost child as multiple elements of the grail myth encourage audiences to ask more than the right questions. If the child is the healing power in ourselves that we periodically seek, in keeping with the grail myth analogy, a sense of *purity* in this quest, longing, identification and utilisation of the inner child is crucial.

The lost child, the searchers *and* the lost child as searcher

In most Australian lost child cinema when thinking about more literal or physical rather than psychological forms of lostness – the missing, abandoned or abducted – the child at the heart of the narrative is rarely found. Similarly the focal lost child, whether recovered or constituting the heart of the narrative mystery, serves as a referent to other even more lost/traumatised children. In applying the idea of the lost child as multiple elements of the grail myth, our cinema can be further understood as stories told from two, and later three, distinct perspectives: the child itself, those searching for the child and the protagonist as both lost child and searcher.

In the less prolific category of films that take the perspective of the lost child, the children are often recovered or find their way home: a few notable examples are *Walkabout*, *Lost in the Bush* (dir. Dodds, 1973), *Manganinne* (dir. Honey, 1980), *Rabbit Proof Fence*, *Australia* (dir. Luhrmann, 2008), *Hounds of Love* (dir. Young, 2016) and *Looking for Grace* (dir. Brooks, 2015). An exception is the documentary-drama *The Back and Beyond* (dir. Heyer, 1954) – the reenactment of an actual case where two young sisters on a remote homestead vanished in the desert, setting off for help after their mother's death. For Collins and Davis, the 'most poignant moment in this depiction of their story is when the girls cross their own tracks. At this point, the older girl, like us, realizes that they have been travelling in circles' (Collins and Davis, 2004, p. 144). Protecting her little sister while reconciling their fate, the girl doggedly continues, presumably to their deaths. In contrast, *Lost in the Bush*, based the case of the three Duff siblings lost in the Wimmera in 1864 and shot in the Wimmera town of Horsham Western Victoria, all the children were eventually discovered by Aboriginal trackers; a recovery that signposts the anxiety surrounding less fortunate settler children. As a story that epitomises the colonial lost child tradition, the film was created for schools by the Victorian government, suggesting a need to educate and reaffirm the lost child ethos.

The *lost in the bush* scenario is deepened in *Manganinnie* to incorporate a sense of spiritual kinship between a lost colonial child and her indigenous Tasmanian guardian, Manganinne (Mawuyul Yanthalawuy). After her family is murdered by settlers, Manganinnie lures the small girl, Joanna (Anna Ralph), from her family in the hope that this mesmeric child, with her mysteriously symbolic alabaster skin and flaming red hair, will lead her back to her devastated people. After rearing the child in Aboriginal culture and survival skills, Managinnie returns her to her family before dying. Having fulfilled her role as grail-child and in keeping with the indigenous pyre burning of the dead, Joanna, still draped in animal pelts, sets alight the family barn where Manganinnie's body has been laid. As the fire intensifies, Joanna sees shapes dancing with the flames – Manganninie's ancestors returning to claim her. In this act, the child adopts her healing role as grail – restoring and reuniting. The curator's notes on the film, like the majority of lost child films, again draw links between the central characters and the lost that they point to beyond the text. Although the film is not a factual account of Truganini, one of the last and most prominent indigenous Tasmanians, he notes that, 'this gentle and visually stunning film reminds us of events which led to the end of the full-blood Palawa line in 1876 with the death of Trugernanner (Truganini)' (Kuipers, 2018).

Collins and Davis, in their chapter 'Lost, Stolen and Found in *Rabbit Proof Fence*', briefly discuss Roeg's *Walkabout*, a film centring on two British schoolchildren abandoned in the desert and rescued by an Aboriginal boy, who is later found dead – draped from a tree. As with nearly all lost child films, the central characters highlight the even more deeply lost: 'As others, including Pierce and Dermody, suggest, the Aboriginal boy is the true lost child of this film. For in the logic of this narrative, there is no place for Aboriginal people in modernity other than as subject of a European romantic longing for an ideal primitive past' (2004, p. 143). In *Rabbit Proof Fence*, the factually based story of three indigenous sisters abducted under a government programme to raise 'mixed-blood' children in designated native settlements, the children escape and retrace the route to their mother via a rabbit proof fence. The two surviving girls, one having been recaptured, even though found, refer us back to other children taken from their families, and the stolen generations of Aboriginal children discussed in Chapter 4 (see Collins and Davis, 2004). In Luhrmann's *Australia*, although the focal Aboriginal child Nullah (Brandon Walters) is eventually taken by authorities and subsequently rescued, he refers us to the thousands of unrecovered stolen children captured from their families under ruthless policies that continued into the early 1980s. *Hounds of Love* is based on the notorious case of the Perth serial killers David and Catherine Birnie arrested after their final abductee, a young teenager, escapes to testify her ordeal. The rescued girl Viki (Ashleigh Cummings) and the notoriety of the actual case thirty years earlier involving four previously murdered victims, one a fifteen-year-old child, is another example of lead characters referring us back to the irretrievably lost. *Mystery Road*, a narrative tracing the last hours of a murdered indigenous teenager, reveals a string of abused and murdered girls in a small outback community.

This common theme in lost child films, where the central retrieved/surviving child characters suggest deeper loss on a larger scale, other lost children in the text, or traces of the lost child in more mature characters, like the naive and somewhat emotionally callow parents of the missing and returned Grace (Odessa Young) in *Looking for Grace*, suggests that we are almost compelled (perhaps directed by the complex) to repeatedly acknowledge the omnipresence of lost children, their grail-like mystique and ultimately their *unfound* nature: as Froud writes, 'The figure of the child is at once ever-present and instantly retrievable, in memory at least, but simultaneously lost forever: the child who haunts history and our self' (Froud, 2017, p. 119).

The searchers

In films that follow the searchers, rather than the lost child her/himself, audiences are not privy to the child's perspective. The child is rarely recovered. It is a grail romance without the object of the quest ever being claimed, and the notion of a Perceval-like protagonist acting as the hero, along the lines of Vogler's inspired twelve-step 'hero's journey' scriptwriting model, is either removed entirely, or when seemingly identified, ultimately thwarted. Lostness in these screen texts also takes the form of those at the heart of the search, and/or the parents of the missing child who we come to discover are emotionally lost, disoriented and/or abandoned. The most noted in this category is Peter Weir's iconic *Picnic at Hanging Rock* (1975), an adaptation of Joan Lindsay's 1967 novel set in 1900 and held in the cultural imagination for its romantic reworking of the *lost in the bush* theme, its stylised imagery, musical score, sexual undercurrents, play with the temporal and metaphysical and the launching of Weir's international career. The subject of critical analysis since its release, the film tells of three adolescent Victorian schoolgirls, with the angelically constructed Miranda (Anne-Louise Lambert) the most enigmatic, and their mathematics teacher who vanish after climbing Hanging Rock in Victoria's Macdeon ranges during a Valentine's day school excursion. Although one of the girls is discovered unconscious, the teacher and the remaining two students are never found.

The story has recently been adapted for theatre by playwright Tom Wright, in a Malthouse/Black Swan State Theatre Company co-production with theatrical runs in Australia (2016–2018), Edinburgh at the Royal Lyceum Theatre (2017) and London (2018) with the Barbican couching the publicity in terms suggestive of the cultural complex: 'Retelling this classic tale, which has haunted the Australian psyche for years, fires the darkest reaches of the imagination' (Barbican Centre, 2018). The play has also been chosen for the 2018 Victorian Certificate of Education (graduating secondary school year), Theatre Studies Playlist. Having built momentum with theatrical adaptations, FremantleMedia Australia produced a miniseries based on the original story with exteriors shot on location at Hanging Rock. The series screened on the cable network Foxtel after previewing at the 2018 Berlin Film Festival.

For Pierce, the film and novel want 'the human dimension of the lost child story to be reduced to a puzzle without an answer', and the mysterious disappearance of the girls to symbolise 'the anxious suspicion that Europeans do not belong in this country; that therefore they should go back to England, or escape into another time, or simply vanish' (1999, p. 164). This idea of settler disappearances as a symbolic form of retaliation by the land and its liminal energies is further explored by Michael Bliss as he considers the fate, not only of the girls but the headmistress Mrs Appleyard (Rachel Roberts), who after expressing her personal losses and fears of financial ruin to a fellow staff member, is found at the base of the rock – a presumed suicide:

> What appear to be violent and disturbing events in the director's films (e.g., the disappearance of the girls in *Picnic*) actually represent an attempt on the part of natural forces to reestablish a sense of order. Read in this way, the film's denouncement, with Mrs Appleyard dead and the school (presumably) disbanded, becomes a return to normalcy.
>
> *(Bliss, 2000, p. 48)*

Bliss reads the film as not only a disruption and return to the natural order of the land, but also as an imposition of 'mathematical precision, order, and rationality', that like the ego in Jung's thinking, cannot sustain a sense of supremacy over unconscious forces (p. 50). The school is constructed as a symbol of British imperialism and Victorian inflexibility with its draconian curriculum, austere regimes and emotional repression. The character of Miranda, who seems to rise above this artificiality, is constructed as a grail-like figure; a beacon for the other girls and later those involved in the search. Often shot as if glowing with her long blond hair and pale face highlighted by the sun and the landscape, she is likened in the film to 'a Botticelli angel': ethereal and atemporal, an element of the unconscious, carrying an intuitive sense of wisdom and foresight – an archetypal lost child who all wish returned to them. Miranda becomes the pivot for intricate networks of loss and grief in the film. For Bliss, her summation of life and her disappearance as 'a dream within a dream' is a state that 'does not represent to her a condition of anxious unreality but one of super-reality that makes the empirical world seem pale by comparison' (p. 57). Like Joanna in Manganinnie, Miranda appears to have a spiritual kinship with the land and its ancestors. The monolithic rocks she slips between and eventually come to *claim* her are frequently captured in upward shots where they are transformed into timelessness and sacred faces.

From a more sociological and historical perspective, the *Miranda Must Go* campaign influencing the screen remix or mash-up *Terror Nullius* (2018) by the art collective duo Soda_Jerk, advocates that the idea of *Picnic at Hanging Rock* as a literary text and iconic feature film creates a white and therefore racist sense of cultural memory/story about *lost in the bush* mythology. The campaign argues on their website *Miranda Must Go* (2018), that actual Aboriginal deaths and losses in the Macedon area have been both unacknowledged and replaced by a myth of white vanishing: 'The region in which Hanging Rock is located, like the rest of Victoria and Australia, was settled by European invaders who through introduced diseases, violence and forced occupation, killed or displaced the original Aboriginal inhabitants'. They ask, 'Whose absences matter?' and also remind us that the site, traditionally of the Kulin Nation, is of deep significance to 'the Wurundjeri, Taungurong and Djadja Wurrung' (*Miranda Must Go Campaign*, 2018). While this activism is culturally relevant and justified, we might also consider *not* vanquishing Miranda, but mobilising her as both a referent for the more deeply lost and a figure, of-and-not-of colonial culture. With a similar fascination for the landscape as Joanna expressed in *Manganinnie*, the toddler Emily in *One Night the Moon* was so enchanted by the full moon that she wandered from the family home. Set in 1932, her father refused to allow Aboriginal men onto his land, despite police providing him with their best tracker who eventually recovered her broken body with the help of the child's mother. These lost children serve as conduits or psychopomps, able to bridge indigenous and non-indigenous worlds; their Perceval-like purity allowing for a transcendence of their imperialist heritage. Like *Picnic*, *One Night the Moon* became a multiplatform event – a musical film with a spin off soundtrack that was adapted for the stage (Melbourne's Malthouse Theatre) in 2009.

This idea of grail-like purity is also captured in the next most prolific *lost in the bush* film, Fred Schepisi's *A Cry in the Dark* also known as *Evil Angels*. The film was preceded by the telemovie *The Disappearance of Azaria Chamberlain* (dir, Thornhill, 1984) and John Bryson's book *Evil Angels* (1985). In a similar fashion to *Picnic at Hanging Rock*, the film was followed by the staged opera *Lindy* (Henderson, 2002) and the miniseries *Through My Eyes* (creators Cavanaugh and North, 2004). An interpretation of the actual disappearance of infant Azaria Chamberlain at Uluru (Ayers Rock), Schepisi's version reproaches the vitriolic Australian public and in particular the media, who at the time doubted the innocence of Azaria's Seven-Day Adventist Church parents, particularly her mother, Lindy, in the disappearance. Camping at the base of the rock with their two children and nine-week-old daughter, the Chamberlains left the tent where the baby was kept unattended for a brief period of time. This was enough for a tourist-acclimatised dingo (wild dog) to carry the infant off into the bush. The search for the child and the source of her disappearance became a national obsession. While Azaria's remains were never found, her then pregnant mother was imprisoned in 1982 for murder and six years later the conviction was overturned by the Northern Territory Court of Criminal Appeal. The case shifted from a national obsession, to a nationally shameful miscarriage of justice.

In Schepisi's shaming of Lindy's accusers for their prejudice of religious practices and the Chamberlain's non-media savvy expressions of grief and trauma, the infant at the centre of the drama ultimately became a grail-like symbol, guiding a sense of public tolerance and acceptance. For Pierce, in his lost child study, the film also addresses the lostness of the infant Lindy delivered while in Berrimah gaol (Darwin, Northern Territory); 'A guard tells her that "she's yours to hold for one hour, but that's all I'm afraid"' (p. 178). One senses from the film, its multimedia spin-offs, the actual case and its aftermath for the Chamberlains, that Lindy herself, the woman beneath the public show of composure and strength of religious conviction throughout the ordeal, was perhaps ultimately the most displaced. We see this idea of the lost child's mother not only as lost herself, but also as a lost child in the films *Looking for Grace* and Farrant's *Strangerland* where Catherine's (Nicole Kidman) adolescent children wander into the desert from their rural home. Only one returns while the other is presumed to have taken a lift in an unknown car. The narrative follows Catherine and her husband Matthew's (Joseph Fiennes) search before turning inward on Catherine's own inner lost child.

Lion – *lost/searcher synthesis*

While Pierce, Davis and Collins have drawn attention to more pivotal pre-2004 lost child texts mentioned above, the latest to be added to this influential list is Garth Davis' 2016 biopic *Lion*. The film was adapted from Saroo Brierley's 2013 memoir *A Long Way Home* – a story that retraced how he became separated from his Indian family at five years old, his journey through the streets of Calcutta, subsequent adoption by a Tasmanian couple, and the quest, via Google Earth, for his birth mother and siblings. In this narrative, like *Predestination* and *Oranges and Sunshine* touched on in Chapter 4, the central character is a synthesis of lost child and searcher, both lost and found, both Perceval and the grail. These contemporary versions of the lost child talk more to the cultural complex and its fundamental archetypal core. Here the lost child, while developed/amplified physically into an actual character, is also clearly understood as an internal aspect of the self that one needs to both locate and liberate, with this return and emancipation forming the therapeutically cyclic pattern discussed by Hillman in his analysis of the orphan archetype (1975/1991). *Lion* may well have been placed in Chapter 6 alongside the discussion of *Predestination*. Both texts adopt the child and searcher's perspective in one character, but *Lion* aligns itself more directly with the *lost in the bush* and grail narratives, where the raw physicality of a lost struggling child is juxtaposed with the archetypal lost child as both a driver of potential healing and individuation.

A product of Screen Australia, The Weinstein Company, See-Saw films, Aquarius films and Sunstar Entertainment, *Lion* begins with aerial shots of the lush Tasmanian coastline merging into the rugged topography of rural India before honing in on Khandwa where the story of Saroo's early life begins. For Tara Judah 'Moving across epic spaces with ease, *Lion* also tells the story of psycho-geographical proportions, whereby the weight of one person's experiences is set against the Earth's grandeur' (2017, p. 8). This capture of the Australian landscape as a pivotal character in itself is central to classic *lost in the bush* cinema, whether the setting is actually the rural inland or landscapes cinematically likened to a similar sense of beauty, expanse, atemporality and awe. There is always the sense that *we* are the uninvited who, rather than conquering the land, as in settlement myths, are merely observers, trying to navigate and orient ourselves.

Davis follows the five-year-old Saroo (Sunny Pawar), as he wanders from his poor rural home one night to follow his older brother Gaddu (Abhishek Bharate) who makes money by lifting heavy bales from trains. Saroo, though, falls asleep at the railway station; waking to find himself alone and his bother gone, he climbs onto a stationary train looking for Gaddu and eventually falls asleep. When he wakes he has travelled 1,600 kilometres East of Khandwa, to Calcutta in West Bengal. Speaking only Hindi rather than Calcutta's Bengali, Saroo navigates the streets of Calcutta in an attempt to return to his mother and brother. He escapes one dangerous situation after another, acting as a referent for the street children he meets who have not been as artful in avoiding paedophile networks that lure homeless children, and corrupt and sexually brutal guards at orphanages where hundreds of 'rescued' children are housed. Throughout his ordeal in India, before being adopted by John and Sue Brierley (David Wenham and Nicole Kidman) in Tasmania, Pawar, as Saroo, is captured on film as an adorable innocent, lost yet resilient and resourceful in his quest. Here, as later in adulthood, he becomes the searcher – a Perceval character – as well as the literal lost child as subject, then later, object of the film.

When we move to the adult Saroo (Dev Patel) twenty-five years later, the younger Saroo is fashioned as a grail-like memory and his increasingly isolated and tormented adult self becomes a mixture of Perceval and the ailing Fisher King. While the adult Saroo's anxious quest is ostensibly focused on finding his birth family by tracing memories of Indian landmarks and train speeds to create a search radius via Google Earth, it is also clear, with the interlocking flashbacks of himself as a child, that he is searching for identity and belonging. The historical child becomes internalised as an elixir – a healing memory, archetypal projection and grail. Not only is the little Saroo a balm for his adult self, but also a grail-like figure for his adoptive mother who like the mothers mentioned above and further developed in Chapter 5, becomes a poignant example of both the inner lost child and the wounded Fisher King.

We first see the adult Saroo, as Patel emerges from the surf, shot against the waves and sun – the 'beautiful boy' as his mother Sue describes him. Later in the film during his restless quest and self-imposed isolation, he returns to his mother, now lonely and saddened by his abandonment and the self-harming and aggressive behaviour, suggestive of childhood trauma, of her second adopted Indian son, Mantosh (Divian Ladwa). In explaining her decision to adopt, Sue tells Saroo of a time when she was twelve years old, living a troubled life with her alcoholic father – 'he wasn't a good man' she says, 'he was out of control'. She remembers standing near her house looking into a nearby field and having a vision of a 'brown skinned child' beside her – 'for the first time in my life I felt something good, I knew it was guiding me and I knew it was going to be fine. It was as if at that moment I could see my future'. In discussing Cooper's analysis of *The Road* as grail story, it was argued that unlike Perceval, Australian lost child/grail stories are not quite at the developmental point of identifying who the grail/child serves. In understanding that the lost child/grail/archetypal core of the complex potentially *serves us* on an individual and collective level, urging us to look inward, we might argue that through the characters of Saroo and Sue, *Lion* is aligned with this purpose. Perhaps even more explicitly than *Oranges and Sunshine* or *Predestination*, director Garth Davis has validated the lost child as a guiding image. The unprecedented decision by the Australian Academy of Cinema and Television Arts' (AACTA) to award (then) nine-year-old Sunny Pawar with 'Best Lead Actor', suggests not only the skill of Pawar's performance as Saroo, but possibly his ability to carry the depth of the archetypal projection. Simon Burke at fifteen years old was the second youngest performer to receive an award in this category for also playing a displaced child in Schepisi's *The Devil's Playground* (1976) – a boy not physically lost, but struggling to free himself from sexually repressive seminary training.

At the BAFTA (British Academy of Film and Television Arts) awards, Dev Patel won Best Supporting Actor for *Lion*. The film garnered twelve 2017 AACTA awards, including Best Film, Best Direction, Best Lead Actor and Best Supporting Male and Female Actors (Nicole Kidman and Dev Patel). The same year Emma Booth won for Best Actress in a film, playing the serial murderer in another lost child film of 2017, *Hounds of Love*. The same year Nicole Kidman also won Best Guest or Supporting Actress for *Top of the Lake: China Girl* (dirs. Campion, Davis and Kleiman, 2017) and Hugo Weaving took Best Lead Actor for *Seven Types of Ambiguity* (Ivin, Kokkinos and Saville 2017) – both miniseries revolved around missing children. As of May 2017, *Lion* was the highest grossing Australian box office Australian film in 2017 taking $29,545,626.00; it was overshadowed only by *Crocodile Dundee* (dir. Faiman, 1986) $47,707,045.00, *Australia* $37,555,757.00, *Babe* (dir. Noonan, 1995) $36,776,757.00 and *Happy Feet* (dir. Miller, 2006) $31,786,164.00, with *Australia* and *Babe* seminal Australian films that centralised the lost child (Screen Australia, 2018).

The sheer volume of Australian films dedicated to the lost child, similarly themed television productions not discussed in depth here and the multimedia evolution of texts such as *Picnic at Hanging Rock*, *One Night the Moon* and *Evil Angels*, demonstrates the ongoing necessity to revisit and reinforce the archetype. As the core of the cultural complex, intensified through cinema and projected in our storytelling as actual children, the lost child is central to the formation of identities within Australia and on the global stage; suggested most recently with *Lion's* six academy award nominations. In a less geographically bound assessment, Froud sees the lost child as symbolic of a 'simultaneous mortality and immortality. The effect on the individual and society disrupts established identities but also encapsulates images of our past and visions of possible futures: a snapshot and also a "negative"' (p. 125). This idea of a 'negative' also applies to the ghostly internal lost child and its various screen manifestations/projections.

This chapter has framed notions of lost child trauma (Collins and Davis) and quest narratives (Dermody) into a more specific grail-oriented framework, with the child, as in Cooper's analysis of *The Road*, as both grail (the searched for subject/object/healing element) and Perceval (the searcher and eventual guardian of the grail/child). After a history of films from the missing child and the searchers perspective, with the outcome of *rescued* and *irredeemably lost* respectively aligned to each category, what we are now seeing appears to be films that embrace both viewpoints, and in doing this they position the child as an internal grail: the core of a complex that we, as a culture, periodically mobilise as a way of responding to the question of who the lost child serves. Talking to ourselves in this way through the arts, by returning, massaging and rechannelling the motif, suggests a developing awareness that this pivotal lost child serves an entwined group identity that can be allegorically thought of as a mixture of wounded king, Perceval and grail.

3
CELEBRATING DEFEAT
The blooded child of war and sport

A significant aspect of the lost child complex in Australia relates to the way heroism has historically and culturally been understood as an uncomfortable fusion of youth, defeat, sacrifice and loss. The complex takes a decisively collective hold when looking at the nation's nostalgic and contemporary relationship to war, whether from a pacifist perspective or a more politically aggressive stance based on the propagandistic idea that nationhood could only have been achieved through the 'blooding' of young men. Many who enlisted in both world wars were little more than adolescents killed and wounded in countries other than their own at the bidding of the then British Empire and later North America. Like colonisation, heroism that was historically built on the defeat of military recruits is an aspect of the lost child complex that like more traditionally constructed histories of lost innocents, emerges from collective trauma. While it might seem a stretch to focus on the 'glorious dead' – a term inscribed on plaques in Victoria's Shrine of Remembrance to commemorate and immortalise fallen soldiers – I would argue that these men, or 'our boys over there' as they were affectionately known, clearly carry the archetypal symbolism of the displaced child. This is patently demonstrated in Australian war cinema with its almost uniform concentration on the sacrifice of naïve youth in offshore campaigns. The dead and critically wounded in foreign and unfamiliar battlefields serve as stark reminders of the disillusion that must have been felt by boys who thought that manhood was a gift of war. Before looking at the more formative films in this branch of lost child cinema, it is important to contextualise Australia's relationship to the history of war as a way of understanding its centrality to the complex. In highlighting the interconnectedness of heroism and defeat, it is also necessary to discuss the close cultural and screen associations between war and sport: two arenas of competition that share a focus on youth, nationalism and for some, irreconcilable loss.

Nationhood built on war and loss

As Marilyn Lake and Henry Reynolds (2010) suggest, Australia's sense of nationhood has been disproportionately built on the Australian and New Zealand Army Corps (ANZAC) legend of overwhelming defeat and suffering. The slaughter of Australians during the 1915 Gallipoli campaign in Turkey (8,709 men killed) is now memorialised as a public holiday (April 25) with simultaneously televised dawn services and/or parades in each state (Australian War memorial, 2018c). Veterans and lost heroes of the first and second world wars, and the Vietnam, Korean, Iraq and Afghanistan campaigns, are rolled into Anzac Day commemorations, but always with the Gallipoli defeat as its centrepiece – a failed British instigated assault on Turkish forces. The increasingly commercialised site of the massacre, the Gallipoli Peninsula (Gaba Tepe, referred to as Anzac Cove), caters to school groups and tourists who take the pilgrimage each year. In a similar sense of memorialisation and adventure, the Kokoda trail in Papua New Guinea, a notorious stretch of tropical jungle where Australian servicemen fought the Japanese (1942), has also become a tourist experience. Film and television didn't popularly embrace these and future military losses until the 1970–1980s New Wave, which took its cue from theatre productions like the controversial anti-Anzac celebrations *One Day of the Year* first performed in 1960 (Seymour, 1962) and the trauma induced xenophobia of World War II veterans in *The Floating World* premiering in 1974 (Romeril, 1975). No matter how earnestly popular culture attempted to address the futility of war through the arts, the collective attachment to heroic death and defeat outshone the political comments on Australia's British, now North American, 'poodle' status when it comes to military engagement.

The tall poppy syndrome and defeat as heroism

The symbiotic nature of lostness and defeat, particularly when represented and celebrated in popular culture, can be connected to a particular Australian marker of worthiness: a tendency to call out seemingly unwarranted group or individual adulation – *the tall poppy syndrome* (TTPS). The advent of social media and the selfie obsession, where self-promotion, self-celebration and the Wohol initiated entitlement to fifteen minutes of fame, somewhat undermines, but also ironically preserves, the egalitarian basis for TTPS. And yet, Australians are still known for celebrating defeat and cutting down high achievers characterised as non-deserving to a far greater degree than they celebrate the kind of heroism or celebrity born of unscrutinised success, embedded in the victory/winning complex that appears to drive North American culture. One might even suggest that an unexpected manifestation of TTPS swept North America in the 2016 presidential election of Donald Trump as a way of cutting down perceived elitist liberals and more pro-liberal focused news outlets. Yet in direct contradiction, Trump voters propelled a 'winning', driven, inexperienced, skittish and relentlessly self-aggrandising multimillionaire to power. Generally speaking, it would seem that Americans do not share the egalitarian sensibility of Australians, despite this nod toward TTPS. Through a seemingly irrational relationship to the promise offered by *American Dream* thinking and the victory complex (Chapter 7), TTPS doesn't seem to be as rooted in the US cultural psyche as it is in Australia. To try and understand the factors that contributed to this suspicion of self-promotion, as well as the attraction of loss and defeat, it is worth tracing the history of TTPS.

N. T. Feather dates the origin of the syndrome to the elder Tarquinius, the last king of Rome (535–509 BC). In a lesson to his son Sextus Tarquinius, he equated the clipping of robust poppies in his garden, to cutting down (or back) the competition to realise and maintain power (Feather, 1994, p. 2). The metaphor shifted from trying to explain how power might be preserved, to a way of perceiving unwarranted glorification. The media further drove this practice that is not unique to Australia, but culturally exercised often against Australians themselves – whether residents or ex-pats working abroad. From a linguistic perspective, Peeters sees the tall poppy as a 'key word' – words/phrases that have cultural resonance – 'which, when studied closely in terms of its currency, its incidence in collections, etc., reveals a great deal about the real nature of egalitarianism, one of Australia's often named cultural values' (Peeters, 2004, p. 1). He argues that TTPS in the early twentieth century referred largely to staff that businesses saw as more viable to retrench because of their high wage bracket, but is now directed at those considered socially successful, 'who, for one reason or another, are deemed not to deserve the respect that they no doubt, think they do deserve' (Peeters, 2004, p. 8).

Perhaps the most significant link for this chapter is the syndrome's connection to the Flanders Poppy of the first world war; manufactured mementoes worn on Remembrance Day and Australia's Anzac Day, that according to Richard Ely, have 'come to symbolize the warrior cut down in a good cause, and so could be easily extended as a symbol of hero-martyrs' (Ely, 1984, p. 105, quoted in Peeters, 2004). The idea of cutting inflated individuals down to size and the cut down (expendable perhaps) war martyr, have an odd synergy: one seemingly deserving of demotion, the other an unwitting victim, yet both lost, defeated and therefore, in an odd Australian twist, heroic.

In her work on the historic Australian lost child, Torney refers the image and associated cultural and personal emotions attached to the defeated war dead, back to the ubiquitous nature of the lost child:

> The mystique of the disappeared or the young dead applied to both explorers and lost children, in the same way that the dead of World War One came to be remembered – 'They shall not grow old, as we that are left grow old:/ Age shall not weary them, nor the years condemn,' asserted Laurence Binyon in For the Fallen, words recited still at every Anzac day service.
>
> *(Torney, 2005, p. 224)*

This raises another important aspect of Australian culture more generally. The concept of youth, abiding in the state of youth, and immortalising the young via early death, have become problematic tropes deep in Australian culture that seem indicative of the complex. Peter Dodds McCormick's 1878 lyrics and music *Advance Australia Fair*, adopted and tweaked as the national anthem in 1984, works to impose a self-concept of eternal youth, with the words 'sons' replaced by 'all' – 'Australian's all let us rejoice for we are young and free'. This romanticism of liberty and becoming is also accompanied, in a rarely sung final verse, to a now much challenged umbilical relationship to England: 'Britannia then shall surely know, Beyond wide ocean's roll, Her sons in fair Australia's land Still keep a British soul' (McCormick, 1944). Those immortalised or frozen in youth on the battlefield and those lost in the bush remain young and become free in death, joining them with contemporary Australians who are called by the national anthem to superficially imagine themselves as youthful. But something more unconscious than nationalistic is going on here. The very archetypal nature of the lost child that links a culturally imposed sense of identity with something deeper, trauma related and interwoven in personal and collective consciousness, arguably fosters a need to return to the inner child as a means of understanding vulnerability and facilitating a sense of healing.

Positioning the nation as a child or adolescent, needing a formative rite of passage to propel it into adulthood, Reynolds notes that World War I was framed and celebrated as a test of both manhood and nationhood.

> The *Sydney Morning Herald*, declared that the nation had cast on one side the ideas and ideals of adolescence and 'assumed the serious responsibilities of Man's estate'. The Hobart *Mercury* was similarly convinced that at Gallipoli, Australia 'had taken up the duties of manhood'. Australians had become a 'blood brotherhood in the best sense'.
>
> *(Lake et al., 2010, p. 30)*

Becoming then was embodied in the youthful soldier who would presumably be tested and 'found' through war, as would the nation itself. Ironically, this figure achieved the greatest cultural capital in defeat and death, when one considers the industries, memorials, commemorations and artistic works – photographs, cinema, television, literature – depicting, and dedicated to, the nostalgia of martyrdom. Rather than a symbol of manhood, the blood brothers of Gallipoli and ensuing campaigns became symbols/images of the lost child. As Torney writes of cartoons produced to symbolise the nation, the figure of the child played an important role in signalling the maturation of the country:

> Initially used to represent Australia's patriotic support of England and the Empire, the image of the boy grew and evolved over the next thirty years, achieving manhood at Gallipoli. He came to represent the healthy self-sufficiency of the colonial 'child' from its 'parent' England.
>
> *(Torney, 2005, p. 37)*

Given the repeated homage to defeat, the colonial child seems not to have gown to manhood through war, as early film and media related marketing at the time suggests, but remained caught in an intricate internal struggle with separation, abandonment and misplaced parental loyalty. Australian New Wave and Post New Wave cinema managed to link an internally intricate sense of separation anxiety from the UK and the need to be initiated through war, with the romanticism and related heroism of loss: death, emotional numbness and/or post-traumatic syndromes.

The glorious dead on screen

In *Celluloid Anzacs: The Great War Through Australian Cinema* (2007), Daniel Reynaud acknowledges the myriad of social and media related influences contributing to Anzac-centred cinema; 'press, live theatre, Government propaganda, foreign war films, war memorials and monuments, and the oral histories of . . . returned soldiers' (p. 2). From 1915, argues Reynaud, early Australian war cinema was utilised as a government vehicle for recruitment during this non-conscription period, with short and feature films such as *Will They Never Come?* (dir. Rolfe, 1915), *Hero of the Dardanelles* (dir. Rolfe, 1915), *For Australia* (dir. Luke, 1915), *Murphy of the Anzac* (dir. Mathews, 1916) and *The Spirit of Gallipoli* (dir. Gategood, 1928) promoting the concept of the returned war-wounded soldier as the lionised hero responsible for birthing the nation. Despite political assistance in releasing these films, the realities of the physical and psychological wounds of returned and imprisoned soldiers (eventually numbering 156,000), and what would amount to 60,000 deaths in action from a population of only 416,809 enlisted men during this campaign, defused the propagandistic romanticism of the Anzac hero (Australian War Memorial, 2018d).

With disillusionment came the shift in focus from the war hero as middle and upper-class, to a figure embracing the working classes and the 'bush' forged mateship of earlier cultural mythologies (Reynaud, 2007). This everyman soldier, or every-boy turned man through the baptism of war, was a dominant theme in the limited cinema made during World War II, which included *Forty Thousand Horsemen* (dir. Chauvel, 1940) and *The Rats of Tobruk* (dir. Chauvel, 1944). The term *digger*, meaning soldier, already in circulation but most likely popularised after the Gallipoli campaign of trench warfare and defeat, was now synonymous with the national Anzac legend. During this early period of Australian war cinema, representations of the lost child are clearly absent. The notion of bush-boys made men through battle is a thematic constant, but because of the governmental censorship that dominated the release of war films during these periods of military engagement, any taint of defeat or irreconcilable loss was considered problematic. This is not to say that the cultural complex was inactive during this period, in fact it would likely have been at its peak, but cultural projections of the archetype appear to have been aggressively suppressed. It wasn't until the advent of conscription in 1965, and the Vietnam war, when compulsory national service (previously limited to Australia and the South-West pacific) was extended to include international service, that our war films took a more critical and cynical turn (Australian War Memorial, 2018b).

The concept of war heroism on screen in the 1970s to the present day is combined with an acknowledgement of the futility of war, highlighted particularly during the Vietnam campaign and applied to depictions of Australia's military involvement from the Boer war on. *The Odd Angry Shot* (dir. Jeffrey, 1979), based on the semi-autobiography of William Nagle's deployment to South Vietnam in the 1960s, is an example of the kind of cynicism that challenges the notion of heroism as lostness and failure. The play *One Day of the Year*, an attack on the national sacredness of Anzac Day celebrations and the seemingly alcohol-fuelled commemoration of those fallen in war, was first banned in 1960 and two years later reworked for television by director Rod Kinnear and producer John Sumner (Lake et al., 2010, p. 86). The approaching Vietnam years saw a significant twist in thinking about how heroism should be honoured and how Australian culture needed to reshape itself; 'Rather than feting the returned soldiers as heroes, students mocked them as relics from a past they wished to leave behind' (Lake et al., 2010, p. 84). With this sentiment, strengthened by Vietnam losses, *The Odd Angry Shot* concentrated on the tedium and futility of the Vietnam campaign through a group of men bound by mateship and political naivety.

Through a self-conscious telegraphing of egalitarianism, the core principle of male bonding and the making of heroes on screen, the film positions the average soldier as working class, economically struggling and ultimately fodder for the military elite. Yet, while cynicism pervades the narrative and one might distil some heroism in the characters' eventual acknowledgement of their doomed campaign, they show no sympathy or understanding for the plight of the Viet Cong; all are seemingly duped by the propaganda of Washington. One might also expect a more disillusioned reaction to the American soldiers that the lead characters befriended, but this turns into another form of mateship. The eventual bonding of the Australians and Americans points to the actual future relationship of these two countries and mirrors the pull of 'Empire'; a relationship that recognises Australia's unflagging need for a parental energy that assuages an ever present fear of abandonment and consequentially, lostness (see Gyngell, 2017). *The Odd Angry Shot's* two returned soldiers sipping beers in the returned soldiers' club while taking in sea views convey a sense of coldness and detachment from their time in service; a palpable numbness at the futile waste of mates killed in action.

The notion of being blooded to manhood/nationhood – responding to the call of 'Empire' propaganda and heroism through adventure in a foreign country, much like – the unfamiliar outback coalesces in perhaps the most formative of Australian war stories, Peter Weir's *Gallipoli* with Mel Gibson as the young, sceptical Frank and Mark Lee as the underage and vulnerable Archie. Both actors exuded the sense of youth, mateship, innocence, egalitarianism, desire for adventure and eventual martyrdom that continues to frame the Anzac legend:

> New social histories such as Bill Gammage's fine study *The Broken Years* (1974) and Patsy Adam-Smith's popular *The Anzacs* (1978), drawing on

soldiers' diaries and letters, paved the way. In particular they would play a crucial role in establishing the innocent young soldier as the face of Anzac, the beautiful boys in the film Gallipoli, Archie and Frank, replacing the reactionary visage of Bruce Ruxton, the omnipresent and vociferous president of the Victorian branch of the RSL [Returned Soldier's League].
(Lake et al., 2010, p. 21)

One of the most popular films of the New Wave, and a seeming influence for Russell Crow's critically received Anzac drama *The Water Diviner* (2014), *Gallipoli* embraces the concepts of separation anxiety, blooding through war as a rite of passage in a personal and collective sense, and the political propaganda tying Australia's future to the survival of the motherland. With each of Britain's colonies under the commonwealth playing the role of abandoned child, eager to please a distant or not entirely good-enough parent, Australia was one of the most enthusiastic of the siblings to demonstrate an over-zealous, and as *Gallipoli* is at pains to suggest, blind and one-sided devotion.

In the 1980s the sentiment had shifted from the intense Vietnam years to a more reflective view of our foreign policy involvement in global warfare. Not only was the futility of various campaigns significant, but also a mixture of separation anxiety that fed into the push for loyalty to Empire, and a blaming and shaming of neglect took central narrative focus. Direct and implied accusations of the British not merely abandoning *her* Australian children, but sacrificing them on the Gallipoli Peninsula like 'the fodder' metaphor in the *Odd Angry Shot*, was portrayed in cinema as an incompetent show of leadership, entitlement and neglect. As Mark McKenna argues, *Gallipoli* along with Australian New Wave films like *Breaker Morant* (dir. Beresford, 1980) and *The Lighthorseman* (dir. Wincer, 1987), were structured around war narratives that pitched the once unquestionable British Empire as the shadowy other, 'reduced to the stereotype of the pompous Pom' (Lake et al., 2010, p. 117); for Torney, 'In the popular renderings of the Anzac story the young Australian soldiers were seen as victims of British military incompetence and callousness. Stories of bravery, stoicism and suffering at Gallipoli and on the Western Front were told as stories of nation-building' (p. 224).

Gallipoli, looks historically, if selectively, to an unquestioning loyalty to Britain, but also injects a more contemporary 1980s pacifist sentiment. Gibson's character Frank becomes the voice of reason over propaganda: 'It's an English war, it's got nothing to do with us' he says. One might argue that Frank eventually enlists in the infantry because of his friendship, or possibly attraction, to the impressionable and younger Archie who is drawn to the glamorous light horse regiment. The relationship between 'the beautiful boys' as Lake refers to the two protagonists, can again be related to the lost child complex. Archie represents all the beautiful boys of both world wars, taken from cities and small towns around Australia who died in the battlefields of Europe and Asia: young and impressionable – drawn to adventure, exotic places and the unknown, with the same romanticism as the lost children of colonial literature and *lost in the bush* cinema – captivated by a seductive and ruthless landscape.

Frank's attraction to Archie's wide-eyed, lost child commitment seems more understandable when viewed through the lens of the complex. It is as if Frank is not only drawn in by the archetypal energy Archie exudes, despite his conscious wariness of it, but he is also drawn to protecting it as an inner sanctuary for both of them. Despite his brotherly, verging on parental claims to Archie, Frank is unable to curb the inevitability of Archie's death on the battlefield – pumped with adrenaline he runs suicidally over the allied trench into a volley of Turkish bullets. It is Archie's blind obedience, in contrast to Frank's determination as a runner for the commanding officers in the rabbit warren of trenches at Gallipoli to avert the final command, that sends Archie over the trench into battle. The actions of both 'boys' take us back to the lost child, the defeated hero, the naive-pure projection of collective vulnerability.

> The idea that a nation has to be 'blooded', and that Australia had been indeed 'blooded' at Gallipoli, was a theme in the Australian official war histories, which helped foster the Anzac legend after the war. The Anzacs were described by H. S. Gullett, an official Australian correspondent who worked with C. E. W. Bean, as 'children of a virgin unblooded country', who at Gallipoli 'fought with all the might and resource of their proud exuberant manhood'.
>
> *(Blackburn, 2016, p. 12)*

Based on Bill Gammage's *The Broken Years* and the diaries of historian and war correspondent C. E. W. Bean (Gammage, 1974; Bean, 1941–1942), *Gallipoli* ensures the underage element of recruitment is brought to the forefront of the drama through Archie. The Australian war memorial lists 125 'Boy Soldiers on the Roll of Honour for the First World War' aged between fourteen and eighteen years, and for World War II the roll of honour recognises the service of seventy-six boys between fifteen and seventeen years old (Australian War Memorial, 2018a). *Gallipoli* acknowledges that birth certificates were not required at recruitment offices if boys had written consent from their parents testifying that they were over eighteen years old. The youngest Australian boy soldier, Private James Charles Martin (1901–1915), enlisted at fourteen years of age and served for one and half months in the trenches of Gallipoli before dying of typhoid complications (Hill, 2001). Anthony Hill writes in his biography of Martin:

> The idea of the boy soldier was all around him. It was there in the junior and senior cadets. Boys could join the new Royal Australian Navy at fourteen to train as soldiers, stokers or signallers, and a year younger as cadet-midshipmen. There were songs about brave little drummer boys marching troops into battle during the wars that won the British Empire.
>
> *(Hill, 2001, p. 22)*

Australian compulsory military training, with boys twelve to eighteen years having to enrol in the junior and senior cadets and eighteen- to twenty-six-year-olds registering with the home defence militia, was legislated in Australia in 1911 and abolished in 1929 (Australian War Memorial, 2018e, also see Barrett, 1979). The war memorial in inner city Melbourne, Victoria, displays a photograph (photographer unknown) of the forty-ninth Senior Cadets – the caption reads:

> Under the Compulsory Military Service scheme, 100,000 Australian boys aged between 14 and 18 were required to attend 64 hours of military training each year. The boys undertook mucketry, field exercises and physical training taught in four whole day drills. 12 half-day drills and 24 one hour night drills. Fines ranging from £5 and £100 were imposed for non-attendance.
>
> *(Victorian War Memorial, Melbourne, Victoria)*

While the practice of accepting underage boys without thoroughly checking for parental consent was more or less unspoken and unlawful at the time of recruitment, this image of the literal lost war child and the young men, who through what in hindsight can be seen as a sense of innocence, is also be enfolded into the archetypal projection. They are, in turn, now memorialised by twenty-first-century children for whom defeat in war is politically and commercially celebrated, and ideas of nationhood hinge on the sometimes unlawful blooding of young men/children (Lake et al., 2010). Hill notes the association of Martin with the children who are now encouraged to see him as a hero:

> In the years to follow, the story of Private James Martin would be recounted to numerous schoolchildren visiting Gallipoli galleries at the War Memorial. His photograph would be published in Anzac histories. Jim Martin would become part of the nation's story. In 1999 his name would be singled out for mention by the Governor-General of Australia, Sir William Deane, at the Anzac Day service at Lone Pine.
>
> *(Hill, 2001, pp. 44–45)*

The defeat and death motif can be viewed in a wider context as entangled with the lost child motif – the nucleus of the complex. The celebration of young James Martin apparently carries with it not a sense of shame for recruitment practices in the face of imminent defeat, but redemption and heroism, as a form of anchoring the significance of the lost child to Australian identity even more securely in the collective memory.

The latest Australian film to deal with the Anzac legacy once again thematically taps into heroism as a form of loss. Similar in concept to Howard Barker's play, *For the Love of a Good Man* (1980), where on the muddy 1920 trenches of post-war Passchendaele, a mother arrives to retrieve the body of her son amid thousands of unidentified corpses, Russel Crowe's directorial debut *The Water*

Diviner (2014) traces the journey of a father, Connor (Crowe), who travels to Gallipoli four years after his three sons were lost in battle to bring their bodies home. The film equally focuses on Connor's mission and the experience of pre- and post-war Turkish troops and their grieving families. Of significance to the lost child in this instance are two pivotal sequences in the film where the brothers, dying in battle, find comfort by returning to memories of their younger selves.

In a flashback scene, the brothers are shot while charging the Turkish forces at night. They find each other among the dead on the field. Henry (Ben O'Toole) the middle child has been shot in the face while Art (Ryan Corr) the eldest and Edward (James Fraser) the youngest, fall beside him seriously wounded. As they lay immobile in the mud, Edward bleeds out for hours and asks Art to shoot him. Removing the bayonet from his rifle and lifting it to Edward's forehead, Art takes him back to a childhood memory, depicted in an early film sequence when their father, Connor, rescues all three from a dust storm – covering them with a blanket and turning the episode into a fantasy of escape on a magic carpet. Conner does this primarily for the small Edward, scared by the storm. He tells him the magic will only work if he closes his eyes. It is a traumatic scene that sentimentally folds into the night-time slaughter at Gallipoli – the smoke of gunfire replacing the dark red dust of outback Australia. As the brothers lie helplessly together on the battlefield, Art recalls the trick of an imaginary adventure for the gravely wounded Edward. Closing his eyes in a repetition of his father's instructions, the younger brother knowingly asks to be taken home – Arts raises his gun and shoots. The scene undermines the early Australian correlation between manhood/nationhood and blooding, by returning these young men to an experience of childhood helplessness and rescue; in this instance, the return harnesses the healing and liberation that the complex can offer, when thinking about this psychological mechanism through Hillman's work on the orphan/child as a place of retreat and renewal, even if that renewal – the idea going 'home' – takes the form of death. It also touches on the idea of the lost child as the healing grail, discussed in the previous chapter, and the archetypal lost child as a *psychopomp* – the guide of liminal spaces – in this scene, directing the boys from one psychological and physical state to another.

The sport-war analogy

Finding Edward and Henry's dog tags at Gallipoli, Connor is given information that eventually leads him to the surviving son Arthur. Accompanying Turkish soldiers to Ankora where they plan to fight the Greeks now invading Turkey's western coast, Connor hopes to reach the town of Aphion close to where Arthur was taken as a wounded prisoner. Stowed away in a freight train carriage, they make space to play Connor's boyhood game of cricket, using a bat and a make-do wicket. As the train is overrun by Greek militia, Connor saves his Turkish companions by hitting the attacking Greeks over the head with his cricket bat. This is yet another symbolic sequence in Crowe's homage to the war/sport analogy with sport as the great unifier. In the spirit of the 1914 football match mythically said to have taken place during the Christmas day truce between the Western Front's German and English soldiers, Connor builds a sense of camaraderie and shared humanity through sport with this small group of former Turkish soldiers. Crowe is also drawing on the sporting theme that underpins the narrative of *Gallipoli*.

As amateur champion athletes who met at the 'Kimberly gift' running competition, a carnival atmosphere opportunely exploited for recruitment to the light horse, *Gallipoli's* Frank and Archie serve as reminders of the guilt imbued recruitment pitches in the first world war to amateur and professional athletes. The federal government at the time also strongly appropriated feature films like *The Hero of the Dardanelles* with its wounded Gallipoli athlete-soldier and *The Enemy Within* (dir. Stavely, 1918) with Australian sportsman Snowy Baker cast as the hero, for recruitment material (Reynaud, 1999). By historically grounding the lead characters, *Gallipoli* also casts shame on the futile sacrifice of such young talent. The opening sequence concentrates on Archie's trainer, Uncle Jack (Bill Kerr), psyching him up for a test sprint – this section of dialogue worked its way into the cultural vocabulary of audiences in the 1980s as a droll motivational drill.

In the final scene of *Gallipoli*, as Archie steels himself into battle, he repeats the mantra, hoists himself over the trench and runs toward the Turkish troops. The image freezes as he is hit in the chest, his 'beautiful' torso arching back with the impact of the bullets. With his captured body foregrounding the bright blue sky of the peninsula, the framing is intrinsic to the classic sun-drenched landscapes of Australian cinema, and therefore, a point of connection between Archie's place of birth and death: 'In Bean's two-volume official history, *The Anzac Story*, published in 1921 and 1924' writes Kevin Blackburn, 'there is a description of Western Australian sprinter Wilfred Harper's own run toward the Turks' trenches at the Nek. Harper, according to Bean, "was last seen running forward like a schoolboy in a foot-race, with all the speed he could compass"' (2016, p. 4).

By comparison *Unbroken* (2014), an account of the American soldier and Olympic runner Louis Zamperini's (Jack O'Connell) journey through Japanese prisoner of war camps, filmed in Australia and directed by North American Angelina Jolie, concerns itself with heroism born of trauma, survival and the eventual liberation. It is not a narrative built around a young dying hero, the epitome of the lost, vulnerable innocent, but a story of triumph against the odds intrinsic to the North American victory complex that tends to underpin its mainstream cinema. A more recent Australian comparison might be the yet to be filmed, 2014 Man Booker winning novel *The Narrow Road to the Deep North* (Flanagan, 2014). Even though the main character, surgeon Dorrigo Evans, survives the notorious Japanese prisoner of war camp attached to the construction of the Thai-Burma railway, his civilian life is troubled with depression, guilt and behaviours driven by post-war trauma. It is not a redemptive narrative. Dorrigo emerges in the final sequences of the book as a feted hero to his country, but to himself he remains a lost child inhabiting the physical shell of an elderly man.

While sport during the World War I was intrinsic to ideas of Australian manhood, Murray G. Phillips stresses that, 'the supreme activity that fused masculinity with national identity was battle' (p. 84). While the UK encouraged the linkage of war and sport, Blackburn argues that it 'did not become part of constructions of national character as it did in Australia' (p. 10). Men associated with sport, in a professional or amateur capacity, were cajoled to enlist and consequently clustered into sportsman battalions. Blackburn cites Martin Crotty's description of how

> Australia's public schools elevated athleticism as 'the embodiment of the hegemonic ideal of masculinity' then 'reconciled' it with a growing militarism by discursively modifying the purposes of sport, investing it with the qualities of preparing boys for war, likening the battlefield to the games field and playing up the connections between loyalty to the team and loyalty to King, Country and empire.
>
> *(Blackburn, 2016, p. 15)*

The sportsman's battalions, led by popular national or more localised sporting celebrities, were strongly supported by various sporting bodies and the government as a means of increasing recruitment from, as the war progressed, a diminishing pool of those willing to enlist (Phillips, 1997).

> With a strong flavour of essentialism, sportsmen were encouraged to believe that manhood could only be fully achieved in the higher order activity of battle. The military units of athletes and the women who helped muster the recruits further emphasised the polarisation of gender identity which, since the development of the ideology of 'separate spheres' in the nineteenth century, portrayed men and women as characterised by qualitatively different traits.
>
> *(Phillips, 1997, p. 91)*

Despite the manipulation of the concept of masculinity/manliness in relation to both sport and war, the use of the term 'boys' in contemporary reportage and commentary when referring to teams of male athletes, dominantly football players, and 'our boys over there', a more historical reference to enlisted soldiers fighting offshore, does not linguistically conjure up associations of manhood and battle, but the gameplay and sacrifice of boys/adolescents.

Confirming the entwined relationship between war and sport for contemporary audiences, each Anzac Day public holiday in Melbourne, after the official ceremony at the war memorial and the returned soldiers parade, a family friendly Australian rules football match, 'the Anzac Day classic' – between teams Essendon and Collingwood – is televised in what might more cynically be seen as a commercialisation of the Anzac legacy. Since 2000, the 'classic' awards an Anzac medal to the player epitomising 'the ANZAC spirit – skill, courage, self-sacrifice, teamwork and fair play' (Collingwood Forever, 2018). It seems appropriate in this discussion of defeat, trauma and loss attributed to the generic early Anzacs, that triple Anzac medal winner – 2000, 2003 and 2004 – James Hird, in his later role as coach of Essendon, resigned from the club following suspension for involvement in the team's performance enhancing drug supplements scandal. Only recently has he publicly disclosed the clinical depression and sense of loss behind his attempted suicide (Buckingham-Jones, 2017).

Mental health issues and a sense of isolation following the voluntary or forced retirement of elite sporting champions, like Olympic medallist Lauren Jackson (basketball), who have spoken publicly about their struggles (*Insight*, 2017), is a related issue now subject to research and media interest with, for example, 46% of Australian elite athletes in a study of 224 subjects experiencing mental health issues (Gulliver et al., 2014). While it is not appropriate in these instances to talk of defeat, the expression of lostness among our elite athletes at the end of their careers, often intensely trained from childhood or adolescence, suggests a return to the inner lost child – a need to acknowledge the complex as not only a stumbling block to development, but also significant to well-being and recovery. As Lauren Jackson revealed in the discussion programme *Insight* 'Game Over' (2017), the professional or elite amateur athlete at the end of their career can temporarily become dependent on the dedicated parenting that allowed them to succeed. Looked at in this way, athletes subject to these setbacks appear cocooned in a sense of childhood or becoming with the end of this short and rarefied period of their life – this return can potentially act as a catalyst for autonomy, providing the opportunity to utilise/abide the lost child archetype as a (grail) source of replenishment.

The Australian Broadcasting Corporation's four-part television miniseries *Barracuda* (2016) adapted from Christos Tsiolkas' novel (2013), seems like an intellectually considered response to the gold obsessed 2012 London Olympic Games Australian swimming team, their brooding behaviour and inability to reconcile unanticipated defeat in the pool. In response to Pippa Grange's *Bluestone Edge Culture Review into Australian Olympic Swimming* (2013) which addressed the Australian teams' 'toxic' culture of bullying, drug and alcohol dependence, and curfew defiance, Brisbane's *Courier Mail* noted 'Swim report missing two words: Grow up' (Balym, 2013). The report noted a disturbing focus on winning gold, failure to support losing swimmers with psychological 'recovery work', emotional instability, a troubling commercial focus on promoting the image of a select group of swimmers and an inability to deal with a sports media who were accused of downplaying not only non-medal places, but also silver and bronze achievements: competitors called it 'The Lonely Olympics . . . as the first week unravelled, the swimmers felt undefeated, alone, alienated and that no one "had their backs" this year' (Grange, 2013, p. 7). It appears as though the culture of this particular team, its management and the Australian media commentators, although ostensibly centred on victory, could possibly have provoked a mindset guided by the lost child. One might argue that in trying to play into the victory complex of North America, without the intricate cultural memory, trauma or embedded collective identity that ties the country to this particular psychological motif, the Australian team, to their detriment, fell into the more shadowy aspects of their own cultural complex.

Set in the late 1990s, the fictional *Barracuda* analyses the bleak layers of the lost child complex through the character of Danny Kelly (Elias Anton), a gifted adolescent athlete selected for the Australian swim team. After becoming world champion in the men's 100 metre butterfly at the age of seventeen, he competes in the final of the Commonwealth Games, but ranks fourth and so misses a medal place. Trained as a swimmer from the age of seven, Danny is privileged in a number of ways: he has the focused dedication of his Greek/Scottish working-class family, a swimming scholarship at a prestigious private school and the loyalty of his coach Frank Torma (Matt Nable). The series tackles a number of social, sexual and gender issues through the lens of competitive swimming, but in relation to sport, loss and heroism, the narrative reaches a culturally significant, and reflective climax. Danny's final defeat at the Games is a harrowing scene. We see this man/adolescent, well-muscled, toned and at the peak of his fitness, break down like a child beside the pool after the race. Heaving and sobbing in front of a crowded aquatic centre, television cameras and his competitors, he collapses beside the pool into the arms of his coach, unable to control his grief. Like the parent of a small boy, Frank cradles him, saying 'you've got nothing to be ashamed of'. It is a sobering and moving sequence, reflecting the pain and confusion behind what one might see as an inability to 'grow up' and a critical denunciation of the still reverberating calls to nationhood – and manhood – through sport and its metaphor, war. Having abandoned swimming Danny is eventually able to use his skills volunteering at a local pool. He finds friendship, perspective and one senses a developing self-awareness as a rehabilitation aide for a wheelchair bound man who he guides through the water in aquatic exercises. *Barracuda* tackles the issue of heroism in defeat, the lost child as a place of retreat, reflection and forward movement, and the way in which the almost infantilising aspect of elite athleticism lends itself to the more shadowy areas of the cultural complex.

In a country first in the world to give women both the right to vote and the right to be elected into government (1902), Australian women in the early war years of the twentieth century were excluded from the war-sport equation on which a sense of nationhood and consequent 'becoming' was built (AEC, 2018). Phillips argues that the active suffragette movement of the late nineteenth and early twentieth century led to a reinvigoration of masculine ideals that became embodied in sport and later war as a backlash to a perceived threat of redistributed 'power and existing gender relations' (Phillips, 1997, p. 81). Denied roles in active service, women's duties during the first world war were largely supportive in nature, campaigning 'tirelessly about venereal disease, alcohol and even the perceived harmful effects of motion films, and as supportive "angels" they rallied themselves into organizations that helped fighting men like the Red

Cross, the Soldier's Comfort Funds and the Sock Funds' (Phillips, 1997, p. 89). Others however directed their energies to a more militant form of bolstering enlistment numbers: 'When appealing to a sportsman's sense of manhood, the recruiters were aided by women from the Amateur Sports Women's Association of New South Wales, which was active in shaming sportsmen to join the proposed battalions. Their slogan was "One Woman, One Recruit"' (Blackburn, 2016, p. 31).

Mobilising the child in Anzac celebrations

Even today with the celebration of nationhood, filtered through Anzac mythology that promoted the ideology of baptism through war, one looks for an equal recognition of female heroism born of defeat. Exceptions to this lack of representation in Australian cinema and television include: *The Martyrdom of Nurse Cavell* (dir. Gavin, 1916) and its sequel *La Revanche* (dir. Lincoln, 1916), and in more recent years the telemovie *Sisters of War* (Maher, 2010) with its focus on a captured nun and nurse in WWII, the film *Paradise Road* (dir. Beresford, 1997) where civilian women captured at sea during WWII were held as prisoners in Sumatra by the Japanese, and the young nurses of the miniseries *Anzac Girls* (Cameron and Watson, 2014). During one of her lectures in Melbourne, historian Marilyn Lake put forward the view that 'Surely it was inappropriate . . . for a modern democratic nation to adopt an Imperial, masculine, militarist event [Anzac Day] as the focus of our national self-definition in the twenty-first century' (Lake et al., 2010, p. 3).

The amount of energy that has been expended on instilling the idea of nationhood through defeat and loss, at the expense of global first achievements that contribute to actual rather than contrived nation building – like the bravery and victory of the suffragette movement – is somewhat astounding. It is a situation that Lake and Reynolds are at pains to validate and at odds to reconcile. When considering the lost child complex, the obsession with Anzac is easier to understand. In the final chapter of her book, Lake talks of the Department of Veterans' Affairs' (DVA) active role in 'militarising our history in schools during the last ten years' (Lake et al., 2010, p. 137). She argues that through relentless retellings of the Gallipoli defeat and related war efforts in our school curricula via materials and excursions promoted by the DVA with governmental support, and the commercialisation of overseas trips to commemorative services at the Gallipoli Peninsula aimed at primary and secondary level students, Australian children are being co-opted as 'the inheritors of the Anzac spirit and its custodians' (Lake et al., 2010, p. 137).

> History has been appropriated in Australia for militarist purposes and comprehensively re-written in the process. The myth of Anzac has been at the heart of the reshaping of public memory through a national story that defines military values as Australian values and overseas battlefields as key

> historic sites. The relentless militarisation of Australian history has effectively marginalised other stories, different historic sites and other conceptions of national values.
>
> *(Lake et al., 2010, p. 138)*

It is ironic that this militarisation of history, largely concentrated around the Gallipoli campaign, ensuing Anzac Day celebrations and the loss of young boy/men, has become, according to Joy Damousi, a source of 'national pride and collective rejoicing' (Lake et al., 2010, p. 109) – a way of consciously and unconsciously embedding the lost child complex deeper into the national psyche. 'We see the Anzacs as we need to see them: an army of innocent, brave young men' writes McKenna 'who were willing to sacrifice their lives so that we might "live in freedom"' (Lake et al., 2010, p. 111). But as Lake takes some time to demonstrate, it is a narrative that has become increasingly foisted on Australian children. In quoting the research of Anna Clarke she notes that, 'Anzac history certainly generates more education funding than any other areas of Australia's past' (Lake et al., 2010, p. 135; Clark, 2008, p. 49). It is therefore almost predictable that the archetypal lost child theme at the root of one of Australia's most dominant complexes is directed toward our children through this amplified and mythologised aspect of history. Lake and Reynolds in their impressive critique of 'the power of Anzac mythology in Australia today and the way that it has come to serve as White Australia's creation myth' (Lake, 2010, p. 1), appear somewhat dismayed by the current popularisation and commercialisation of the Anzac and *his* mythic legacy. But to reiterate, when viewed through the lens of the cultural complex, the co-opting of this narrative of youth, death and deferred becoming is perhaps to be expected. And even, as some might still believe, 'at Gallipoli on 25 April 1915 . . . the Australian and New Zealand Army Corps (ANZACs) made good: a nation was born on that day of death', it was a still birth of sorts – compromised by loss (Lake et al., 2010, p. 2).

The Anzac legend was invigorated with the 2015 centenary of the Turkish landing Gaba Tepe – a 10,000 strong crowd at Gallipoli marking the occasion. Since this remembrance service, subsequent terrorist attacks in Turkey and warnings issued by the Australian government have contributed to a fall in crowd numbers, yet 2018 Australian dawn services continue to draw large crowds with school-aged children significant contributors to the event (Puvanenthiran, 2017). There is a deep reverence in this country for Anzac Day, one cultivated through literature and the media, with film and television in general taking a less controversial approach to history than it did during the New Wave. War might seem a fair distance in the imagination from small children perishing in, or surviving, the outback, but given the extraordinary popularity of the Anzac legend and the culture's investment in reimagining the Gallipoli massacre of young men, boys and adolescents who died in an unfamiliar and disorienting landscape, attempts to reinforce the 'event', particularly when aimed directly at schoolchildren, are inextricably bound to the lost child complex. War focused screen narratives, commemorations, memorialisations and sporting culture itself as an arena of do-or-die competition, almost intuitively incorporates lost children, and the lost child ethos into their versions of sacrifice, regression and defeat.

In thinking back to the previous chapter, one might ask how these lost children, or the inner lost child of war casualties, are factored into the grail myth. We can certainly see trauma and the idea of a quest at the heart of these stories, but it is more difficult to identify the child as a healing agent rather than a source of grief. Two questions needed to be asked of the Fisher King – *who does the grail serve?* and *what ails you?* The first is perhaps easier. The lost child in the Anzac context would seem to serve the culture, and each annual dawn service has the potential to facilitate a sense of healing – a return to the promise of the child and a desire to abide in that energy. But it seems that in our remembrance, mourning and lionising of the 'glorious dead', we have not worked toward exploring the question of *what ails us*; we avoid confronting the specific nature and persistence of this still open wound. In talking of psychological wounds as trauma, and trauma as a resurfacing, almost autonomous component of the complex, what ails us might be the failure to acknowledge the misguided loss and 'blooding' that was imposed on many of 'our boys'. The need to celebrate loudly, commercially and competitively counting the attendance numbers at each Anzac Day as if it were a tourist attraction, does not seem to be about returning to the lost child for succour, but it might, in a very unconscious way, be symptomatic of a wound connected to the suppression of past follies and 'bloody' servitude to a fickle British parent.

PART TWO
Double wounding

4
DOUBLE WOUNDING
Imposing lostness

Jung's concept of the outwardly projected *shadow* revolves around aspects of the personality that are incompatible with ego ideals. If all complexes carry a shadow element, the internal child is a potential source of disavowal. *Trying* to disown the archetypally configured 'child' at the core of the cultural complex and therefore a fundamental aspect of collective and psychological identity can be understood as a form of self-betrayal. I use the word *trying* with emphasis, because one can never be rid of shadows on a personal or collective level, rather, as Jung argued, it is healthier (more responsible) to confront, reconcile and acknowledge this material as an aspect of one's own psyche. While I've discussed the way in which we incorporate notions of the lost child in cinema under themes such as *lost in the bush*, war, sport and a particular Australian inflected understanding of heroism, I argue here that an aspect of lostness is also very obviously located in the historical *rendering* of actual children as lost, displaced, traumatised and damaged. Although there are many variations of these cyclic behaviours critiqued in Post New Wave cinema and television, I'll concentrate, in a fairly condensed fashion, on three main categories of institutional and governmental neglect: the *Stolen Generations* – Aboriginal children taken from their families by political and religious agencies to be placed with institutions and white families; the *sexual abuse of children in religious institutions*; and government *refugee policies*, implemented to the physical and psychological detriment of children.

By inflicting harm in this way, through various governments, institutions and those who have failed to act, acted inappropriately or refused to acknowledge harms done, it can be argued that elements of the collective psyche have been, and still are, complicit in ensuring childhood lostness both externally and internally. It seems like such a profoundly ironic pattern, given Australia's sensitivity to feelings of suffering around ideas of the internal/external lost child, but then again, from a Jungian perspective, these practices are entirely in keeping with how confronting shadow/complex driven material is often misguidedly processed: that is, as will be discussed later, disavowed and projected onto others/ objects (Jung, 1959/1969). It is not uncommon for those who have suffered trauma to release this sense of helplessness by inflicting trauma (Kaplan, 2004; Bloom, 1999). To be both lost and responsible for, or complicit in, endowing a sense of lostness, is, as I will call this condition from now on, a form of *double wounding*. The previous chapter grappled with the question of why the repetitious focus on 'heroic' defeat and loss has become such a cultural fixation – respectful remembrance is one thing, a wound that refuses to close, is another. In a sense, sending 'our boys over there' to offshore wars that involved trauma and sure death, is a form of double wounding.

The history of projection suggests an unconscious pattern established from penal settlement, with the abandoning cruelty that allowed mass human (convict) rejection from the UK (parent) to be cyclically revisited by successive generations as lost child trauma. We see this kind of hostile parental theme in Australian New Wave war films like *Gallipoli* that reimagine British generals reducing diggers to sacrificial fodder. The pattern in contemporary culture is not as distant from the past *affects* of rejection as we would like to imagine. After public, usually media sustained awareness of a particular mass child-related injustice, redemptive action is slow to be taken until there is, as much as is collectively possible, a sobering acceptance of the need to address the situation. Public, governmental apologies are voiced, Royal Commissions are announced to deliver policy recommendations, and then, almost inexplicably another set of harmful circumstances warranting action surface. The cultural complex, it seems, perpetually shifts projections. Although often occurring simultaneously, the three broadly catagorised instances of abuse mentioned above follow this pattern.

Dramatisation of these events in cinema and television are slow to take hold, usually requiring a lengthy period of reportage via news broadcasts, national flagship current affairs programmes like Australia's *4 Corners* or *The 7:30 Report* and feature documentary exposes, before production and distribution of more artistically structured stories and emotionally evolved narratives around these issues are publically screened. While mainstream, independent and indigenous Blak Wave cinema (dated at 2009) has produced a steadily developing body of work focused on the Stolen Generations through documentary and drama (Collins, 2013), we are yet to have significantly increasing dramatic outputs that address institutional, refugee and detention related child abuses. This of course is not to say that as this book is being finalised, such stories are not in the early stages of discussion, development or submission to government funding organisations.

Self-care system

Kalsched's *the self-care system* is related to double wounding – a probable consequence of the need for self-protection and the maintenance of the complex (Kalsched, 1996, 2013). To reiterate from Chapter 1, Kalsched theorises that after severe trauma, the psyche has the potential to split into elements of *wounded* (victim) and *wounder* (aggressive defensive drives). These autonomous terrorising drives misguidedly seek to protect the victimised aspect of the psyche through a fear of 'getting close to the painful *affects* that threatened the soul with annihilation' (Kalsched, 2013, p. 166). An extreme negativity or aggression is therefore able to dominate the inner world of traumatised subjects and drive dissociation and splitting (Kalsched, 2013). Not only can trauma divide an individual's psyche into a problematic binary of this nature but the same processes may take place on a collective level with trauma-induced aggression played out more literally through self-harming and destructive behaviours.

In considering double wounding as an aspect of the Australian lost child complex, it is necessary to return to unconsciously embedded trauma that gives rise to the fixation. The traumatised aspect of the culture can be seen to irrationally offer *protection* by terrorising, in an attempt to eliminate, elements/cues that may trigger the initial trauma. Actual children who are lost or vulnerable children may constitute these cues and are therefore shunted away, hidden from sight and their abuses ignored for long as possible, until the collective psyche is forced to confront the devastating situation it has created.

As well as the idea of protection embedded in Kalsched's *self-care system*, where the traumatic reminders are blocked and aggressively driven away, the Jungian concept of the shadow is also related to the distorted form of defence or autoimmune response that suggests double wounding. Reminders of the lost child are not only diverted, but the whole concept to the lost child, and of course the complex wrapped around the motif, seems to be projected onto external *others* in classically shadow driven behaviour. A culture that so prolifically sentimentalises the vulnerable lost child, while at the same time directing hostility toward it, suggests disavowal: a desire to be free of the complex but inextricably bound to it – 'complexes can have us', we don't have them (Jung, 1960/1969: § 200). As Kalsched argues, the traumatised core – in our instance, the lost child – or *soul* as he calls it, is not to be discarded, but secured (Kalsched, 1996). However, while we appear invested in ridding ourselves of the complex and any association to it, by identifying external objects (children) as triggers that force an unwelcome confrontation with the inner lost child, and in this process rendering these 'external figures' *lost* rather than 'us', it would seem that the collective is engaging in a similar kind of warped preservation that Kalsched attributes to the self-care system:

> the purpose of the self-care system is to keep an innocent core of the self out of further suffering in reality, by keeping it 'safe' in another world. Further, in this innocent core of the self is a sacred something within the human personality that is often referred to as the soul. The defensive system that 'covers the abyss with trance' tries to keep the innocent remnant of the whole self from being further impacted by suffering-in-reality. This protection has survival value for the individual menaced by a traumatic environment, but it proves to be problematic in the long run

because psychological growth depends on a relational process through which the innocent core of the self gradually accrues experience. Dissociative defences prevent this and thus compromise personal development.

(Kalsched, 2013, p. 24)

While Kasched does not read the shadow into his schema, I would like to argue for its inclusion in the complicated and multidimensional reactions to the lost child, because at some level, given the veracity of collective projection, this sense of *soul* is both nurtured *and* relegated to the shadows. It's important to be clear that talking about the cultural complex and the culture it dominates in this way, with its/our capacity to double wound, is not by any stretch of the imagination an excuse for abuse, but a way of grappling with what may underpin and drive such persistent and ongoing behaviour against children that from any logical, moral and ethical perspective, seems incomprehensible.

Ordinarily, according to Singer, 'Cultural complexes also tend to be bipolar, so that when they are activated the group ego becomes identified with one part of the unconscious complex, while the other part is projected out onto the suitable hook of another group' (Singer and Kimbles, 2004, p. 21). He talks about this in projective terms that conjure up images of racism, sexism or cultural disunity – we might think of how Trump's divisive behaviour that incited 'isms' on a group level during his campaign and presidency, encapsulates Singer's point that collectives and individual members of such collectives, when entangled in a complex, 'automatically take on a shared body language and postures . . . like personal complexes, cultural complexes provide a simplistic certainty about the group's place in the world in the face of otherwise conflicting and ambiguous uncertainties' (Singer and Kimbles, 2004, p. 21). This relates to the lost child complex as discussed in this chapter. Much of the population decries the mistreatment of children in all three areas considered below, yet more fear-driven, populist, authoritarian and racially prejudiced factions within the same culture project shadow material onto vulnerable children, rendering them lost. The diverse ways in which the lost child complex is processed by an entire culture though, is of course not this clear-cut or rationally explained, but teasing out theoretical possibilities can help in understanding and potentially moving forward.

Shadow

The shadow is a concept developed in Jung's *Aion: Researches into the Phenomenology of the Self* (Jung, 1959/1969), but as Anne Casement points out, Jung's thinking on this aspect of the personality, experienced on a personal and collective level, was influenced by neuro-psychiatrists like Janet who considered, 'the phenomenon of double consciousness, in which two different personalities co-exist within a single body' (2003, p. 30). Casement further connects the shadow and neurosis, which for Jung takes the form of 'an inner cleavage – a state of being at war with oneself. What drives individuals to this state is the suspicion of being two people in opposition to each other – the shadow and the ego' (Casement,

2006, p. 100). Those who create lost children, potentially shielding their own inner lost child, may well be seen to engage in such a 'cleavage' – for a culture to do this indicates a collective at odds with itself.

Jung's reference to complexes as splinter psyches 'means that parts of the psyche detach themselves from consciousness' (Casement, 2003, p. 34). That is, they act as dominant, independent entities. As in the case of the lost child dilemma, not only can the complex create a cleavage, as Jacobi writes, 'in conflict with the conscious ego, thus placing the individual [and the collective] between two truths, two conflicting streams of will' (1959, p. 15), but the complex itself 'has a dual aspect' (Jacobi, 1959, p. 21). Shadow/splitting can therefore also occur *within* the complex, a turning in on itself, leading to double wounding.

For Jurhgen W. Kremer and Donald Rothberg the collective shadow presents as a myriad of dis-eases, marking all cultures and variously coded into the collective, generational memory: 'Difficult to grasp, contain and evoke in language . . . an immensity of harm inflicted by human beings upon each other and the natural world and to the vast after effects of such harm in subsequent generations and the entire social body' (1999, p. 3). They note that denying responsibility for projection and its repercussions is intrinsic to collective shadow phenomena.

> The collective shadow manifest outwardly in atrocities . . . and the myriad other ways in which individual and collective human potentials are blocked. It may also manifest more inwardly, amid the complexities of each individual psyche, as hatred toward oneself, one's heritage, and one's culture (for both oppressed and oppressor), dissociation, and feelings of impotence, dissociation, the desire for revenge (so that others might experience something like one's own pain) and the continued fear of the 'other' and that which is like the 'other' in one's own being.
> *(Kremer and Rothberg, 1999, p. 2)*

This kind of shadow-driven fissure ensures that the archetypal nucleus of the lost child complex remains marginalised and disowned – orphaned.

Jung equates aspects of the shadow, the collective shadow particularly, with the concept of evil, arguing as Casement notes, that one cannot deal with evil if one has not confronted their own darkness (Jung, 1964/1970; Casement, 2003). It is a sentiment reminiscent of Aleksandr Solzhenitsyn's famous quote from *The Gulag Archipelago*:

> If only there were evil people somewhere insidiously committing evil deeds, and it were necessary only to separate them from the rest of us and destroy them. But the line dividing good and evil cuts through the heart of every human being. And who is willing to destroy a piece of his own heart?
> *(Solzhenitsyn, 1974–1978, p. 168)*

In thinking about the collective shadow in more negative terms, even as it applies in such a damaging way to the double wounding of the lost child in Australian culture, the word *evil* is a too conveniently religiously toned/supernatural concept to apply to human behaviour. It dehumanises criminals . When one designates evil to an individual or group because of acts committed, as do politicians and journalists with unfortunate regularity and often in the face of terrorism, it elevates the perpetrators to the level of untouchable, unearthly and mystical. Something that is not *us*. It seems to be a way of avoiding the root of extreme behaviour: a lazy word, unhelpful in addressing what are very human, if deluded, pathological and non-empathetic, actions. It can stop us accepting the shadow as an element of the psyche and the culture, so it is surprising that Jung should mobilise such a culturally and religiously *loaded* term so freely in his theorisation of the shadow, even if he is quick to justify good and evil as unknowable and as principles 'of our ethical judgement' (Jung, 1964/1970: § 864).

Double wounding within the lost child complex for instance, when expressed as unacceptable actions against children, is not evil, but the cruel consequence of an unaddressed psychological condition. This is where Australian film and television, as mediums for scrutinising double wounding, can help in the process of acknowledging, and consequently claiming, this two-fold aspect of the lost child complex. *Amplification*, in the Jungian sense, takes a more introverted meaning. It refers to the therapeutic practice of exploring one's associations with archetypal patterns/images/symbols/expressions in dreams, fantasy and repetitive ideas, to shine a light on their significance to our individual emotional behaviour (Jung, 1960/1969). Luke Hockley finds parallels in this technique with the way that screen material can act as a catalyst for self-reflection if we take the time to question and expand our associations with the imagery that stimulates our most intense reactions (Hockley, 2014).

Film and television as filters for the recognition of double wounding

This book largely looks at the ways in which the lost child, as a vulnerable aspect of Australian cultural identity, is repeatedly addressed on screen. Here, I look to the darker side, the shadow side of this archetypal knot at the heart of the complex, which has also, to varying intensity, been expressed and exposed in the cinema. Not only does film reveal what was once, and still can be, unacceptable to the collective ego, but as Rushing and Frentz argue, by equating screen content to dreams, 'we are alert to the ways in which they undermine the truth about the cultural psyche even as they tell it – how they prevent us from facing our shadow at the same time that they facilitate it' (1995, p. 48). The following chapter will primarily look at productions that have very consciously set out to expose shadow aspects of the cultural complex rather than bury, excuse or justify them. Kremer and Rothberg draw on the poetry of Jewish Holocaust survivor Paul Celan to underline the significance of artistic 'attempts to deepen and remember language to such an extent that individual and collective suffering can be explored and expressed' (1999, p. 3). They acknowledge that although creators and readers/audiences can be brought to the brink of endurance via this material, such confrontation is necessary 'if there is to be healing, if there is to be awareness and wholeness' (1999, p. 3).

Anne Haebich (2011) argues for art as a sustainable medium for articulating and unravelling the emotional complexity of past trauma so painful that it resists compartmentalisation. She refers to the work of indigenous artists, for whom 'in the toxic environment of verbal attack and counter-attack of the Stolen Generations debate the visual arts provided a potent alternative space for framing the rich layers of their history, and . . . art galleries provided safer and more democratic sites to represent Indigenous views' (2011, p. 106). When thinking about indigenous and non-indigenous film created by those representing trauma as a form of recognition for harms done, as opposed to those affected first-hand or generationally by trauma, the result may not be as cathartic and internally dynamic as it is for survivors. It can though, as Haebich argues of art, be provocative, challenging and in relation to the lost child, layered with *affect* for audiences in general.

The Stolen Generations

The *Stolen Generations*, more specifically, refers to children of indigenous Australian mainland and Torres Strait Islander communities (offshore islands annexed by Queensland – territories of the Commonwealth of Australia), particularly those with lighter skin thought to have *mixed* blood, who were taken from their families by government and religious agencies. These children and infants were placed with European families or orphanages, in misplaced, paranoid and ruthless attempts to foster segregation and biological and cultural assimilation (Moran, 2005). In the opening to the short documentary *The Road Home* (dir. Martin, 2003), we are told that the implementation of Australia's 1883–1969 assimilation strategies in New South Wales were responsible for the separation of approximately 6,000 indigenous children from their families and communities. This poignant student film, from the Australian Film, Television and Radio School, is based on the experiences of Roy Read, an indigenous man who returned to the now deserted Kinchela Aboriginal Boys' Training Home in Kempsy, New South Wales (operational between 1924–1971), after being taken from his family at the age of two. Over its forty-seven years, the government-run facility catered to over four hundred abducted Aboriginal boys (see: Browning, 2017). Read's memories of his infancy at Bomaderry children's home and then Kinchela forty-nine years ago when he was eight years old is haunting and difficult to comprehend. He was lied to about his family, told that he was an orphan, his name was replaced by a number, and he was physically beaten and sexually abused. He explains that the beatings were sanctioned by the authorities who forced older boys to attack children, even their own siblings, and turn a blind eye to the sexual abuse delivered to younger boys in shower blocks. Forced to work on the farming property and then sent to cattle stations, Read ran away from each job assigned to him, 'just because I wanted to go home' he tells us. After eventually finding his relatives, Read began working to rebuild his fractured familial relationships.

This testimony is one among thousands of stories from older men and women with childhoods begun in trauma. The speaking out, media documentation and artistic expressions of loss by indigenous and non-indigenous Australians, all aim to contribute toward collective healing. These narratives, a product of the policies of assimilation under varying state and territory laws, address not just the lost children who testify or create art inspired by their experiences, but also entire generations carrying unspoken childhood and parental trauma from being physically, emotionally and psychologically *forced into lostness and loss* (see: AIATSIS, 2018).

Tilley (2012) refers to settler Charles Tompson's poem 'Blacktown' from *Wild Notes from the Lyre of a Native Minstrel* (1826), as evidence of racial discrimination that prompted the New South Wales government to consider indigenous peoples as lost children who needed rescuing. She further refers to stanzas that encouraged Aboriginal families to place their 'darkling' children in Christian schools 'as part of the dominant ideological climate that endorsed the subsequent creation of the stolen generations' (2012, p. 65). In contradicting Peirce's view of the poem as reconciliatory (1999, pp. 3–4), she argues that 'Blacktown' is 'an example of the metaphoric use of a lost child to reinforce discourses of black displacement and white superiority' (2012, p. 66). Torney discusses other earlier methods of assimilation, dehumanisation and slavery: 'They were hunted and captured like animals and this was recorded quite openly. People wrote of "getting", "acquiring" or "securing" a child' (2005, p. 74). During the push to develop a British colony, Aboriginal adults and their children were murdered, with for instance, children numbering 'among the more than 300 bodies found after the Waterloo Creek massacre of January 1838' (Torney, 2005, p. 75). Aboriginal children were coerced into serving colonisers as translators and trackers – 'sold or traded as commodities . . . there was absolutely no recognition of any special rights to protection and nurturing due them' (Torney, 2005, p. 74).

Drawing on the missionary zeal to inculcate indigenous children into a Christian education, Torney argues that, counter to the Victorian ideas of childhood innocence and purity, young indigenous children were denied protective nurturing. This dismissal, 'culminated towards the end of the nineteenth century in the adoption of the national image of "Young Australia" as a completely white image' (Torney, 2005, p. 75). The Australia policy of assimilation was only repealed in 1973 by the Whitlam Labor government. Stories and memories of this draconian period are still raw and deeply embedded in Australian culture. During the writing of this chapter, I was listening to a podcast with young Gamilaroi/Torres Strait Islander comedian, actor and playwright Nakkiah Lui, popularly known for her work on the television sketch show *Black Comedy* (Shelper and O'Toole, 2014). In conversation with host radio Richard Fidler, she talked of her grandmother's fastidious, compulsive cleanliness – daily bleaching, vacuuming and polishing. Her mother explained that when she was a child, Nakkiah's grandmother was forced into hyper vigilance because she believed, 'if they weren't tidy and clean they [welfare officers] would take the children' (Fidler, 2017).

The recent re-dressing of assimilation policies and indigenous dispossession was most passionately addressed by Labour prime minister Paul Keating. Under the Keating government (1991–1996) the ground breaking 1992 *Marbo v Queensland (No. 2)* High Court ruling restored land rights, taken after the British occupation, to Aboriginal and Tores Strait Islander peoples – legally formalised in the *Native Title Act* of 1993 (AustLII, 2003). The inquiry into the Stolen Generations, the *Bringing Them Home Report: A Report into the Separation of Aboriginal and Torres Strait Islander Children from their families*, was established in 1995 and tabled in parliament in 1997 under the successive Liberal (conservative) party. Newly elected prime minister, John Howard, was critical of the report, refusing to publically apologise. He reiterated his stance in the opening address for the 1997 Aboriginal reconciliation convention: 'Australians of this generation should not be required to accept guilt and blame for past actions and policies over which they had no control' (see transcript Howard, 1997). Howard raised his voice in anger and self-defence to an auditorium of indigenous delegates, many of whom stood and turned their backs as he spoke. After defeating Howard in December 2007, Labour leader Kevin Rudd lead a nationally televised Official Parliament House Apology in February 2008.

The Report of the Northern Territory Board of Inquiry into the Protection of Aboriginal Children from Sexual Abuse (2007), titled Ampe Akelyernemane Meke Mekarle 'Little Children are Sacred', begins with the statement 'In our Law children are very sacred because they carry the two springs wells of water from our country within them' (Wild and Anderson, 2007). Not only were indigenous adults carrying the legacy of their stolen childhood but Aboriginal children of the twenty-first century were found, by the Board of Inquiry (appointed in August 2006), to be subject to sexual abuse. The complexity of such childhood neglect, family turbulence and domestic violence was attributed to 'problems of alcohol and drug abuse, poverty, housing shortages, unemployment' (Wild and Anderson, 2007, p. 5).

Since colonisation, the introduction of alcohol, physical displacement, emotional and psychological trauma attributed to stolen children, and the fragmentation of indigenous culture, escalated. The kind of dysfunction and confusion documented in the report can be clearly associated with an external *rendering/projection of the lost child*. While the report resulted in the government's 'national emergency response to protect Aboriginal children in the Northern Territory from sexual abuse and family violence', also known as 'the intervention', the raft of reforms to be legislated, and policed, were thought by the Australian Human Rights Commission to be rushed, not supported by adequate consultation, disempowering to the very people it targeted and inconsistent with international human rights (Australian Human Rights Commission, Social Justice report,

2007). Once again Aboriginal communities were folded into the shadowy vortex of the cultural complex: 'Paradigms once set in play persist through time; as the official rationales for the recent Northern Territory intervention attest, Aboriginal families continue to be deemed dangerous sites from which to rescue neglected children to be usefully trained and assimilated into settler society' (Haebich, 2011, p. 108).

Quite a bit of time has been taken here to describe Australia's governmental and institutional relationship to indigenous children. This is a gesture toward developing some understanding for international readers of the harms done and the way in which the lost child complex, in its darkest form, has been inflicted on an entire people for whom this archetypal motif was, at most, peripheral to their pre-colonial culture and spirituality. It is also necessary to understand the depth of this trauma on the psyche of the country (Pierce, 1999). Much of the wounds touched on in this chapter, and the lives of children and adolescents affected by Stolen Generation history, displacement and the need for belonging, has been captured by non-indigenous Australian film-makers in works such as: *Jedda, Manganinnie, The Chant of Jimmy Blacksmith* (dir. Schepisi, 1978), *Rabbit Proof Fence, Australia* (see Waddell, 2014) and *Charlie's Country* (dir. Rolf de Heer, 2013), and indigenous film-makers in nationally significant works such as *Bedevil* (dir. Moffatt, 1993), *Radiance* (dir. Perkins, 1998), *Beneath Clouds* (dir. Sen, 2002), *Satellite Boy* (dir. McKenzie, 2002), *Samson and Delilah* (dir. Thornton, 2009), *Bran Nue Dae* (dir. Perkins, 2010), *Here I Am, Toomelah* (dir. Sen, 2011), *Mystery Road*, and *Sweet Country* (dir. Thornton, 2017). Each of these films, embracing the darkness and futurity embedded in the lost child complex, warrant wider discussion, but three in particular represent the cinematic trajectory of this archetypal projection.

Chauvel's 1955 *Jedda*, originally titled *Jedda the Uncivilized*, is marked by racist overtones of mid-twentieth-century Australia. It was the first feature film to star indigenous Australian actors, the first Australian colour film, and the first drama to allude (circuitously), to the issue of removed and displaced Aboriginal children, a largely unacknowledged practice and source of collective trauma for white Australian audiences at its 1955 premiere in Darwin. The melodrama follows the life of Jedda (Rosalie Kunoth), the child of an Aboriginal mother who died in labour. As Barbara Creed writes, 'it is now impossible to discuss *Jedda* without referencing the stolen generations' (2001, p. 210). She highlights the 'deliberate staging of debates about assimilation' between Jedda's adoptive parents, Sarah and Douglas McMann (Betty Suttor and George Simpson-Lyttle), white owners of a prosperous buffalo station in the Northern Territory. Sarah seeks to civilise her indigenous labourers, while Doug finds this antithetical to their 'wild' nature. This conflict sets the scene for a narrative focused on the domesticated and now grown Jedda's seduction, capture and eventual death by the young 'full-blood' Aboriginal, Marbuk (Robert Tudawali) (Creed, 2001).

That the first Australian colour feature is driven by the archetypal lost child, suggests the significance of the complex's hold on Australian white culture and its projection onto indigenous culture. Not only were the central actors, Kunoth-Monks and Tudawali, temporarily accepted into Darwin society as glitterati/national celebrities at a time when the Star Theatre premiering the film was segregated, but the displaced character of Jedda – a threshold figure as Creed points out, neither familiar with her tribal heritage nor emotionally assimilated despite her upbringing – symbolised the folding of indigenous Australians into the lost child complex (Fox, 2010). While Creed sees *Jedda* as a contradictory text in relation to its positions on assimilation, she ultimately reads the character of Jedda as '*a* stolen child and a stolen woman – but in both contexts her captivity is subordinated to the imperative of upholding the myth of white superiority that the dominant culture seeks to maintain at any cost' (p. 229).

Collins and Davis' *Australian Cinema After Marbo* (2004), the title referencing the historic *Marbo v Queensland* land rights case noted above, detail Noyce's *Rabbit Proof Fence* as a response to the *Bringing Them Home Report*. Charting the true-life 1931 story of three stolen young sisters, who followed a 2,000 kilometre rabbit proof fence from where they were taken and kept in isolation to be trained as servants, back to their original home, Collins and Davis classify Noyce's classic as '*the* film of the Stolen Generations' (p. 133). They see it as a Hollywood genre driven 'vehicle for retracing the past', by reclaiming lost child mythology and employing 'rhetorical elements of testimony and witnessing . . . best understood in terms of international screen studies debates about memory, history, trauma and film' (p. 133–4).

Samson and Delilah, by indigenous writer and director Warwick Thornton, follows the emotional connection of two Aboriginal adolescents living in a small Northern Territory settlement. After Delilah's (Marissa Gibson) grandmother dies, she fends for herself and Samson (Rowan McNamara), a young man with addiction problems, by moving to urban Alice Springs. Despite addiction, physical injury and ostracism by the urban community, this largely dialogue free, yet emotionally complex narrative, draws Delilah out as a symbol of futurity, survival and integrity. Delilah confronts her challenges, moving from the city to the outback with a seeming knowingness of its capacity to give rather than take life. This return to land, home and belonging reads as a patent rejection of the Alice Spring settler culture that in this portrayal signifies physical and spiritual decay for its indigenous fringe dwellers. What we see in this exquisitely shot film is both a haunting of imposed lostness and a reclaiming of the potential of the lost child as a source of regeneration – a theme linked the grail myth thinking revisited in the following chapter. In contrast to *Jedda*, where imposed lostness leads to death and *Rabbit Proof Fence*, where the text is informed by a three-act Hollywood trajectory to best harness the story and generate *affect*, *Samson and Delilah* offers a different rhythm, style and sense of timeless endurance. It reflects the outback land itself and the resilience of those who most authentically inhabit/ed such spaces. Its beauty and sense of woundedness is not driven by conventional (European influenced) narrative structures, and with the archetypal lost child at its heart, in both its positive and negative bipolarity, it is a film to be deeply felt and experienced, rather than understood through melodramatic or heroic frameworks. Indigenous film-makers like Thornton, Tracey Moffatt and Rachel Perkins, also reflect Haebich's belief that visual artists and their work have the capacity to break,

> the endless cycle of dry debate in the public arena, they are blazing a trail for a nation seeking to come to terms with the haunting shadows of its past in a critical global context. At the same time they are looking to the future in staking their claim on the ways that the histories and experiences of the Stolen Generations will be remembered by generations to come through imagination and creativity that goes far beyond the limitations of the archive and dry academic debate.
>
> *(Haebich, 2011, p. 122)*

Royal Commission into Institutional Responses to Child Sexual Abuse

The emotion of Australian lost child narratives for indigenous and non-indigenous Australians was unambiguously laid bare with the public exposure of practices and assimilation policies leading to the Stolen Generations. Public outrage at injustice against children resurfaced on a national level shortly after prime minister Rudd's parliamentary 'Apology to Australia's Indigenous Peoples' (February 13, 2008) with the increasingly public testimonies of abuse, much of it sexual, in secular and religious, education institutions, orphanages, organisations and detention centres. Once driven by investigative journalism, these cases were documented through sworn testimony at the public hearings of the *Royal Commission into Institutional Responses to Child Sexual Abuse* (*RCIRCSA* as the commission will be referred to) established by former Labour prime minister, Julia Gillard, on November 12, 2012 with a funding provision of '$434.1 million over four years (including $66.8 million in 2012–13 and $43.2 million in capital funding)' (Biddington, 2013).

Aligned with counterpart inquiries in the United Kingdom – *Commission to Inquire into Child Abuse* (Ireland 2000–2009), *The Historical Institutional Abuse Inquiry* (Northern Ireland 2013–2017), *Public Inquiry into Historical Child Abuse in Scotland* (2015–), *Independent Inquiry into Child Sexual Abuse* (England and Wales, 2015–) – the central focus of the RCIRCSA was to 'inquire into institutional responses to allegations and incidents of child sexual abuse and related matters' and consequently prepare recommendations including 'policy, legislative, administrative or structural reforms' (RCIRCSA, 2017). The RCIRCSA handed down its final seventeen volume report in December 2017, reporting a total of '42,041 calls handed, 25,964 letters and emails received, 8,013 private sessions held and 2,575 referrals to authorities (including the police)' (RCIRCSA, 2017). This response, in a small Australian population of (then) 24.6 million, demonstrates the depth of lost child wounding that has been allowed to continue because abuse was unreported, reported and dismissed, and/or swept under the carpet by knowing and colluding authorities.

Cinema and television has only more recently become a vehicle to document, address and rethink abuses that the RCIRCSA raised. Tori Garrett's film *Don't Tell* (2017) is based on the literary account of a woman, given the pseudonym 'Lyndal', who fought the courts for recognition of her childhood abuse by a Housemaster when she was a boarder at Toowoomba Anglican primary (pre-secondary) school, Queensland. Her tenacity enabled her to sue the church (Roche, 2011). When the perpetrator was charged in 1990, he committed suicide forty minutes before his court appearance, having previously abused over twenty children. On his death, the school failed to pursue any of these cases. Lyndal's 2001 victory ushered in national reforms and background checking, well before the establishment of RCIRCSA (Miko, 2016). Both this development and the RCIRSCA hearings led to workplaces, Australian universities included, making Working with Children Checks compulsory for all staff.

In an article written with my La Trobe University colleague Timothy Jones for *Media International* (2016), 'The spoken and unspoken nature of child abuse in the miniseries *Devil's Playground*: The Royal Commission into Institutional Responses to Child Abuse, the Catholic Church and television drama in Australia', we discussed how events raised in the RCIRCSA, particularly its focus on a string of paedophile priests teaching in Catholic schools (primary and secondary) in the small regional diocese of Ballarat, Victoria, was reflected and portrayed in *Devil's Playground* (dirs. Krawitz and Ward, 2013). This miniseries, set in 1988, is a spinoff of director Fred Schepisi's semi-autobiographical Australian film classic *The Devil's Playground* (1976). While Schepisi's work concentrates on a child's sexual awakening while training for the priesthood in 1953, the television series takes a darker turn from this quite tender focus on a child's sexual exploration, to the predatory and abusive sexual crimes against children by priests. Tim and I were quite critical about the inadequacy of the miniseries to confront the pathology of child sexual abuse. Here are our concluding thoughts:

> Through various techniques of distance and 'palatable' characterisation, *Devil's Playground* manages to contain and package trauma for popular consumption. By structuring the series as ahistorical thriller, it resists the Church's discourse of moral failure. Clerical sex offences are unambiguously represented as criminal acts. Yet, these unspeakably horrific sex crimes are safely distanced in the past and displaced geographically. The series sympathetically explains, rather than challenges, the inadequacy of religious institutional responses to allegations of offending. It confirms contemporary outrage at past offences. And, yet, by depicting [the characters of] Andrassi [a Bishop] and Quaid [a reoffending paedophile priest]

as engaging in struggles of conscience, it turns away from the horror of the dissociated psychopathic cleric and the malignant and passionless self-preservation of Church hierarchs.

(Waddell and Jones, 2016, p. 91)

Drawing on the intricacies of the screen text, we argued that the character of Bishop Vincent Quaid, played by Don Hany, uncannily resembled an actual identity in the Ballarat abuse cases, George Pell, who it has been claimed in RCIRCSA testimony, ignored sexual abuse cases reported to him, moved to distance the church from culpability, and limited victim compensation claims (Waddell and Jones, 2016). Pell was Bishop of Melbourne from 1987–1996, Archbishop of Melbourne in 1996 and Cardinal, housed in the Vatican, from 2003. Church protection of this kind of pathology is of course transnational, exposed by Tom McCarthy's biographical film *Spotlight* (2015) centred around the Boston Globe's pursuit of paedophile priests, and Amy Berg's *Deliver Us from Evil* (2006), a chilling documentary film focused on the Irish born, American practicing paedophile priest father Oliver O'Grady – climactically revealed as a disturbing example of double wounding when probed about his own familial sexual abuse and inculcation into abusive practices as a child in Limerick.

What is unique to Australia, shedding further light on the country's dominance of lost child pathologies, is that since our article, and as I write this chapter, Pell, having taken a leave of absence from his role as Vatican treasurer or Prefect of the Vatican Secretariat and one of the pope's most senior advisors, returned from Rome to stand trial for historical sexual abuse allegations prepared by Victorian police (Kirchgaessner, 2018). The Pell trial is more far reaching than one man's guilt or innocence – it exposes the direct and indirect harm imposed on hundreds of children and their families. It suggests a split and confrontation within the cultural complex, much like the evolution of Stolen Generation healing: an example of how collective lost child energy constellated by survivors and their champions is working to contest the damage inflicted on children that rendered them once, and for many, forever, lost to childhood trauma. Two more relevant issues raised through the RCIRCSA are the migration of children from the UK to commonwealth countries including Australia (1930s–1770s), and children held in custody in the Northern Territory.

The migration experience of child orphans has been publically discussed and written about over a number of decades, but the traumatic sexual abuse of these children, now adults, at the hands of various Australian institutions and religious organisations, has been further scrutinised by the RCIRCSA and the UK *Inquiry into Child Sexual Abuse*. Jim Loach's 2010 UK-Australian co-production, *Oranges and Sunshine*, is a biopic following the experiences of Nottingham social worker Margaret Humphreys (Emily Watson), who discovered that many of the children transported to Australia through migrant schemes funded by the British government were not in fact all orphans. Children were placed in care by living parents, and the 'stolen' children of young single women were often told that their child had died. English child migrant John Hennessy, for instance, testified at the RCIRCSA that Irish nuns banished his twenty-four-year-old unmarried mother, forcing her give birth in an English convent. She was consequently told her child had died. Raised as an orphan, Hennessy was sent to Western Australia in 1947 at the age of eleven, and underwent a childhood of sexual abuse at the hands of the Christian Brothers and more senior boys at Bindoon Boys Town: 'I feel exhausted telling my story to ineffectual parliamentary inquiries' Hennessy wrote in his statement. 'Senators listen and weep at the account of a lost child, beaten and raped, but what has changed? I feel there is no real justice' (Hennessy, 2014, p. 22).

Humphreys traces the cases of surviving adults from this scheme who were placed in governmental and religious 'care' – many were sexually abused and/or forced to work in harsh labour-intensive conditions. *The Leaving of Liverpool* (1992), an Australian Broadcasting Corporation and British Broadcasting Corporation co-produced miniseries directed by Michael Jenkins, canvases the journey from Liverpool and the injustices in Australia that migrant children under this programme received. David Hill, former chairman and managing director of the Australian Broadcasting Corporation, himself a child migrant placed in care from 1959, was one of the most public voices testifying at the UK *Inquiry into Child Sexual Abuse* in 2017 and filed a submission to the RCIRCSA as an advocate for fellow child migrants (Hill, 2015). Although not personally abused at the New South Wales farm school managed by the Fairbridge Society where he was sent, Hill wrote *The Forgotten Children* (2008) and claimed that 60% of those sent to Fairbridge were sexually assaulted (Symonds, 2017).

In 2010, the year *Oranges and Sunshine* was released, former UK prime minister Gordon Brown apologised to those affected by the British initiated scheme. While harm was done in separating these children from their families, their trauma was further impacted by the behaviour of select religious and government authorities in Australia now being called to account. It was only on October 22, 2018, ten months after the RCIRCSA handed down its report, that the current Liberal government, under prime minister Scott Morrison, formally apologised to victims and survivors of institutional child sexual abuse in Canberra's Parliament House. Both Morrison and opposition leader Bill Shorten called for the commission's recommendations to be enacted.

While the RCIRCSA canvased extensive instances of sexual child abuse, a separate *Royal Commission into the Protection and Detention of Children in the Northern Territory* was established in August 2016. The Australian news flagship programme *4 Corners* aired an episode, 'Australia's Shame' (2016), detailing graphic sexual and violent assaults by prison guards on child and adolescent inmates at the Don Dale Youth Detention Centre in the Northern Territory. Detained children were, among other abuses, asked for oral sex, restrained on specially designed chairs and masked in what is called a *spit hood*, beaten, abandoned in cells, bribed with soft drinks to fight each other, and stripped. The programme captured images and footage of some of these crimes. The following month the Royal Commission was established, and after three periods of extension to collect evidence, concluded in November 2017.

In addition to this in 1992 and 1996 the Western Australian and (in 1997) the Northern Territory Government introduced mandatory sentencing laws for theft that imposed blanket minimum sentences without recourse to circumstance or age considerations. The law also imposes a minimum of twelve months when convicted of home burglary for a third time, no matter how minor or significant – known as Three Strikes and You're Out. The Western Australian Law society issued the briefing paper 'Mandatory Sentencing' that argued: 'Indigenous children in WA are now 52 times more likely than non-indigenous young people to be in detention – twice the national rate of overrepresentation' and further added that such legislation, 'disproportionately impacts upon particular groups within society, including indigenous peoples, juveniles, persons with a mental illness or cognitive impairment, or the impoverished' (Law Society of Western Australia, 2016). Louis Schetzer and Danny Sandor, in a discussion paper for the National Children's and Youth Law Centre, outlined a number of disturbing cases. The first listed below is from Western Australia the second, from the Northern Territory:

> In two years, one 11–13 year old from the north has received two sets of 12 months detention, two 12 month conditional release orders and one supervised release order of six months. He has little family care and was stealing food from houses because he was hungry.
> *(Schetzer and Sandor, 2000, p. 6)*

> A 15-year-old girl was charged after being a passenger in a stolen vehicle. She was convicted of being in unlawful possession of a vehicle, and was sentenced to 28 days detention under the NT's mandatory sentencing laws.
> *(Schetzer and Sandor, 2000, p. 13)*

These penalties have been widely criticised, contested and challenged by various legal organisations, judiciary professionals, youth services, the media and interest groups. The laws added to the considerable government-condoned intolerances against children that I have touched on in this chapter, particularly lost children, or rather children who have been rendered lost by the state, their communities and family units subject to significant hardship and poverty. I will now turn to the most recent lost children – child asylum seekers estranged from their country of origin and rendered lost to illness, abandonment, trauma and a sense of home through inadequate government care. These children, who have tried to enter the country, largely by boat, with parents, guardians or unaccompanied, have been placed in offshore processing centres operationally financed by Australia.

Children seeking asylum – mental health and disavowal

Legislated in 1992, mandatory immigration detention was imposed on those entering the country without legitimate visas, including children, who were subsequently labelled unlawful non-citizens in the Migration Act 1958 (Australian Government, 2017). In 2014 Professor Gillian Triggs, president of the Australian Human Rights Commission, presented the Attorney General George Brandis QC with *The Forgotten Children: National Inquiry into Children in Immigration Detention*. When published, the 324-page report, containing twelve emotional drawings by children of their sadness at being held captive, triggered immediate media attention and calls for the sitting Liberal Government to address the physical and psychological condition and treatment of children in immigration detention.

Among its findings, the eight-month inquiry which canvased eleven detention centres and interviewed 1,129 children and parents in detention, estimated, at the time of release, that Australia held 'about 800 children in mandatory closed immigration detention for indefinite periods, with no pathway to protection or settlement. This includes 186 children detained on Nauru' (Triggs, 2014, p. 10). Many of these centres have since closed, but the findings that most disturbed the media and the Australian public in early 2015, related to the deteriorating mental and physical health, sexual assaults and self-harm of children in prolonged and indefinite detention – claims sourced from the children, their parents, psychiatrists, pediatricians, research and the Department of Immigration and Border Protection itself (Triggs, 2014, pp. 10, 20, 29). Talking publically about their findings placed health workers, educators and support staff at detention centres in a precarious position. Under the Australian Border Force Act 2015, any person performing duties relating to immigration and border protection risked two years imprisonment for disclosing information relating to their work-experiences or professional recommendations. Doctors filed a High Court challenge to the secrecy provisions of the Act in 2016, forcing the government to amend its gag orders on medical practitioners (Hall, 2016).

On announcing the inquiry, the government took a number of measures to ensure that some children meeting specific conditions of age and health were released to the community and offered bridging visas, but many still remained in detention (see Triggs, 2014, pp. 13–14). In keeping with Australia's psychological relationship to the lost child complex, and the projection of that complex onto *others*, Triggs made some damning comments about the country's exceptional position on children deemed unlawful citizens:

> No other country mandates the closed and indefinite detention of children when they arrive on our shores. Unlike all other common law countries, Australia has no constitutional or legislative Bill of Rights to enable our courts to protect children. The Convention on the Rights of the Child is not part of Australian law, although Australia is a party. The Convention

is, however, part of the mandate of the Australian Human Rights Commission to hold the Government to account for compliance with human rights. This Convention accordingly informs the findings and recommendations made by the Inquiry.

(Triggs, 2014, p. 10)

Australia is the only country in the world with a policy that imposes mandatory and indefinite immigration detention on asylum seekers as a first action. While other countries detain children for matters related to immigration, including Greece, Israel, Malaysia, Mexico, South Africa and the U.S.; detention in these countries is not mandatory and does not occur as a matter of course.

(Triggs, 2014, p. 19)

Trigg's statement needs to be amended in light of Donald Trump's 'Zero Tolerance' policy where migrant families, including toddlers, at the Mexican border were removed and detained in June 2018 (Miller, 2018; Solon, 2018). A short, but significant statement in Trigg's report directly taps into what I have been arguing in relation to how the complex influences a sense of the collective self: 'How we treat asylum seekers goes to the core of our identity as a nation' (Triggs, 2014, p. 17).

This chapter has been concerned with the mistreatment of children, how they have been cyclically abandoned, and how this very active mobilisation of one of the nation's most toxic *shadows*, contributes to the discourse of who we are. It reflects double wounding to the point where one can argue that the *other* is us, and that in rendering children lost, they become enfolded into a dominant complex, ensuring, in a twisted way perhaps, a kind of psychological closeness. Following this line of thinking, one can sense the centrality of the lost child to national identity, even if that part of ourselves is deeply unconscious and deeply troubling. The denial that has accompanied reported experiences of child endangerment while in detention, which the Triggs led report brought to light, and the subsequent condemnation of these whistle blowers (and Triggs herself), merely confirms the tenacity of lost child projection/disavowal.

It was reported that Triggs was asked to resign on release of *The Forgotten Children*, by Brandis and Tony Abbott (then prime minister), on the basis of political bias, despite the fact that the report was critical of both the sitting (Liberal) government and the opposition party's (Labour) handling of child asylum seekers. According to *The Guardian*, Abbott was reportedly enraged at the claims that he saw as singularly levelled against his party, and the assumption that the report's release during his tenure (rather than during the former Labour government's) was intentionally manipulative and partisan on Triggs' part (Taylor and Medhora, 2015). The Tasmanian author Richard Flanagan – Booker Prize winner, director/writer of *The Sound of One Hand Clapping* and co-writer of the film *Australia* – felt compelled to champion Triggs and the conditions she and her team exposed. The exert below calls to mind the previous incidents of child mistreatment outlined in this chapter – the cruelty, the silencing of cruelty and the long awaited apology for that silence:

> Gillian Triggs's real crime is that as human rights commissioner she spoke up for human rights with a government that has no respect for them . . .
>
> One day, many years from now, another prime minister will stand up and to a teary gallery and apologise for the damage done to refugees in detention. We will be told that we didn't know then what we know now. We will hear testimony of destroyed lives. But we did know. We always knew. We just chose not to hear and to silence those who tried to remind us of the truth.
>
> *(Flanagan, 2015)*

This warning is reminiscent of Hillman's writing on the consequences of failing to recognise aspects of our heritage, no matter how unpalatable, as the connective tissue that forms our complexes. He argues that such disavowal ensures that we become orphans with no linage or anchor:

> History provides parentage to psychic events, giving them background in race, culture, tradition. When we refuse the historical aspect in our complexes, how history reaches us through our complexes – for it is in them that my race, my ancestors and my historical culture affect me most closely – then we create orphans.
>
> *(Hillman, 1975/1991, p. 44)*

This aligns with Flanagan's sense of exasperation. It is a projecting out – an attempted discarding – of our lost child complex, repeatedly rejecting the history of actively inflicting lostness upon children (material signifiers of the archetype) when they become displaced and burdened by the behaviour of those supposedly acting as figures of authority or guardianship. The lack of compassion involved in such projections involves denying these children their heritage so that they might, in a healthy individuation process, have the opportunity to access, reconcile and abide in their own cultural complexes. The renegade psychopathy that Hillman predicts from such rejection and isolation from a past that has formed who we are, appears to have culminated in all three situations outlined in this chapter: the *Stolen Generations*, the incidents scrutinised in *Royal Commission into Institutional Responses to Child Sexual Abuse* and the *abandonment of child refugees*.

Like the Stolen Generations and the children traumatised by events exposed in the RCIRCSA, the treatment of children in immigration detention magnifies collective shadow projection – the *making of* lost children and their adoption of the complex likely to result from such trauma. We have always known in Australia, as elsewhere in the world, that naming child cruelty incurs both wrath and denial. Two and a half years after the release of Trigg's report, halfway through 2017, Abbott's successor, Malcolm Turnbull, refused to extend Triggs' contract as Commissioner. She nevertheless won the Australian Voltaire, freedom of speech, award in 2017 (Wahlquist, 2017).

A significant part of the controversial phone conversation between Trump and Turnbull on January 28, 2017, satirised on the North American sketch programme *Saturday Night Live* (2017), involved confirmation that the government's November 2016 agreement with former President Barack Obama to resettle 1,250 refugees from the islands of Nauru (including children) and Manus, would still be confirmed. At the time of writing this book the agreement has not been fully honoured and the Manus Island detention centre, with considerable resistance from the remaining adult male refugees who believed it unsafe to be housed elsewhere in Papua New Guinea, officially closed (October 31, 2017). It would seem that is where Trump's 'altruism' ends in light of his now repealed policy to remove small children from their parents at the Mexican border.

Given such recent developments in policies regarding the treatment and detention of children seeking asylum and refugee status, it seems that the film and television industries are still in the formative stages of processing their approach to the issue. Screen material is richest on the internet/social media, current affairs programing and documentary film, where children are rarely the sole focus and refugees feature more than asylum seekers: *Letters to Ali*, 2004 (dir. Law, 2004), *Chasing Asylum* (dir. Orner, 2016), *Molly & Mobarak* (dir. Zubrycki, 2004) and *Go Back to Where You Came From* (SBS television, 2001–2015). While Australian cinema has tackled story-lines of immigration, the struggle of refugees and the hardship of resettlement in such an environmentally alien and at times unwelcoming country – *Silver City* (dir. Turkiewicz, 1984), *The Sound of One Hand Clapping*, *Home Song Stories*, *Lucky Miles* (dir. Rowland, 2007), *Unfinished Sky* (dir. Duncan, 2007) for example – television drama, rather than film has more comprehensively addressed contemporary refugee and asylum seeker narratives.

The most recent example, the miniseries *Safe Harbour* (dir. Ivin, 2017), aired on the Special Broadcasting Service (SBS), Australia's radio and television multicultural broadcaster, dramatically tackles the issue of asylum seekers seeking refuge in Australia through treacherous boat passage organised by 'people smugglers', mainly from Indonesia. The deaths of many families, including children, prompted the Abbott government to adopt the controversial and ruthless policy of containing those arriving by boat in detention centres offshore; a move that virtually stopped the people smuggler trade, but also 'relieved' the government of processing and resettling arrivals onshore (Parliament of Australia, 2017). *Safe Harbor* dramatises the struggle of asylum seekers, through the story of a group of friends, who, while holidaying on their yacht, encounter refugees aboard an unstable boat incapacitated through engine failure. Unable to take all eleven survivors aboard, they tow the boat, but as a storm approaches they are forced to turn back toward Indonesia where the boat departed on its way to Australia. The towrope is severed, the boat is cast adrift and a child dies as the storm sinks the rickety vessel. The four-part series uses the mystery of identifying the person who cut the rope to delve into the traumas, tensions and struggles of resettlement for the surviving Iraqi family of refugees who lost their child at sea.

Sunshine (created by Cameron and McCredie, 2017) is a crime mystery miniseries, focused on the psychological consequences and overcoming of racism for a South Sudanese community of aspiring basketballers. Set in the outer western suburb of Sunshine (Melbourne, Victoria), *Sunshine* addresses the complications of refugee integration, political asylum and the struggles of the South Sudanese community, rarely represented in Australian screen story-telling and too often negatively profiled in the news media. With a similar lost child core, the mystery threaded through the four-part series is built around the assault and sexual predation of a fifteen-year-old wealthy local girl who remains unconscious until the disclosure of the crime.

Marking Time, a 2003 miniseries written by John Doyle and directed by Cherie Nowlan, focuses on the blossoming relationship between two adolescents in a racist, rural town – 'Hal' (Abe Forsythe) the son of the local school teacher, and the Muslim Afghani schoolgirl 'Randa' (Bojanna Novakovic), hosted in the community with her father as asylum seekers escaping the Taliban. As the series closes, and Randa and her father find that they will not be granted refugee status, both are deported. The series climaxes with Hal leaving the country on a mission to find Randa. *Marking Time* was aimed at the xenophobia roused by the government's refugee policies, which in 2003 hadn't reached the level of severity and public scrutiny of more recent years. In the 2004 Australian Film Institute Awards, the series won in seven categories, including four Acting for Television awards, Best Direction in Television, Best Screenplay in Television and Best Telefeature or Miniseries. We have not, as yet, come close to telling fictional, or biographically driven stories that attempt to illuminate the plight of small children in detention centres and offshore camps, as outlined in the *Forgotten Children* report. I am sure this will come, as did the films by indigenous and non-indigenous film-makers that continue to shine a light on the Stolen Generations. When such stories reach our screens, they will signal, as they did with attempts at indigenous reconciliation, a conscious acknowledgement of the damage that projections of the lost child complex can inflict: projections that suggest repression, fear, disavowal and failure to individuate.

These darker aspects of the lost child complex that suggest a doubly wounded country/collective at odds with itself, address, as Triggs intimated, the soul of the culture. In borrowing Kalsched's self-care system of psychic splitting where the inner wounded/victim is terrorised by a misguided 'protective' aspect of the psyche, we might think of double wounding as a version of this, where the inner lost child is so vulnerable that protecting it implies a form of burial or disavowal: a fear of acknowledgement because of the *affect* attached in rousing this wound. The lost child then can be projected outward in a reckless form of protection from the trauma of confrontation. The idea of the complex's capacity to generate double wounding is not of course a defence for the kind of behaviours discussed in this chapter, but a way of trying to wrestle with the nature of the complex and its potential to shape a sense of collective identity: 'Projections change the world into a replica of one's own face' (Jung, 1959/1969: § 17).

While many Australians remain not simply dissatisfied, but angry at the inaction of past governments and institutions for their responses to the Stolen Generations, institutionalised child sex abuse and the treatment of refugee children, racist and hard-hearted undercurrents that resist the kind of shift needed to confront cultural shadows are, of course, not unique to this country. Encounters potentially leading to reconciliation though, are a prerequisite for individuation – genuine inward reflection can facilitate change, as we'll see in the following chapter.

5
INNER AND OUTER TWINNING
Parent as lost child/lost child as parent

Deeply problematic governmental and institutional initiatives and behaviours that impose lostness on children is an expression of the complex that can be related to similar and yet quite divergent forms of double wounding. This chapter looks at cinema where the concept of the lost child, and lostness itself as an archetypal motif, is profoundly embedded in parental figures. It is not simply that these parents carry an unevolved inner child, but they are trapped *in* and *by* their childhood: disturbing memories readily enough recalled, but inadequately felt, and so remain 'ghosts in the nursery' as Fraiberg, Adelson and Shapiro describe these intrusive inner presences (1975, p. 387). While aspects of the parents' inner child might be fleetingly glimpsed, their projections onto actual children render innocent others, lost through no fault or misdirection of their own. Both directly and indirectly they create the conditions for their own children's lostness through *parentification* – the endowment of caregiver and/or guardian roles. Through this behaviour we are able to see a dual form of victim/protector *twinning*. The inner child of the parent appears to be nurtured by the corporeal outer child, and the corporeal parent finds nourishment through the child's prematurely developed inner parent. I'm going to focus in depth on four films that exemplify this aspect of the lost child in Australian cinema as a way of more intimately exploring this psychological exchange: Jennifer Kent's gothic horror *The Babadook* (2013), Glenda Hambly's *Fran* (1985), Richard Roxburgh's *Romulus My Father* (2007) and Tony Ayres' *The Home Song Stories* (2007).

Each film won in multiple AACTA award categories with *The Babadook* taking out best Film, Direction and Original Screenplay; *Fran* – best Lead Actress, Supporting Actress and Original Screenplay; *Romulus My Father* – best Lead Actor, Film, Supporting Actor and Young Actor; and *The Home Song Stories* winning in eight categories – best Original Music Score, Lead Actress, Direction, Cinematography, Screenplay, Production Design, Editing and Costume Design. The critical success of these core lost child films speaks to the skill of cast, screenwriters and crew, as well as the tendency of the lost child complex to be generationally embraced as a storytelling vehicle able to tap into the sore-and-sweet-spots of a culture.

These texts have been selected because of their sensitive and insightful approach to the character of a vulnerable parent who is helplessly and traumatically struggling with demons (literally and figuratively) and the child/children on the receiving end of their shadow, who to some degree serve as multiple grail projections. These popular films avoid sentimentality and moral judgement. The emotionally *stuck* adult who has difficulty with their own inner chaos and the effect this turbulence has on their child is dealt with empathetically. What is particularly moving about each work is the central child's resilience in the face of traumatising parenting. The films variously focus on the socio-economic, emotional and mental health issues of sole parenting, and while women take the dominant focus in this discussion, there is no investment here in 'mother-blaming'. What interests me are the ghosts that haunt each story.

The child/ren drawn into such family dynamics, although clearly depicted as lost in a physical sense, demonstrate an extraordinary buoyancy. Many take on parenting responsibilities, demonstrate stability in the face of emotional turmoil and become aspiring heroes in a quest to defeat the anxieties destabilising their parent/s. The situational lostness they experience through abandonment or neglect runs parallel to the inner dislocation of those who, almost against their will, have placed these children in such precarious situations. The children tend to adopt a grail-like quality in their ability to provide a degree of guidance and healing to the inner lost child of their emotionally fragile mothers.

Childhood ghosts and parentification

Selma Fraiberg, Edna Adelson and Vivian Shapiro's seminal paper 'Ghosts in the Nursery: A Psychoanalytic Approach to the Problems of Impaired Infant-Mother relationships' (1975), approaches issues of neglect and rejecting motherhood from the interdisciplinary perspective of psychoanalysis, developmental psychology and social work. Although *Romulus My Father* is the only film in this section to deal with the kind of mother-infant abandonment this paper focuses on, and here neglect appears to be more couched in postnatal depression, Fraiberg, Adelson and Shapiro's work provides a relevant perspective to each of the films and the concept of the parental inner lost child. Drawing on two complex case studies of rejecting mothers to illustrate their approach and findings, they argue that the repression of childhood trauma, 'provides motive and energy for repetition' of pathological parenting, where the parent adopts the aggressive behaviour they were subjected to as children (Freud, 1936/1966, p. 419). In attempting to tap the source of this repression, avoiding *history as destiny* thinking, they found, 'that memory for the events of [the parents'] childhood abuse, tyranny, and desertion was available in explicit and chilling detail. What was not remembered was the affective experience' (p. 419). Although these parents could readily recount events of their abuse in ways that were detached, even cynical, they were unable to access the painful feelings experienced at the time. Acknowledgement of the *affect* of lost/traumatic childhoods eventually allowed them to empathise with their own children's need for affection: 'In each case our therapy has brought the parent to remember and re-experience his childhood anxiety and suffering, the ghosts depart, and the afflicted parents become the protectors of their children against the repetition of their own conflicted past' (Fraiberg, Adelson and Shapiro, 1975, pp. 420–421).

These emotionally detached memories, or 'ghosts', can be thought of as inner lost children. Such presences make appearances overtly or covertly in *Fran*, *The Home Song Stories* and *Romulus My Father* – while more recent trauma haunts the world of *The Babadook*. Although we are witness to parental neglect and the physical abuse of the children in these films through repression and repetition, we are more explicitly subject to their parentification – a role that is either enforced on the child, or adopted through compassion and necessary. In this way we see the inner child parented by the inner adult *at the same time* as we see the outer child reaching toward, and almost intuitively acknowledging, its twin buried in the parent.

Parentification was primarily defined by Ivan Broszormenyi-Nagy and Geraldine M. Spark as a term that 'implies the subjective distortion of a relationship as if one's partner or even children were his parent. Such distortion can be done in a wishful fantasy or, more dramatically, through dependent behavior' (1973/1984, p. 151). They emphasis that such relationships need not be uniformly classified as pathological, but intense parent/child role reversals have been thought to not only affect childhood development, but also trigger more problematic conditions – narcissism, anxiety, shame and depression (Jurkovic, 2014; Katz, Petracca and Rabinowitz, 2009; Earley and Cushway, 2002). Gregory Jurkovic goes so far as to claim that, 'the childhood of destructively parentified children is lost' (2014, p. xiv). His thinking is more clearly aligned to the behaviour of characters in the films under discussion here rather than the more benign forms of role assignment and loyalty gestures within the less dysfunctional families: 'pathological parentification is a discriminable category of maltreatment in its own right. In addition to being part of the spectrum of problems subsumed under the label "child maltreatment", severe forms of parentification may have specific etiologies, sequelae, intergenerational transmission patterns, and treatment responses' (p. xx).

Pathological parentification as we'll see, can also suggest ghosts in the nursery, for 'parents who are classed as high on parentifying measures will attempt to address their loss of emotional nurturing as a child through their own children' (Earley and Cushway, 2002, p. 173; also see Broszormenyi-Nagy and Spark, 1973/1984; Jurkovic, 2014). The tendency for generational repetition of child abuses, repression and parentification, hinted at in *Fran* and *The Home Song Stories*, can also be applied to films not included here that might be considered to fall under the category of inner/outer lost child twinning. Although parentification is not as overt in *The Babadook*, the child emerges as a potential hero driven by a need to protect his mother, and even when fearful of her shadow possession, he is still intent on saving her from the spectre of past trauma.

Grief and possession

Kent's gothic horror, *The Babadook*, is a rare genre film in Australian cinema. Developed from her earlier black and white short *The Monster* (2005) it pays homage to classic possession films like *The Exorcist* (dir. Friedkin, 1973), *The Sinning* (dir. Kubrick, 1980), *Repulsion* (dir. Polanski, 1965), the *Nightmare on Elm Street* franchise originally created by Wes Carven (1984–2010), haunted house clichés and adolescent/child poltergeist possession. It is also deftly aligned with Robin Wood's influential Freudian reading of the 1960–1970s American horror film as a genre driven by a *return of the repressed* where children often feature 'as the monster or its medium' (Wood, 1986/2002, p. 29). Added to these more obvious pop culture references, Kent draws on early German expressionism and silent film surrealists like George Méliès and Segundo de Chomón: we see Amelia (Essie Davis) as the sole parent in this basically two-handed mother-son narrative, try to sooth her insomnia by watching interwoven genres of television and silent film including short sequences of Chomón's *La Maison Ensorcelée* – The House of Ghosts (1908).

The story centres on a fraught mother plagued by her six-year-old son Sam's (Noah Wiseman) night terrors and obsession with fighting monsters. She is left as sleepless as a new mother with what might at first be thought of as prolonged postnatal depression. Sam is seemingly driven to rage and convulsions by these creatures, particularly the figure from a pop-up story book, *Mr Babadook*, and yet he is equally possessed by the need to protect and save his mother. In order to sleep, relieve her stress around the child's relentless behaviour and regain some semblance of normal functioning, Amelia is prescribed sedatives for the child. As Sam begins to adopt a regular sleep pattern, reducing his anxiety, Mr Babadook begins to haunt Amelia, drawing her to erratic, hallucinogenic trips where the walls appear to secrete cockroaches and leading her into uncontrollable filicidal rage toward her child. She even strangles the family dog in a fit of mania. The increasingly demonic possession of both child and then mother takes place at the time of Sam's birthday, a distressing anniversary that Amelia never celebrates. We discover that on the day of Sam's birth, her husband, driving her to hospital, crashed the car. Amelia witnessed his decapitation. The psychological intrigue of repression and trauma driving the tensions between Amelia and Sam, and then its materialisation as a dominating shadow, make *The Babadook* quite an exceptional film in a culture reluctant to cinematically play with psychology and, even more pointedly, maternal rage. Amelia's feelings 'develop an energy that becomes something that splits off from her and then starts to control her' says Kent (*The Babadook*, 2014). In referencing Kubrick's *The Sinning*, where a possessed father attempts to kill his wife and child, Davis adopts a compassionate view of her character; 'It's about facing your trauma and grief . . . and you have to live with that . . . and in a way nurture it, to have any kind of balance' (*The Babadook*, 2014).

Kalsched references *Mourning and Melancholia* (Freud, 1917), reiterating Freud's insistence that 'that loss of the loved object must be actively grieved one step at a time and that a failure to spend adequate time doing this . . . leads to depression. . . . In Dante's poem we see the terrifying inner world that results from such untransformed mourning' (Kalsched, 2013, p. 100). This haunting is brought to life in the monstrous materialisation of Amelia's failure to acknowledge her grief and form a genuine attachment her son – screaming when in the possessed state, 'You don't know how many times I wished it was you and not him who had died'. We don't see this lost child aspect of the complex in Amelia, in a departure from the three other films – her own childhood trauma is not the source of her parenting dilemma. But like *Fran*, *Romulus My Father* and *The Home Song Stories*, *The Babadook* suggests the danger of projecting the untransformed energy of loss onto children.

As Amelia reads Sam *Mr Babadook*, the text of the pop-up book clearly stresses the importance of acknowledging the shadow, living with it and incorporating it into a more individuated sense of identity: 'You can't get rid of the Babadook' she recites, but if 'you know what it is to see' you can befriend this 'special one'. Although Kent is reluctant to reveal and so impose any detailed psychological framework, allusions to the Jungian shadow literally and figuratively shape the film. Images in the storybook of large black silhouettes encroaching on a sleeping child and an Amelia-like mother figure become reflected in the action of the film. We see shadows of the Babadook's outline on the walls and ceilings of Amelia and Sam's gothic terrace house, a set designed from a colour palette of dark blues, greys and black. The hauntings take place at night, with the Babadook shadow only diminished by the switching on of lights and the occasional glow of the television screen. Amelia finally confronts and stares down the Babadook demanding to know what it wants. Sam then straps her with rope to the floor of the basement where she stores precious memorabilia of her husband. This scene, where the Babadook is goaded into submission, borrows from the frenzied bed-tying sequences in *The Exorcist*, even culminating in Amelia vomiting a black blood-like substance as if expelling an internal shadow. At the end of the film, Amelia and Sam celebrate his birthday together, sharing it with the subdued Babadook that they now keep in the basement and periodically feed with worms. This conclusion neatly folds into a Jungian reading of reconciliation. Casement's summation of this necessary step is not just an uncanny synopsis of sorts for Kent's film, but also for Wood's earlier analysis of American horror:

> The conflict that ensues from confrontation with the shadow in both alchemy and analytical psychology must eventually result in a union or coniunctio, the term Jung borrows from alchemy. It is a struggle that has

to be lived through and experienced and cannot be abolished by rational means or repression, as the latter means that it lives in the unconscious, and, in that way, is all the more subversive to the conscious personality.

(Casement, 2006, p. 101)

In tackling the necessity of reconciliation with what one finds unbearable, Zen teacher John Tarrant writes that 'the courage with which we bear our darkness frees others from having to carry it for us' (Tarrant, 1998, p. 170). *The Babadook* provides a revisited mythological fantasy of this psychological pathology, so apt for the horror genre – even the silent surrealist films that inspired Kent's vision of Amelia's repression and its material manifestation add to the texture of the unconscious nature of uncanny imagery, often mobilised through horror: Freud's *unheimlich* and *heimisch* (strange and familiar) tension able to arouse the repressed (Freud, 1919/1955). As Barbara Creed has so prolifically outlined in her body of work on the psychoanalytic punch of the genre, disavowed and externalised psychic material, seemingly beyond articulation or identification, can indeed shape the monster that confronts the possessed subject (see Creed, 1993, 2005).

Fran

From the blurred margins of supernatural/psychological possession and projection, the following films use social realism to address the inner lost child. The children made lost in these texts are unable to fully, or safely, experience their own youth – it is as if in the process of rescuing the hapless parent by adopting the role of primary carer, the child sacrifices/loses her/his own childhood. Before looking at how this reverse role-playing is imagined in the memoirs *Romulus My Father* and *Home Song Stories*, it is important to first consider Glenda Hambly's *Fran*, one of the first films to make a significant contribution to this sub-genre of lost child stories. Made in cooperation with the then West Australian Department of Community Services, *Fran* was primarily developed from a documentary project centred on child fostering for Perth's department of community welfare: 'They were trying a new policy called permanency planning where if your children were fostered out for long periods of time, in order to give them permanency, they were going to allow them to be adopted by the new foster parents' says Hambly (*Fran*, 2010). Although the policy wasn't endorsed, she restructured her research of women potentially affected by the controversial strategy, into a feature film. Hambly didn't appear to consciously create a drama about the particular form of parent/child lostness discussed in this chapter, but *Fran* is a blisteringly relevant portrayal of an emotionally and psychologically unanchored woman, struggling with parental responsibilities and seemingly incapable of protecting her three children from the cycle of abandonment and abuse.

Fran Carter's (Noni Hazlehurst) inability to provide a more stable life than she experienced as a child appears intricately bound to her failure to confront, reconcile and nurture her internal child, revealed to be increasingly directionless as the narrative unfolds. The character returns us sharply to the cultural complex, for it is in this kind of internal wilderness, intensified by poverty and violence, that the displaced child thrives – passing from generation to generation. In this sense *Fran* is central to this book's argument that Australian cinema echoes the culture's archetypal obsessions and its desire for self-reflection.

As the narrative takes us through Fran's sense of abandonment, we come to realise that the journey we take with her is one she has repeated may times in the past as a mother and the child of neglectful parents. Dependent on support from others, unable to hold down a steady job and driven to attempted suicide on a number of occasions, Fran is frequently alone and deserted by the emotionally inaccessible men in her life – her own father, her husband and her new paedophile boyfriend Jeff (Alan Fletcher) found to have been abusing her eldest daughter Lisa (Narelle Simpson). She also intermittently abandons her own children to spend nights and later an extended holiday in Northern Australia; behaviour that, coupled with Lisa's abuse, forces the welfare agency to remove her children. Fran's inability to address recurring problems and learn from her mistakes suggests an unwillingness to confront the deeper and more painful issues of her life since childhood. Because of this, she often behaves with the impulsivity, immaturity and limited awareness of consequences that one expects and tolerates of children, not adults. It is as if she is immobilised *in* and *by* her own childhood – unable to individuate. As Hazlehurst says in the audio commentary to the National Film and Sound Archive's preserved release, 'This was a woman who had absolutely no ability to make the right choices as far as her children were concerned because of her own background. That's what I liked about it – it was the cycle of dysfunction' (*Fran*, 2010).

Snippets of Fran's dialogue, presented as throw away lines, alert us to the depth of this instability. Her unsettled upbringing is introduced four minutes into the film with a friend's use of cleaning bleach – 'I can't stand it', says Fran, 'the standard issue in every institution I was ever in'. She describes herself as being sexually 'fair game' to school boys when she was a child, running away from home at fifteen years old and spending her childhood in and out of foster homes: 'they put me mum away when I was five, she's an alchy [alcoholic]'. Fran talks of her promiscuous mother and a father she never knew. Her dialogue implies a suicidal past where she was forced to rely on the invalid pension, and yet she resists applying for the supporting mother's pension because of its requisite monitoring of her movements. Fran's snatched recollections are largely disassociated from emotion, consistent with Fraiberg, Adelson and Shapiro's findings that good-enough parenting by those who have been traumatised is only possible when *affect* accompanies the memories of childhood abuse.

Like a rebellious adolescent, she appears to construct welfare itself and more compassionate social workers within the system, as parents; lying to them, not wanting to be beholden to their conditions, and yet depending on their constant presence for random backup support. The undeveloped side of Fran is also transparent to her paedophile boyfriend Jeff who not only abuses Fran, but her daughter Lisa – the one on whom the mothering role of cooking and caring for the other children often falls. Both children and adults are parentified in this triadic relationship – Fran appears to seek parental affection and attention from Jeff, and they parentify Lisa as a caregiver and sexual object respectively: 'If one adult parentfies another – for example, a mate – the distortion usually occurs through a fantasied, often unconscious, regression of the self to a childlike position' (Broszormenyi-Nagy and Spark, 1973/1984, p. 152). Jeff's instinctive tapping into the archetypal core of Fran's almost intractable lost child complex, and then taking full advantage of this weaknesss, is a form of unconscious cruelty that she masochistically invites and encourages to the detriment of her own, and her children's, well-being – most particularly Lisa.

The behaviour is reminiscent of Fraiberg, Adelson and Shapiro's first case study of a woman they call Mrs March and her baby Mary. The mother was observed to be ignoring her baby's cries, as if she hadn't heard them,

> This is a mother whose own cries have not been heard. . . . The mother's distant voice, her remoteness and remove we saw as defenses against grief and intolerable pain. Her terrible story had been first given factually, without visible suffering, without tears. . . . She had closed the door on the weeping child within herself as surely as she had closed the door upon her crying baby.
>
> *(Fraiberg, Adelson and Shapiro, 1975, pp. 395–396)*

Fran's traumatic past, with its hinted sexual abuse, remains unfelt; as if her cries, like Mrs March's, had been unheard at the time and are still unfelt on a conscious level. She brushes off Lisa's sexual abuse by Jeff as lies, never considering the child's pain or trauma, much as she fails to emotionally experience her own childhood suffering. As with Mrs March, '*When this mother's own cries are heard, she will hear her child's cries*' (Fraiberg, Adelson and Shapiro, 1975, p. 396 emphasis as original). But one senses that Fran will never hear her own sorrow, and even when she talks about previous suicide attempts, there is no sense that the associated emotion has ever been deeply addressed. Lisa therefore will similarly not be heard.

While the *Babadook* and *Fran* can be placed in distinctive yet almost opposing film traditions – social realism and gothic horror – like all artistic genres, their boundaries are porous. In Aviva Briefel's analysis of *The Babadook*, a text dominated by a mother providing exhausting reassurances to her son, the film becomes a vehicle through which director Jennifer Kent 'uses horror conventions to provide an unprecedented critique of the burdens of maternal responsibility' (Briefel, 2017, p. 3). Briefel's position that the monster, Mr Babadook, becomes an analogy of the overwhelming fears of parent-child intimacy, also resonates in Hambly's construction of Fran:

> As Kent shows through the character of Amelia early on, the parent may be as terrified of the destructiveness of intimacy as the child is – in the

first part of the film, she flinches at Samuel's insistent, oedipally tinged embraces – and such a fear can lead to a denial of the real or imagined monsters that occupy their worlds.

(Briefel, 2017, p. 21)

Although we don't see allusions to fictional creatures, the calculated gothic touches of the mise-en-scene, or terror externalised in screams, murderous intent, and blood-letting, we are witness to a darkness in Fran that clearly exposes a fear of mature intimacy and its perceived destructive ramifications.

Fran's most genuine sense of loving revolves around her children, and yet this intimacy is often self-sabotaged. In a sequence quite early in the film when her children return from school trying to embrace her, Fran, in a drunken stupor from a day alone confronted with the repetition of housework, itself a metaphor for the cyclic and exhausting mess-clearing of her own life, yells and physically pushes them away as if repulsed by their affection, leaving Lisa to adopt the parenting role. She frequently abandons them, rejecting their neediness when it thwarts her attempts at independence, and in denying Jeff's abuse of Lisa, once again subjects her children to the prospect of being fostered.

Fran's maternal ambivalence is not constructed as monstrous, and yet the synergies between her and Amelia's trauma become increasingly transparent. The pull of Fran's own inner child demanding recognition, and her inability to profoundly address past traumas, is perhaps the most poignant thread in Hambly's work. At least in a Jungian sense, Amelia confronts, acknowledges and nurtures her shadow, but one senses Fran will always be in thrall to her phantom orphan. The false intimacy she finds in her sexual relationships with men, who, as her friend Marge (Annie Byron) reminds her, are invariably shallow, transitory and violent, can be read as a deflection from more genuine and fear-provoking closeness; an avoidance of intimacy with her children and her own deprived inner child. Trauma is suggested as the monster driving Fran and Amelia; the result of memories that have been randomly recalled and yet not deeply confronted because of the psychologically tormenting weight they carry. As Hambly and Kent show us, repression and disavowal allow for the shape-shifting of trauma into shadow material which can attach itself malignantly to the lost child core of the cultural complex.

Memoir

The final two memoir-based films touch on the parental projections of lostness and psychological instability through parent/s and child. Based on the memoir of philosopher Raimond Gaita, now public academic and Professorial Fellow at the University of Melbourne, Richard Roxburgh's *Romulus My Father* is the story of Rai's (Kodi Smit-McPhee) journey through the fraught co-dependency and separation of his migrant parents. Like the child Tom of *The Home Song Stories*, Rai whose memoir we watch unfold, takes on the role of narrator. Raised in the small Victorian town of Frogmore, primarily by his Romanian speaking Yugoslav father Romulus (Eric Bana), the film, beginning in 1960, addresses his German mother Christina's (Franka Potente) sense of restlessness, postnatal depression and eventual suicide. There are many ways to read Roxburgh's work, particularly the profound father-son affection and enduring bond at the heart of Gaita's original text and the film, but for the purposes of this chapter, the relationship Roxburgh creates between Christina and Rai demonstrates a more poignant sense of partentification and loss: 'I was always afraid Richard Roxburgh would romanticize my mother. . . . But I don't think he does' says Gaita to Australian author Helen Garner as they retrace the landscape of Gaita's childhood where the film was shot (Garner, 2007, p. 43).

> 'This,' says Gaita in his quiet, neutral voice, 'must be where they shot the bit with the pram' – a scene in which the boy Raimond, trundling a pram that contains his baby half-sister, pursues his disturbed mother as she leads a stranger into a shed and has sex with him against a wall, while the frantic boy watches the encounter, with its violence and degradation, through a crack in the corrugated iron.
>
> *(Garner, 2007, p. 43)*

Standing beside him at Christina's gravestone marked *She Suffered Deeply*, Garner notes that Christina was not yet thirty years old when she died.

Following a similar trajectory as Christina, the single mother Rose (Joan Chen) in writer/director Tony Ayres' autobiography *The Home Song Stories*, also takes her own life. Marrying an Australian sailor, Rose, a Shanghai nightclub singer, and her small children May and Tom (the childhood Ayres) move from China to Melbourne. Her years of drifting from man to man, frustration at the confines of parenthood and suggested bipolar mood swings, link her to Fran. Although Fran survives, rather than ending with a sense of resolution, Hambly suggests that the loss of her children to the welfare system will inevitably launch her on another downward emotional spiral. In the final shot of the film, as Lisa is being held by welfare before her foster home placement, she gazes in a mirror as she brushes her hair: Hambly holds this image as if to force the question of whether she will perpetuate the cycle of familial dysfunction or defy it. The accounts of Fran, Christina and Rose's struggles with lostness, motherhood and economic survival under trying circumstances that lead to their dependence on men, also reinforces the trauma attached to their archetypal lost child. As we'll see later, this becomes most explicit when toward the closing scenes of *The Home Song Stories*, Rose recounts the suffering of her own childhood to a now adolescent May (Irene Chen) as both recuperate in hospital after suicide attempts.

Unlike *The Babadook*, the children in *Romulus My Father* and *The Home Song Stories*, while distressed by their mother's erratic behaviour, become her central source of stability. The occasional neglectful and physically abusive behaviour of the mothers here, more so than Fran, takes on a sense of ghostliness, as if Rose and Christina were somehow possessed by a force beyond their control, as is Amelia in *The Babadook*; Rose, jealously slapping and raging at May's attraction to men while her own beauty fades, and Christina physically and emotionally abandoning her second child to Romulus' friend Mitru (Russell Dykstra), Rai's helpless infant half-sister Susan. As she limply holds the baby, refusing to feed or change her nappies, the once beautiful and whimsical Christina sinks into herself, becoming almost lifeless. Rai adopts a parenting role, comforting the baby, and as Garner remembers from the film, wheeling her in the pram. Susan is eventually placed in an orphanage. The sons, and authors of these stories, Rai and Tom (Joel Lok), do not seem to suffer the physical brunt of their mothers' instability with the same force as their sisters, but through intermittent abandonment, are nevertheless tied into the lost child complex.

The terror of degrading intimacy to a destructive energy, raised by Briefel earlier, which can lead to a lack of insight into, or disavowal of, the inner demons it gives rise to, is reinforced in the films discussed here by the overwhelming and distanced love each of these mothers show to their children. With the exception of Christina, it is possible to interpret the love/rage ambivalence, particularly toward the daughters, as an outward projection of the lost child – a violent external rendering of lostness, a repetition of callous treatment in childhood, and an inability to address or accept/nurture their own impoverished inner child. 'Even among families where the love bonds are stable and strong' write Fraiberg, Adelson and Shapiro, 'the intruders from the parental past may break through the magic circle in an unguarded moment, and a parent and his [sic] child may find themselves reenacting a moment or a scene from another time with another set of characters' (p. 387). Only in *The Home Song Stories* and *The Babadook* is there a sense of final confrontation with traumatic pasts. Fran alludes to her childhood frequently, but refuses to confront the feelings inherent in the shadows it raises, and so in keeping with the allegory of *The Babadook*, feeds her demons – we are not clear about Christina's past, there is no suggestion of childhood trauma, but one senses a history of untreated mental illness and instability compounded by her move to Australia with Romulus and four-year-old Rai. Like *The Babadook*, the closing sequences of *The Home Song Stories* allow us to witness the trauma at the heart Rose's story.

As Rose and May recover in hospital from suicide attempts – May's overdose prompted by her mother's brutal behaviour – Rose tries to explain her past. In flashback sequences, overlaid with Rose's monologue, we are told of her childhood as the youngest daughter of loveless family who arranged her marriage to a cruel older man. At seventeen Rose became pregnant; 'But I was a child myself, I didn't know how to take care of a baby' she says, 'so my first daughter, your elder sister died'. She lost another baby when she was eighteen years old, and then fell in love with her husband's younger brother. The scandal drove the couple to Shanghai where they lived an impoverished life. When her lover committed suicide Rose was pregnant with May: 'It was always you' she tells her, 'you always save me'. After this episode Rose begins to decline and eventually dies after an attempt to hang herself, but one senses that this confession or confrontation with the lost child releases both daughter and to some degree, mother.

Rose's child/adolescent past is never revealed till this point. Her promiscuity and caprice, previously couched as part financial necessity and part escape, is given a poignant depth in this monologue. We are now permitted, as she permits herself, to *feel* the traumatic source of her need for continual acceptance and affection without shame or judgement. The cathartic moment has parallels with Fraiberg, Adelson and Shapiro's case studies. The authors see Mrs March's tentative disclosure of her emotionally deprived childhood as 'the beginning of new insights. . . . As she was helped [by her therapist] to re-experience loss, grief, the feelings of rejection in childhood, she could no longer inflict this pain upon her own child' (p. 400). 'Annie', the sixteen-year-old parent in the second case study, is able to recall brutal events but not their *affect*. Through therapy she eventually begins to allow herself 'the permission to feel along with remembering' (Fraiberg, Adelson and Shapiro, 1975, p. 408).

The Fran-Lisa, Christina-Susan, Rose-May dynamics hint at a cyclic repetition of lostness, and yet in each film, including *The Babadook*, these children, along with the narrators Rai and Tom, appear to have resisted, even escaped the shadow aspects of the complex. Because each child was forced to confront, and protect their mothers, they appear to have accepted and nurtured not only their parents' archetypal lost child, but their own sense of material and emotional lostness. There is a suggestion of resilience in *Fran's* final shot of Lisa in the mirror – an image of defiance and nurturing; Amelia and Sam's care and feeding of the basement bound Babadook; Rai and Tom's ability to reflect on their challenging pasts without sidestepping the associated pain; May becoming a school psychologist; and Susan removed from welfare to be cared for by Rai and his father Romulus. This is of course also intertextually layered by the national celebrity of Raimond Gaita and Tony Ayres, a literature and philosophy graduate, now a successful director and producer. While Ayres, through the character of the adult Tom, tells us in voice-over at the end of the film that, 'we never talk about our mother, neither of us knows what to say', the film opens with an expression of his need to confront what might be thought of as a form of ghosts in the nursery – 'If everyone has one story which defines them, shapes who they are, then this is mine . . . I write over and over trying to understand her, and all the things she did'.

Grail child and wastelands

Each of the children here also follow the pattern of characters in more literal lost child cinema discussed in Chapter 2, as combinations of the grail-bearer, Perceval and the grail itself. The sense of a romantic quest, intrinsic to *lost in the bush* narratives as noted by Dermody and further identified here as grail quests, can been modified in this instance with the grail not as an object of healing or a healing quality to be *searched for*, but a sense of restorative support readily accessible and identifiable to the parent in the form of parentified children. While one might experience a sense of questing in *The Babadook* to identify, confront and sooth the inner monster/shadow, the lost child within Fran, Christina and Rose are not as clearly alluded to as archetypal complexes that need to be retrieved and challenged. Because they are never acknowledged as lost, and so in need being claimed, their inaccessibility is key to the story. Fran and Rose reveal the ghosts of these inner children, but each spectre is placed firmly in the past rather than challenged as the unshakable psychological drivers of their behaviour. Unlike *The Babdook*, these inner energies are never brought to the surface so that their woundedness can be understood and soothed. The actual children of these women come to represent that which they cannot grasp in themselves – a grail-like form of salvation. What we see is a twinning, with the outer more evolved child, reaching to the inner child of the parent in a form of protective partnership.

As argued in Chapter 2, when Australian lost child stories are couched as quest narratives, particularly grail quests, the expectation that heroism should focus the action seems misplaced, belonging to more Vogler-inspired, victory driven frameworks common to North American cinema (discussed in Chapter 7). While the *lost in the bush* genre (modernised to include urban and transnational environments as in *Lion*) varies in its degree of climactic, frustrated or enigmatic conclusions, *child-as-grail* quests are intrinsic to its structure. In the collection of films discussed here, and an entire sub-genre that falls into this pattern of parents rendering children lost through their own sense of arrested development, unpredictability and displacement – *The Sound of One Hand Clapping*, *Here I Am*, *Shame* (dir. Jodrell, 1988) and *High Tide* for instance – the child at the heart of the drama, despite their lack of anchorage and parental stability, becomes a source of redemption and/or futurity. It is as if the parents seek a sense of becoming in their children: a wish to not necessarily be rescued themselves, but to ease their own inner lostness through their child's ability to rise above the chaos that they have facilitated. What we discover in these stories, is the resilient twin of the parental lost child.

The notion of the child as grail and grail-bearer is therefore linked to a form of parentification that idealises the child (Jurkovic, 2014, p. 6). 'Mothers with histories of early abuse will have specific difficulties in developing a representation, or model, of themselves as a safe and caring parent and may have wishes and needs that they hope an infant will fulfil' writes Louise Newman in her paper linking Fraiberg, Adelson and Shapiro's findings with borderline personality disorder. 'For example, a mother who has been neglected and emotionally deprived may hope that her child will care for her and meet all her emotional needs' (2008, p. 217). While parentification has raised concern for positive childhood developmental, Louise Early and Delia Cushway in their overview of the literature balance the tendency to focus on the maladaptive outcomes of partentification with its potential to broaden a child's understanding of relationship: 'Parentified roles could therefore function as precursors to the development of appropriate adult responsibility taking. It is feasible on this basis that a continuum of parentification exists from appropriate to inappropriate caretaking' (2002, p. 170). When thinking back to Chapter 2, in relation to Cooper's association of McCarthy's *The Road* with grail mythologies, the father in the novel and film is revealed to be a form of elder Fisher King, 'wounded and infected by that which is destroying the land' and his son, a combination of grail-bearer and grail (Cooper, 2011, p. 226). The parents discussed in this chapter similarly adopt the combined role of wounded elder Fisher King, incapable of healing themselves, and guardians of the grail (when applying the child-as-grail metaphor) in the protective love they show. As the wounded king entrusted Perceval, the youngest of King Arthur's knights, with healing his wounds, so the mothers in these films parentify in order to survive.

The story of the wounded king who guards the grail, his kingdom a potential wasteland, and Perceval the pure of heart who after a failed attempt, relocates the king and voices the appropriate questions – *who does the grail serve?* and *what ails you?* – in order for fertility to be assured, is useful in thinking about the mythical and psychological import of the films discussed above. The King's realm was earlier referred to a potential wasteland. The harsh environments depicted in this chapter are far from the apocalyptic wastelands of *The Road*, but they nevertheless portray barrenness, actual and latent, generated by a mixture of emotional, socio-economic and psychological circumstances. The idea of a potential wasteland in the wounded Fisher King mythology was tied into Chrétien de Troyes's earliest version of the story. Later authors embellishing and reshaping the original were more explicit in describing a wilderness directly associated with the King's wound – either a supernatural punishment, or a consequence of war and illness laying the land to ruin (Marino, 2004). Similar to the ruin of the environment and potentially the King's subjects, the wasteland experienced in these films is haunted. When looking at the lost child complex, each film plays with the notion that a mixture of innocence and integrity is needed to restore fertility. All the principal children carry an essence of the grail's purity and Perceval's sense of duty and compassion – May, Rose's child to the only man she loved who *saves* her and is forced to curb her erratic behaviour; Sam in *The Babadook* who invents devices to protect his mother and eventually ties her to the basement floor as means of forcing a confrontation with trauma; Lisa who keeps house and nurtures a mother unable to care for herself; and Rai who tries to protect both his parents from self-harm while positioning himself as the point of connection and futurity between them. By acknowledging and acting on the *right questions* of what ails their parents, they altruistically serve as conduits for, or beacons of, potential healing.

The dominant or intermittent worlds Fran, Amelia, Rose, Christina and Rai's father Romulus create for their children are precarious, heightened by near poverty, the struggle to support their families and tender moments of optimism that are inevitably undercut by disappointment. We might interpret this as a form of wasteland that these children navigate, and from which they resiliently emerge. Their presence can be read, as Cooper writes of grail narratives in general, as a way of interpolating 'images of fertility into a world characterized by infertility' (p. 226). And deeper within their wilderness is the impoverished inner child of the parent – lost and, with the exception of Amelia, largely unrecoverable.

There are clear parallels in Rai and Tom's stories with Davis' biopic, *Lion*. All three films position the narrators/protagonists as both *grail-lost child* and *seeker* of the grail-lost child in their quest to recover memories of their parents and in the process their vulnerable childhood selves. The third element of *grail guardian*, which Perceval ultimately becomes, can also be seen in the reflective way these characters come to terms with, and potentially abide in, the experiences and perspectives of the retrieved child they present to us. One might argue that all three stories are more about the becoming of the child, than the redemption or retrieval of lost parents.

The idea of adult characters being haunted and regressed through an inability to reconcile the pain of their own childhood is looked at further in the following chapter. The difference is that in this next discussion of how the complex can manifest, adult characters do not parentify or render their own or other children lost. They are more clearly caught in their own displaced pasts – worlds that they inhabit affectionately and uncomfortably with a tacit understanding that while it is important to move on, it is also important to return.

PART THREE
Inner children and the victory complex

6

STUCK IN THE PAST

Lost child as earworm

Specific or fleeting memories of childhood, triggered by spaces, smells, emotions or even colours, have a curious correlation with earworms – those songs that get stuck in your head on a continuous loop, or pop up spontaneously at pertinent times as if to tell you what you are *really* thinking of a situation/person. In this revisitation of the lost child, I'm going to look more intimately at films where the seemingly autonomous complex claims and haunts adult characters, returning them to their childhoods with a tenacity, that like the earworm, is difficult to shake. Often unable to move beyond the restricting limits that the complex places on their reflections, perceptions and behaviours, they remain caught by, yet resist disavowing, the child – they hold on to it as a tangible reality. Although the memories are uncomfortable, there appears to be some security in the familiarity of these phantoms. The stories of those who do manage to move forward in their lives, despite harsh histories punctuated with periods of displacement and isolation, provide useful allegories for understanding that although the archetypal lost child cannot be purged and should not be ignored, it is necessary to draw it into a relationship built on mutual coexistence. Something like singing the earworm out loud.

Many films fall into this category of childhood memories that haunt, as distinct from narratives that concentrate on, or even marginally draw attention to, actual lost children. This small sample of work where those tangled in the complex either rise above their past or remain trapped within it, include adaptations from the novels of celebrated Australian authors – Man Booker Prize winner Richard Flanagan's *The Sound of One Hand Clapping* (1997) and Nobel Prize Laureate Patrick White's, *The Eye of the Storm* (1973). Australian adaptations of popular North American fiction – Newton Thornburg's *Beautiful Kate* (dir. Ward, 2009) and Robert A. Heinlein's *All You Zombies* renamed *Predestination* by the Spierig Brothers (2013) – along with *Charlie's Country* (2014), jointly scripted by its director Rolf de Heer and lead actor David Gulpili, are also representative of this particular sub-genre of lost child cinema.

Of these texts, the reworked science-fiction labyrinth *Predestination* best condenses the sense of capture by the lost child complex in the way that it incorporates all the central elements of the above films – memory, haunting, affection for, and attempted rejection of the inner child, as well as the need to flee the past while recognising the impossibility of escape. It becomes clear that no central character remains unscathed, yet many emerge more knowing and reconciled. In being forced to confront lost childhoods, unlike the characters of the pervious chapter, there is a sense that they have made a significant shift in their relationship to the complex. This dilemma of confrontation and the need to appreciate the importance of reconciliation is most powerfully illustrated in twin brothers Peter and Michael Spierig's noir, American accented, yet intrinsically Australian themed thriller, filmed in Melbourne and funded by Screen Australia, Screen Queensland and Film Victoria.

The personal and collective return to childhood

When characters return to their childhood, often through flashbacks and voice-over sequences, they tend to act on a distorted replay of memory that suggests a changed relationship their younger, often damaged, selves. The archetypal core of the complex triggered by thoughts and images of childhood does not change – it is the subject's relationship to the complex that brings about development or regression. For Hillman the orphan/lost child motif constitutes a '*psychic condition in need*', itself not developing as does the literal child, but like liminal or threshold energies and symbols, functions to facilitate growth and transformation (1975/1991, p. 26 emphasis as in the original). In his work on alchemy, Jung puts forward the idea that relationship between the subject and any archetypal undercurrents that intrude in her/his life by opposing 'prevailing views', involves raising these patterns and their projections to consciousness through the *transcendent function* so that their possible meanings can be explored and psychological change is possible (Jung, 1963/1970: § 257). This might be thought of as *birthing* or awakening another aspect of the personality.

Films that adopt themes of returning to an internal lost child, echo the basic principles of psychoanalysis and related practices. Hillman identified the way that psychology, 'turns to the child in order to understand the adult, blaming adults for not enough of the child or for too many remnants of the child still left in adulthood' (1975/1991, p. 28). There is though, a positive therapeutic quality to the films discussed in this chapter. They have not been deliberately chosen for this reason though, but because they best illustrate the many Australian narratives that employ the device of child/childhood return as a means of understanding the present, making peace with the pathologies of lostness and appeasing fragmented disturbances from the unconscious (and their *affects*). These kinds of memories, or hauntings, are attached to events and images of childhood and the archetypal child that seeks recognition: '*Our cult of childhood is a sentimental disguise for true homage to the imaginal*' (Hillman, 1975/1991, p. 22 emphasis as in the original). As Hillman stresses, the abandoned, or in this case lost, child is returned to periodically throughout our lives, and each encounter provides the opportunity to rediscover and uncover unconscious and threshold material that can guide psychological development.

> By giving voice to the abandoned child it is always there, and must be there as an archetypal necessity. We know well enough that some things we never learn, cannot help, fall back to and cry from again and again. These inaccessible places where we are always exposed and afraid, where we cannot learn, cannot love, and cannot help by transforming, repressing or accepting are the wilderness, the caves where the abandoned child lies hidden. That we go on regressing to these places states something fundamental about human nature: we comeback to an incurable psychopathology again and again through the course of life yet which apparently does go through many changes before and after contact with the unchanging child.
> *(Hillman, 1975/1991, pp. 19–20)*

The lost child, like Hillman's abandoned/orphaned child, makes itself known in psychotherapy largely through dreams 'where we ourselves or a child of ours or one unknown, is neglected, forgotten, crying, in danger of need' (Hillman, 1975/1991, p. 13). Similarly, if cinema and the artistic offerings of popular culture function as a form of collective dreaming, and like dreams become conduits for unconscious material/energies, then the cyclic and repetitive appearance of the lost child in Australian cinema indicates a significant archetypal impact on the culture. One that like the characters' memories in the films below, needs to be addressed and examined through amplificatory processes. Textual screen analysis might be seen as an academic twist on this therapeutic practice of dialoguing with unconsciously surfacing material, given that all involved from creative practitioners to local audiences are not only involved in the process of dreaming the child, but also *are* the child (Hockley, 2014): 'With the child's return comes childhood. Both kinds: actual with its memories and imaginal with its reminiscences. We have come to call this memorial factor with its two kinds of remembrances: the unconscious, personal and collective' (Hillman, 1975/1991, p. 22).

Another offering by Hillman in relation to this collection of films, is his insistence that the '*notion of consciousness inherently necessitates repression of the child*' (1975/1991, p. 23, emphasis in the original). He sees the ego playing the role of responsible parent, able to reign in the child that remains an imaginal presence existing on a deeper psychological plane within the Self, and also carries a sense of soul, or what might be called life essence. This child therefore remains submerged in the psyche beyond the defining and critical eye of the parental ego. In this way the adult characters in each of the films, at a point of identity crisis, are forced by external circumstances, usually the death or illness of a parent, to return to their childhood homes and their consequent childhood memories. In accessing the child in this way, they are temporarily released from their critical ego/parent selves and by reinvigorating the more resilient inner lost child, are more open to personal transformation through a nurturing of the actual lost child that they imagined her/himself to once be.

Linked to the concept of cultural memories discussed in Chapter 1, personal memories also focus on reminiscences formed from selective images, film-like rewinds and narratives of a childhood self – accumulated, distorted, possibly fabricated and influenced by experiences from the point of the childhood episode/s to the present. The recalled *playback* is therefore not a replication of actual events, but a reconstruction, comparable perhaps to an edited, voice-of-god narrated and story-boarded documentary. As Nelson and Fivush understand autobiographical memory, the very act of expressing one's history involves the acquisition of 'language ability, narrative understanding, temporal concepts, self concepts and consciousness, and social psychological concepts – as well as being embedded within social cultural discourse models, and that each of these individual and social processes follows a variable course of development' (2004, p. 489). The act of organising personal history into coherent accounts or episodes is the product of social and artistic awareness and observation, that allows for the integration of culturally learnt models of storytelling. In arguing that the child 'learns to tell about personal experience in the social forms valued by the community and acquires a more coherent form that aids in the retention of a whole episode, and not just fragments of scenes', Nelson and Fivush also suggest that the ability to express our own story appears to be tightly woven into our awareness of cultural processes and our interpellation, or internalising of cultural ideals and values embedded in communal storytelling (2004, p. 490). *The Home Song Stories* and *Romulus My Father* are examples of how remembering is not necessarily linked to a detailed recall of facts, but under the more forgiving description of 'memoir', they become explorations of both the *affect* attached to traumatic events and the behaviour/motivations of significant others – parents in these cases. This kind of distance allows for a more reflective perspective of past experiences.

The organisation of memories takes place on a personal and collective level, much like the cultural complex itself. Individual and cultural expressions of lost children – as memories, recorded events or fictions – like the psychological personal and collective *affects* associated with lostness, are inextricably entwined. It might be more descriptive and helpful to consider the adult reflections of childhood in the films discussed, as not a reviving of the actual child each of the central characters imagines themselves to have been – tempered by the learnt cultural processes of storytelling – but the inner or archetypal child projected and merged with such recollections. These images and/or fragmented snippets of the past present as more symbolic and therefore beyond any definitive understanding. The child of the past and the inner child never totally reveal themselves – our experience of them is a life-long unravelling as we return to the child, again and again. Like the longed-for object at the heart of any complex, they can never be obtained.

Remembered children do not ultimately become fully realised characters, capable of being enfolded into a reliable and cohesive narrative. They remain unknowable in their role as core phantasms of the complex, symbols and conduits for transformation: like the more unsettling aspects of the complex as Jung saw it, they 'behave as real disturbers of the psychic "economy"' (Jacobi, 1959, p. 9). This is not to say that the nature of the complex is adversely disruptive, as Freud assumed it to be in his estimation of the Oedipal complex as a personal and sexually configured form of repression (Jacobi, 1959; Freud, 1922–1925). It is possible to suggest that the recollections in these films act as a form of amplification for an intrusive symbolic/actual child fusion: as a psychological interlacing of personal experience and the archetypal, the complex is clearly on show (Jacobi, 1959, pp. 8–9). Each character serves as an example of the relationship between individual experiences of the child *and* lost child complexes. This intertwining is intrinsic to the national expression of the complex which cannot take hold culturally without also being experienced to a greater or lesser degree on a personal level (Singer and Kimbles, 2004). In looking to film as a conduit (or expression) of this psychological condition – and a way of amplifying or interpreting the various personifications of the lost child complex – it can be suggested that audiences (and even those involved in the film-making process) are repeatedly drawn to the lost child theme because it is likely to have resonance on a personal level.

To look a little more closely at the personal aspect of the complex, Jacobi argues that a number of ego driven 'attitudes' to the complex are likely to be experienced; 'total unconsciousness of its existence, identification, projection, or confrontation' (1959, pp. 17–18). In stressing that only confrontation ultimately leads to a clearer understanding of the condition, audiences are made aware of the adoption of each 'attitude' as the personal narrative unfolds, but confrontation does not always lead to a more positive relationship with the complex. Instead of assisting in the individuation process such encounters may act as catalysts for disavowal. This is most pointed in the characters of Dorothy, also referred to as Princess (*Eye of the Storm*), and the Barkeep (*Predestination*). Even though the various traumas that enabled the complex in its unconscious form to overwhelm these characters are brought to the surface, it does not necessarily mean that the emotional tensions behind these confrontations automatically subside: as Jacobi writes, 'Only the emotional experience coupled with the understanding and integration of its content can resolve it' (1959, p. 16). But is this resolution a realistic outcome? It is perhaps more appropriate to suggest that one learns *to live with* the situation. Hillman argues of the abandoned inner child, that this *living with*, involves a shift in the relationship one has with the archetypal/symbolic root of the complex. Of the films below, only in *The Sound of One Hand Clapping*, *Beautiful Kate* and more poignantly *Charlie's Country*, we do experience a combination of the emotional and the intellectual as critical to assimilating and easing the frictions of the lost child complex. Although stripped of its more disturbing influence, the child still remains in symbolic form as a fragmented, unknown and enduring presence.

The Sound of One Hand Clapping, *The Eye of the Storm*, *Beautiful Kate* and *Charlie's Country*

Tasmanian Richard Flanagan won the Man Booker Prize in 2014 with *The Narrow Road to the Deep North*, a novel inspired by his father's experiences as a POW forced into hard labour by the Japanese army on the infamous Thai-Burma railway. A noted Australian author before this award, *The Sound of One Hand Clapping* (1997) was Flanagan's second novel winning the Victorian Premier's Prize for Best Novel 1998, Vance Palmer Prize for fiction, the 1999 ABA Australian Book of the Year Prize, Adelaide's National Fiction Literary Award and Australian Booksellers Book of the Year. Flanagan's novel was adapted to a screenplay and in 1998 he directed the film version. This is not currently easy to access online or through DVD, but it is a highly relevant example of lost child cinema – a *searcher of the grail* and *grail* combination (as in *Lion*) symbolised in the character of Sonja Buloh (Kerry Fox) who confronts her troubled childhood as the daughter of Slovenian immigrants traumatised by the second world war. Pregnant, long estranged from her family since the age of sixteen, and deserted by her mother at the age of three, the thirty-six-year-old learns the nature of her mother's disappearance, a scene we see early on the film as she walks into a snow storm and never returns. Thinking she'll abort her pregnancy, Sonja returns to Tasmania to revisit her alcoholic birth father Bojan Buloh (Kristof Kaczmarek) in an attempt to try and reconcile her past. The film moves between past and present, abandonment and reconciliation, trauma induced callousness and forgiveness. While the adult Sonja features throughout, her infant, childhood and adolescent selves become the central focus of the story.

This Australian lost child theme of returning to childhood through memory flashbacks and a need to come to terms with the erratic behaviour of a parent, is echoed in later cinema, particularly *The Home Song Stories* which also focuses on the emotional complexity of the immigrant experience. *The Sound of One Hand Clapping* however, touches on the pattern of rendering children lost through an inability to reconcile one's own adult traumas, rather than an inability to confront those of the inner child, as discussed in relation to *double wounding* and parenting behaviour driven by ghosts in the nursery. Coupled with this sense of loss, the harsh Tasmanian landscape, Australia's most southern state, becomes a source of beauty and challenge. It is exquisitely shot by cinematographer Martin McGrath and we are reminded not only of its challenging winter climate, but also its haunted past. Just two years before the film was released, Australia experienced the most violent mass shooting at Tasmania's historic convict prison site, Port Arthur. Families were randomly targeted including small children. It so emotionally rattled the country, that strict gun laws were introduced by then prime minister John Howard with overwhelming public support. Thousands of weapons were recalled under a buyback scheme and destroyed (Phillips, Park and Lorimer, 2007).

Patrick White's novel, *The Eye of the Storm*, reworked for cinema by Fred Schepisi, provides another sharp example of the adult as both an embodiment of the lost child and wounded bearer of an irreconcilable lost child complex. Published in the same year as White's elevation to Literature Laureate in 1973, the novel is described by journalist and author David Marr in his biography *Patrick White: A Life*, as a narrative where the characters 'are haunted by their inability to love *enough*' (1991, p. 511). Christopher Ricks in the *New York Review of Books* (1974) notes that the novel adopts King Lear-like overtones and metaphors through its central protagonist, the narcissistic matriarch Elizabeth Hunter who summons her inheritance-hungry children to her deathbed (Ricks, 1974). As well as the film inevitably compromising on the descriptive detail of White's 600 pages, comparisons also do not do justice to the particular pathos that Schepisi and actors Geoffrey Rush and Judy Davis bring to Hunter's two *lost child complex-beleaguered* middle-aged adult children, the fading and impotent London-based actor Basil (Rush), and Paris-based Dorothy (Davis), formerly married to royalty. Her nickname 'Princess' appears to be less about her social standing, than her inability to move beyond a privileged, yet developmentally thwarted and emotionally starved childhood.

The lure of a significant financial legacy forces the siblings back into the malignantly maternal relationship they fled overseas to escape. Predictably the mother Elizabeth (Charlotte Rampling) triggers their regression to 'self-object' status – children that exist, from Elizabeth's narcissistic perspective, as objects to gratify her ego rather than subjects valued in their own right (Jacoby, 1990). Basil and Dorothy are therefore forced into an imposed childhood position of powerlessness and puppetry that continues to drive their complexes. On returning to Australia they revisit the home where they (one suspects) have always unconsciously remained developmentally caught: an imprisoning childhood space, shaped and maintained by their mother's pathological self-absorption. The form of sexual flirtation that Elizabeth imposes on the adult Basil, that he in turn uses to mollify her, suggests that this behaviour was well understood, and may have begun earlier in Basil's childhood or adolescence. This form of sexualisation, an aspect of parentification more abusively presented in *Fran*, can also contribute to an understanding of Basil as developmentally 'challenged' (Broszormenyi-Nagy and Spark, 1973/1984; Earley and Cushway, 2002).

From these two texts dealing with the complexity of child-parent relationships and their enduring influence on adult children whose fragmented childhood memories interweave with the archetypal child motif that drives and disrupts their lives, Rachel Ward's 2009 adaptation of Newton Thornburg's *Beautiful Kate* (1982) looks to the sibling relationship of fraternal twins Kate and Ned Kendall

(Sophie Lowe and Ben Mendelsohn). Forty-year-old novelist Ned returns to his cantankerous dying father and younger sister Sally (Rachel Griffiths) on their South Australian sheep station 'Wallumbi'. Here Ned relives memories of his difficult childhood with an aggressive father, the early loss of his mother, his incestuous relationship with Kate, Kate's death in a car accident with his brother Cliff (Josh Macfarlane) at the wheel, and the string of events that led to Cliff's later suicide. Ned's young fiancé, Toni (Maeve Dermody), a close physical facsimile of his sister, reluctantly joins him on the trip back to the drought-affected farm. In this intensely family driven narrative, she focuses us on Ned's unresolved and ongoing adolescent desire for his sister. It emerges that Cliff also experienced the guilt Ned carried since childhood, but to a more intense and unbearable degree. The adult Sally suggests to Ned that Cliff hanged himself because Kate drew both of them into a sexual relationship.

The film is poignant in its reluctance to cast moral judgement on Kate's behaviour. Sally's tactful final estimation of her sister as a 'messed up little girl' summarises all we know of Kate in flashbacks – a child without a mother, parented by an emotionally distant and bullying father, and sister to two sensitive brothers that she relied on for a distorted sense of intimacy and control. The final scene of the film shows Ned throwing a pile of old family artefacts on a bonfire: a baby's pram and the pages on which we saw him write about his relationship with Kate throughout the film. The sense here though is not that he is relinquishing the past, or reburying the memory of his sister, but purifying or baptising the lost children that still capture his imagination: developing a new compassionate and self-forgiving relationship with these memories that spin around his lost child complex. There is a repetition of the adult writer trying to capture and understand both himself and the disturbed women/girls lost to him in *Beautiful Kate* and *The Home Song Stories*, where the adult Tom, much like the adult Ned, tells us 'I write over and over trying to understand her'. The poster used to promote *Beautiful Kate* shows the upper naked torso of Sophie Lowe set against a black background. The body is masked by Lowe's long hair draping her shoulders and muted shadows – only one side of her face is highlighted. For Australians in particular, the image references the work of artist Bill Henson. His similarly moody photographic collection of naked adolescents inhabiting what can be interpreted as an uncomfortable liminality between childhood and adulthood, became a source of moral controversy – a subject also taken up by David Marr in *The Henson Case* (2008). For director Rachel Ward, 'Bill Henson was very much my aesthetic template – I wanted you to be . . . taken into this other world' (Nettheim, 2017–2018).

The oppressive parenting in the preceding three films can also be woven into De Heer's *Charlies Country* (2013) when considering the governing authorities, police and the legal system, as surrogate or metaphorically negligent guardians. The character of Charlie (David Gulpilil), a displaced elder in the Arnhem Land reservation, Northern Territory, is a lone character who seeks the traditional nomadic freedom of his ancestors; a way of survival denied him by a state that controls settlement sites and hunting permissions. Charlie, who speaks his thoughts in the Yolngu Matha language, has few possessions but has kept an old black and white photograph of himself as a child performing with traditional dancers and musicians for Queen Elizabeth II on the steps of the Sydney Opera house when it was publicly opened in 1973 (Australian Government: Department of Home Affairs, 2018). As authorities repeatedly curb his need to live and hunt in what he refers to as his 'Mother Country', he periodically revives the pride he felt in his artistic ability and the memory of being selected as a representative of his people – a recognition of indigenous culture in the year that the policy to keep Australia 'white' through discriminatory immigration practices was eventually dismantled. The aging Charlie is clearly shown as lost to his own land, homeless and desperately trying to revive a sense of self-respect. After trying to return to the country of his childhood, hunt and live without restraint, he is eventually taken to Darwin hospital in a depleted and malnourished state. Charlie is a man rendered lost. At the hospital a treating doctor says to him, 'I believe you were found in the bush' – Charlie responds by telling him that he was born in the bush, not found.

This film could have been developed further in Chapter 4 along the theme of *double wounding*, but the focus on Charlie's return to the photograph of himself as a boy at key moments in his troubled life make it more appropriate for this discussion. Charlie lovingly returns to the image and his childhood memories as a form of comfort. The unreconcilable aspect of this inner child – free, nurtured, honoured and gifted – is that its essence seems lost and unattainable. The photograph is large and creased. The film opens with Charlie examining the image. It sustains him as he tries to return to his Mother (country). We don't see the full black and white image of the Opera House, the Sydney Harbour Bridge in the background, the crowds and the troupe of dancers, for the first hour of the film. It is revealed to us as Charlie lays ill in his makeshift hut, deep into the bush, away from the remote Arnhem Land community where he lives.

He is asked repeatedly to teach traditional dance to the young boys in his community, but refuses until the end of film where we see children gather around him in a circle as he tells them of his experiences dancing with other boys for the Queen. In the final sequence the young boys perform traditional dance in body paint against firelight. It is as if Charlie has awakened the inner child once lost to him – recapturing a sense of belonging and union with his ancestors. Gulpilil and de Heer's film could well be thought of as a grail myth with the central character, as in *Lion*, fulfilling and embodying the multiple roles of *seeker of the grail* (lost child), *grail* and *grail keeper* in Charlie's steadfast need to abide in the inner child. There is also, of course, a sting in the tail of the line 'dancing for the Queen'. An allusion perhaps to subservience under British rule – the repeated phrase casts a shadow over his treasured photograph.

Predestination

Of all the films mentioned and others addressed in specifically themed chapters of this study, *Predestination* best depicts the spiralling entanglement of past, present and future selves that constellate around a deep love of, and enduring connection to, an unanchored inner lost child. The film focuses on re-visiting one's self in formative developmental stages. Like T.S. Elliot's *Four Quartets*, such re-encounters allows for a more informed and compassionate understanding of the self: an exploration from 'where we started' to a knowing of the 'place for the first time' (Elliot, 1971, p. 59). I have previously tackled the concepts of memory, identity and self-discovery through intricate textual studies of *Memento* (dir. Nolan, 2001), *Mulholland Drive* (dir. Lynch, 2002) and *The Others* (dir. Amenábar, 2001) (Waddell, 2006), all of these films, coincidentally, are led by noted Australian actors (Guy Pierce, Naomi Watts and Nicole Kidman respectively). *Predestination* though is entirely uroboric (even more so than *Memento*): a cyclic, a-temporal story of surrendering, discovering and rebirthing oneself.

The story begins in a 1970s bar. The character of the Barkeep (Ethan Hawke) meets 'John' or 'the unmarried mother' (Sarah Snook), a moniker John uses as the writer of magazine confession stories. John tells the Barkeep of his start to life as a female baby left on the doorstep of the Cleveland Orphanage in 1945. As a young woman, 'Jane', he is inducted into Space Corp., a unit that trains girls strong in mathematics, science and athletics for government service. But Jane was expelled on becoming pregnant to a man who deserted her during the early phase of their relationship. After her caesarean section the surgeon tells her that she has two sets of immature reproductive organs. While anesthetised, her uterus and ovaries were removed and a male urinary tract constructed. Further surgeries force Jane to accept her male body – 'John' – but over time her resentment builds for the man who left her. The Barkeep asks John, that if it was possible to confront this man, without any ramifications for what may occur, 'would you kill him?'

The Barkeep, however, is working undercover for the Temporal Bureau, a secret organisation that allows its agents to move back and forward in time to prevent crime. His final mission is to eliminate a terrorist called the 'Fizzle Bomber'. The Barkeep reveals this to John, but also gives him the opportunity to go back in time and meet the man to whom he became pregnant. The Barkeep teleports both himself and John back to the time when John met Jane (his former self). This future and past self fall in love and begin a relationship. In a hermaphroditic play, John comes to realise that he fathered Jane's child. The Barkeep abducts the baby from the hospital, time travels back to 1945, leaving her on the doorstep of the orphanage. What we discover is that the central characters of the baby, Jane, John, the Barkeep and eventually the Fizzle Bomber, are all versions of the same person at different periods in their life. Without describing the minutia of the byzantine narrative, the question that guides the film relates to the possibility of changing the past – if this is possible then could we change the future? In taking John back to Jane, the Barkeep's attempt to confront him/them with the father of the child in the hope that he would be killed, therefore fails. In short he does not succeed in eliminating himself – a self that also becomes the terrorist Fizzle Bomber he is assigned to liquidate.

The notion of the uroboros is mentioned in *Predestination* and a number of times in Heinlein's 1959 short story. A pagan symbol of eternity, imaged as a circular snake or sometimes a dragon with its tail in its mouth, it is frequently mentioned by Jung in his studies into the mercurial world of alchemy. He refers to the uroboros as a symbol of the Self (rather than self) – both the core around which the various components of the psyche are regulated *and* a concept of wholeness or completion of the individuation process (Jung, 1959/1969; Jung, 1963/1970). While there is something of the alchemical in *Predestination* and its uroboric theme, the film has no pretension to the optimistically achievable wholeness of individuation in Jung's psychology. The future is bleak, returning to the past at will sets the conditions for psychosis, and although the past self is mourned and loved as a thing of beauty, the present self is disappointing and the future-self becomes a threat to be eliminated. The child in the tail-chasing cycle however, remains divine – virgin-birthed, abandoned and rescued only to be reborn. It is therefore the child that sits at the heart of this uncomfortable rotation. Relegating it to the status of orphan, as the barkeep does in his abduction of the infant, merely sets in motion an eternal cycle of rebirth and rediscovery. In a hauntingly relevant passage to *Predestination's* idea of the inner child *as shadow*, Jung also sees the image of the uroboros as symbolic of 'the integration and assimilation of the opposite, i.e. of the shadow. This "feed-back" process is at the same time a symbol of immortality, since it is said of the uroboros that he slays himself and brings himself to life, fertilizes himself and gives birth to himself' (Jung, 1963/1970: § 513).

I am not as interested in untangling the narrative of *Predestination*, as I am in exploring how the question posed above – if we could change the past, can we change the future? – relates to the lost inner child complex. As the archetypal core of the complex doesn't change and it is only our *relationship to it* that evolves, the past cannot similarly be altered. Only our *relationship* to formative incidents can shift. The memories and images that attach themselves to these key events are subject to tonal and emotional change. Such a re-evaluation from a more matured perspective has the potential to positively influence one's sense of identity and futurity. Hillman talks about the constructive potential for personal and collective relationships with the complex in his discussion on the archetypal/symbolic nature of the lost child: 'the abandoned child is both that which never grows . . . and futurity springing from vulnerability itself. The complex remains . . . that which becomes different are our connections with these places and our reflections through them' (Hillman, 1975/1991, p. 20).

Throughout *Predestination*, particularly in the Barkeep's various ploys to eliminate his past self, change is thwarted. He is doomed to an eternal return and yet one senses at each opportunity to destroy himself – whether as John meeting Jane, the Barkeep meeting the baby, or the Barkeep meeting the Fizzle Bomber – he not only learns a little more about himself, but learns to love the parts of himself he rejects: 'you're beautiful', John tells Jane, 'someone should have told you that'. When as the Barkeep he eventually meets his future aging self, the bomber tells him: 'If you want to break the chain you have to not kill me, but try to love me again'. This suggests that in killing *himself*, he will simply be set back on the path of endless return that begins and ends with an attempted purging of the child.

The inner child as *stuck* and *embodied*

The idea of purging or neglecting the inner child, and regarding it as a wound to be either healed or disavowed, also shapes the character of Dorothy and to some degree Basil in *Eye of the Storm*. Basil, who describes the pair as 'Mummy's two great disappointments', is more open to returning to the childhood-liminal space and resuming a playful yet calculating relationship with his ill mother. He also unsuccessfully attempts to draw his emotionally distant sister to him in a sibling pact of nurture and woundedness, that one suspects they shared as children. On visiting his once large country family home with Dorothy as a form of respite from their mother, he tells the young caretaker couple who attempt to accommodate them in suitable overnight rooms that, 'I'm more comfortable in the children's room'. The child in Dorothy that we see in these scenes remains neglected, and yet there are glimpses of her struggle to either reconcile her childhood hurt or dismiss/repress it: 'Our parents and childhood, our parents' life', she says to Basil, 'is it better to lock loveless misery in a box buried deep in the closet with the other remnants of childhood, or is it better to take it out and examine it in a more forgiving light?'

The last scenes of the film show Dorothy in her favourite Paris restaurant spoiling herself with delicacies. It is as if she has returned to a more artificial maturity and independence in an attempt to separate herself from the memory of her isolated childhood and the imaginal lost child she harbours. Rather than consciously integrating this aspect of her psyche as Basil, however clumsily, attempts to do, her relationship to it remains dismissive; a mirroring of her mother's relationship toward her as a child. Hillman is again helpful at this point, for his understanding that when the ego attempts to dominate the inner child as a metaphoric parent or mature adult existing in a fantasy of autonomy, the lost child becomes ostracised and its emotions relegated to otherness (1975/1991, p. 13). He argues that commonly:

> a restoration of the mythical, the imaginal and the archetypal implies a collapse into the infantile realm of the child. Our strong ego-centred consciousness fears nothing more than just such a collapse. The worst insult is to be called 'childish', 'infantile', 'immature'. So we have devised every sort of measure for defending ourselves against the child – and against archetypal fantasy. These defences we call the consciousness of the strong mature and developed ego.
>
> (Hillman, 1975/1991, p. 23)

The pattern we have been exposing shows a vicious circle. Abandoning *of* the child in order to become more mature and the abandonment to the child when it returns. Either we repress or we coddle this face of our subjectivity. In both cases the child is unbearable: first we cannot support it at all, then we give way to it altogether.

(Hillman, 1975/1991, p. 43)

These defences, in part, contribute toward the often 'stuck-ness' of the lost child motif. The lost child may be embraced rather than disavowed, but it is still difficult, impossible for some even, to sift through the problematic *affect* it provokes.

In Australian cinema, where adult characters either deliberately ignore or are unable to separate from the lost or literal past memories of childhood, it is clear to see the complex at work. *The Sound of One Hand Clapping* and *Beautiful Kate*, *Oranges and Sunshine* (Chapter 4) and *The Dressmaker* (dir. Moorhouse, 2015), a film revolving around the return of a fashion design icon to her estranged outback community – a separation driven by unresolved childhood trauma – are more redeeming examples of reconciliation with the inner child. When looking at films that concentrate on this aspect of extended childhood disorientation, this archetypal material becomes a burden carried by adult characters. It is as if they wear the archetypal image, inflected by past woundedness, in and through their bodies, whether it be the sexually needy child/woman mother (Nicole Kidman) of two missing teenagers in *Strangerland*, the sexually 'held' Dorothy in *Eye of the Storm*, the Oedipally challenged Charles (Norman Kaye) in *Man of Flowers* (dir. Cox, 1983) or the violently rebelling and reacting boy/men in *Head On* (dir. Kokkinos, 1998), *Erskinville Kings* and *Animal Kingdom* (dir. Michôd, 2010), to mention only a few examples of how *affects* associated with the complex can extend to a problematic embodiment of the displaced child.

'If we are anywhere most the victim of childishness, or more at war with it' writes Hillman, 'it is in the body, treated as an enemy, as an inferior to be disciplined or indulgently coddled' (1975/1991, p. 41). The return to the childhood state through an almost involuntary physical return to bodily memories is clear in *Beautiful Kate*. Although in this text the subjects are young teenagers, rather than prepubescent children, Ned's desire for Kate determines his choice of sexual partner (the Kate look-a-like, Toni) and his sexual behaviour. In the few scenes of the couple having sex, Toni is facing away from Ned – her long blond hair, small body shape and obscured face, enough to evoke Ned's adolescent arousal. Geoffrey Rush and Judy Davis, as Basil and Dorothy in *The Eye of the Storm*, adopt physical gestures of ungainly playfulness and tight-bodied fearfulness respectively, that allows for a clear imagining of them as children pandering to and defensively protecting themselves from their narcissistic mother. In all of the five films highlighted in this chapter, the protagonists are circumstantially forced back into their childhood environment, or remain situated within it as in *Charlie's Country*. This uncomfortable familiarity becomes the catalyst for more intense encounters with the inner lost child.

In terms of embodiment, developments in neuroscience and virtual reality technology can contribute to the way a return to an uncanny environment might transform us to a particular state of mind and physicality. While embodiment of the inner child and its representation in film may seem a far cry from neuroscience, it is worth taking a moment to consider the connective potential of these areas. The virtual environment has some resonance with the dream environment. These two states allow one to directly experience another body. In the dream, we can find ourselves literally in the body of another or ourselves at a previous or future age. When memories are experienced on a physical as well as imaginary level, we can be transported to a past incarnation of ourselves, whether or not that is an accurate or culturally modified representation of who we were. This might even be extended to an intense identification with screen images and characters that are able to trigger versions of the spectator's childhood self.

Inspired by Jaron Lanier's 1980s work on shifting self-concepts when placed in a virtual body, Mel Slater and Maria V. Sanchez-Vives examined the possibility of changed behaviour and thought, when participants of their study were virtually endowed with bodies markedly different to their own. Their experiments on adults given the virtual body of a child demonstrated that, 'adults inhabiting a virtual child's body overestimate the size of objects and demonstrate implicit attitude and behavioural changes that seem more child-like, but in an adult body the same size as that of a child, they do not exhibit such changes' (Slater and Sanchez-Vives, 2014, p. 24, also see Banakou, Groten and Slater, 2013). They placed thirty adults in the virtual body of a four-year-old child synching up the real bodies with those technologically created to form an illusion that the artificial body was theirs. Their aim was 'to determine whether embodiment in a young child's body would influence perception of object sizes and attitudes about the self' (Slater and Sanchez-Vives, 2014, p. 28).

These findings that brain flexibility allowed the participants to adapt to a more behaviourally child-like self, also took into consideration that the autobiographical memories of the participants might also have been aroused 'to determine perception and other mental processing' (Slater and Sanchez-Vives, 2014, p. 28). Although this was considered, social factors such as expectations of what it is to be a child were thought not to have affected the experimental illusion of adopting a virtual body as one's own, and as a consequence, adopting attitudes and behaviours aligning with that body type. They therefore concluded that, 'the brain is apparently able to drive attitudes and behavior of individuals according to their level of body ownership with respect to the type virtual body in which they are embodied' (Slater and Sanchez-Vives, 2014, p. 28).

This idea of virtual body ownership is sutured into Jennifer Haley's Olivier award-winning play *The Nether* (dir: Jeremy Herrin, 2014). Set in the future, a late-middle-aged man adopts the body of a young female child who functions as a willing pedophilic object for others entering the Victorian-set reality space. This child-like, virtual, persona becomes more viable to the player's sense of self than his actual material existence. Of course this text could also be explored through the paradigm of the adult-as-lost-child, being enthral to the complex on a psychological, and, when experienced more intensely, a physical level. This is an extreme arena of fantasy, but the idea of the complex entwined with notions of embodiment and a regressed sense of self is also evident in the films under consideration here.

Predestination though cleverly problematises the notion of lost child embodiment by playing with a revisitation of bodies literally arrested in their developmental state: the young Jane, the re-gendered John, the newborn, the barkeep and the psychotic Fizzle Bomber. Each can be imagined as a vertebraic section of the snake-shaped uroboros – always present and intrinsic to this spinal curved metaphor of the life-cycle. While there is no overt sense of lost child performativity, the baby surrendered to the orphanage serves as the core around which each incarnation of the central character pivots, as if these personas were each surrendered or displaced, unwillingly to another time and identity – lost to the connective threads joining them together as one circular organism, they become *an* eternally reproducing person.

The character/s in *Predestination* are all somehow inextricably attached as agents of the Temporal Bureau, which functions as a controlling parental 'body'. Acting outside of the Bureau's charter is a capital offence. One might argue that the agent(s) therefore, never achieve independence. Rather their temporal movement back and forward to revisit their former/future selves and play with the possibility of changing the future by changing the past, leads to no actual transition or escape from their circular fate. The mysterious device that enables their movement to and from time zones is enclosed in a violin case and always kept close. It is made clear that any attempted abuse of this object, such as jumping back and forward in time too far or too often, will lead to psychosis. Once the object is abandoned at the end of the film when the Barkeep shoots the Fizzle Bomber (himself), we don't see an emergence into a state of selfhood, but oblivion and a suspected return to the cyclic beginning with the baby. In this way the central character is an eternal embodiment of the lost child, searching for independence, but always the agent of an organisation that does not allow her/him an independent life.

In keeping with both Hillman and Jung's thinking, the negative influence of the complex can be alleviated by an active shift in the relationship between ego/parent and complex/child. For Hillman, the child should remain *lost* rather than *repressed/disavowed* in the process of psychological development. He talks of a unification of the child and the adult, so that the adult is 'perennially a child' who periodically returns to, or seeks out this aspect of their psyche as a way of nurturing and attending to it – a process of acknowledging the existence of 'the child contained' (Hillman, 1975/1991, p. 46). This eternally vulnerable element also contains the potential to help develop a greater sense of insight into one's character and therefore serves the individuation process.

In arguing that contained within the 'pathology is also the futurity' Hillman touches on the unresolved dilemmas that *Predestination* and the lost child complex present (1975/1991, p. 19). As the Barkeep cyclically attempts to obliterate his past self, extinguish the lost child and ultimately carry out the Temporal Bureau's (parent/ego) command to kill his own destructive pathology in the form of the Fizzle Bomber, we are repetitively reminded of his love for Jane, John, the baby and himself – as the Fizzle Bomber tells him, 'If you want to break the chain you have to not kill me, but try to love me again'. This might then be read as a warning against disavowal and attempted obliteration. This kind of toxic or neglectful tie to the lost child and the complex that forms around it is not helpful in alleviating the challenges it presents. To love it again and again, as cautioned in *Predestination*, is the most effective way to make peace with this troublesome and yet healing aspect of the psyche. The hermaphroditic play in the film – the birthing of one's self – talks to such an attempt at self-inter-(dis)course.

The films discussed above and the idea of the child as an unreconciled aspect of the past is a characteristic of the lost child complex that Australian cinema returns to again and again. This repetition might be thought of as a collectively unconscious way to not eliminate this element of our selves, but change our relationship to it – recognise the inner child as both lost and found. Rather than containing it in the past, *Predestination* asks us to think of our split selves (our complex) as ever-present versions of 'soul' or life essence that should not be killed off through neglect, but loved again. This inward spiralling can either be seen as a path to individuation or a stifling earworm-like loop. Having drawn so much on Hillman's philosophies of the inner child/orphan in this chapter, it seems appropriate to close on this final quote:

> By giving favour to this idea of the child that is not meant to grow, we might imagine the child's abandonment and need for rescue as a continuous state, a static necessity that does not evolve towards independence, does not evolve at all, but remains as a requirement of the fulfilled and matured person.
>
> *(Hillman, 1975/1991, p. 31)*

7

THE VICTORY COMPLEX

Nostalgia for the American dream
and the art of the win

The lost child, just one among a variety of complexes that influences history, place and character, can never independently capture a country or a people, but it has significantly contributed to the complexity of interwoven Australian identities. When trying to compare the motif with complexes that dominate other cultures, it is hard to go past North America for a more diametrically opposed comparison. *The American Dream* (or the *Dream* as I'll refer it) – the entitlement to, and capacity to realise, personal success – has matured since the silent film to become an ideological driver of mainstream American cinema. The concept departs dramatically from the emotions, philosophies and wounds associated with the archetypal lost child, for the very suggestion of being 'lost' is anathema to the *Dream*. There is certainly grief and vulnerability involved in narratives that pursue this fixation, but I'd argue that the sense of *loss* and *being lost* are deployed more as plot devices for the discovery of true potential. Loss is a state to be railed *against*. Unlike Australian cinema, popular film in the United States tends not to embrace lostness in itself as an opportunity for reassessment and self-understanding. In 2007, while challenging North America's involvement in the Middle East and emergence from the cold war, former Soviet president Mikhail Gorbachev argued that the country was in the grip of a *victory complex*. Reinforcing this evaluation, *Washington Post* and *Rolling Stone* journalist William Greider renamed this compulsion to succeed, the 'winners complex' (2009, p. 29). If there ever was a psychological obsession that could *have* a people, guide a way of life and overshadow more minor cultural neuroses, this is it.

The unacknowledged shadow, on a personal or collective level, acts as a magnifying glass that forces us to bear witness to shortcomings that are disavowed. As Singer argues, the shadow sits alongside, 'archetypal defenses of the group Self . . . I do not see these energies/structures as fixed entities but as potential, dynamically shifting channels in the collective psyche through which huge *affects* and energies may pour when aroused' (Singer, 2016, p. 38). Although the USA's victory/winning ethos is motivational and optimistic, it has arguably found its shadow in Donald Trump. After gliding down a gold-plated escalator at Trump Tower to announce his presidential bid (June 16, 2015), Trump's (self) motivational – some might argue incoherent – speech played on the galvanising nature of the complex: 'Sadly, the American dream is dead' he proclaimed, 'but if I get elected president I will bring it back bigger and better and stronger than ever before, and we will make America great again' (Trump, 2015).

Post-election, Trump's compulsive need to 'win' dominated his presidency. In the climate he attempts to create, 'losers' are deemed *persona non grata*. If one doesn't actually win – and publicly at least Trump couches political decisions, criticisms and opinions of others in these terms (I don't think I have to list the endless volley of tweets as evidence) – defeat is either transmogrified into a victory or victory is simply fabricated (Politifact, 2018). Watching the 2017–2018 White House administration unfold from Australia, a country dominated by American screen media, I was even more aware of just how culturally different we are, and of the long shadow that obsessional winning casts. Yet, whatever form it takes, the cultural complex *has* both of us: 'it does seem apparent that Alpha dynamics not only fuel our country' writes North American Jungian analyst Jacqueline West, 'but that *they have us in their grip*' (2016, p. 242).

It seems inevitable that when this book is released, the dignity once ascribed to the American presidency will have taken yet another hit. It is almost synchronistic that the 2018 Golden Globes were dominated by Oprah Winfrey's rousing equality and empowerment speech. A celebrity and a brand that epitomises the rags-to-riches *Dream* with the mantra 'live your best life', Oprah was, for a brief moment, called on by social media audiences to run for office in 2020. The *New York Times*, Trump's bête noire, reported the day after the awards ceremony;

> Ms. Winfrey's speech accepting the Cecil B. DeMille Award for lifetime achievement was directly about the #MeToo movement [promoting the outing of, and accountability for, sexual abuse] and the arc of civil rights struggles. But with its talk of 'tyrants' and 'history' and 'a new day,' it had the music and lyrics of the kind of acceptance speech that ends with a balloon drop.
>
> The moment has inspired a mini 'Oprah 2020' boomlet of speculation in political media. Even NBC saluted Ms. Winfrey with a tweet, since deleted: 'Nothing but respect for OUR future president'.
>
> *(Poniewozik, 2018)*

The film *Three Billboards Outside Ebbing Missouri* (dir. McDonagh, 2017) garnering four awards at this event and later in the year winning two Academy Awards for Frances McDormand and Sam Rockwell, is significant in the Globe's annual salute to achievement (winning) and, in 2018 anyway, political oratory. The narrative is ultimately driven by the protagonist Mildred's (McDormand) frustration and revenge for the unsolved case of her teenage daughter's rape and murder. The corrupt, racist and violent police officer, Dixon (Rockwell), evolves from a red-neck bully, plucked straight from Hillary Clinton's 'basket of deplorables' (her controversial catch phrase for Trump's more xenophobic and bullying supporters during the 2016 presidential campaign), into a character redeemed by self-reflection. In a poignant suicide letter left by his boss, Chief Willoughby (Woody Harrelson) – the brunt of Mildred's scorn – Willoughby in effect encourages Dixon to be his best self, seeing in him redemption and potential. As politically contemporary as *Three Billboards* appeared in its explicit depiction of racism, struggling small town America and the sexual abuse of women, it was a revisioning of the *Dream*, with Dixon and Mildred eventually united through a shared recognition of their better selves. Their acceptance of the futility of beating-up on, defeating and so winning against external enemies who served as projections of their own inner torment, was inevitably tied to the victory complex. A salient message for Trump perhaps. It is a film, that as Hockley argues of the psychological power of cinema, and by extension screen culture, 'does not offer an escape from the real world. Rather, it provides a means through which to descend into one's own inner life' (Hockley, 2014, p. 151).

The victory complex and ego inflation

On October 3, 2007 at Kentucky Center's Whitney Hall, Gorbachev was reported to have assessed North America's penchant for claiming military and political triumph, as actions driven by a 'victory complex' (Smith, 2007). In his book *The New Russia* (2016), he reaffirmed this belief in the USA's proclivity to self-congratulation:

> The US political elite, having claimed victory in the Cold War, drew the 'appropriate conclusions' from this delusion. Overconfident about its power, it embarked not only on military intervention in the Yugoslav conflict, but launched missile strikes against Iraq. It's 'victory complex' did nothing for relations with Russia.
>
> *(Gorbachev, 2016, p. 317)*

While Gorbachev's phrase suggests a psychological theme in United States' thinking (military at least), if not a complex in the Jungian sense, the US/Coalition led military installations grouped around the Bagdad International Airport in 2004 after the 2003 invasion (Operation Iraqi Freedom), were actually named the Victory Base Complex (VBC), while Saddam Hussein's occupied Al-Faw Palace or Water Palace attached to this cluster was renamed Camp Victory.

Greider's *Come Home, America: The Rise and Fall (and Redeeming Promise) of Our Country* (2009), devotes a chapter to the Winner's Complex where he adopts a convincing position on the victory complex as a collective psychological disposition, perhaps not in directly Jungian terms, but as a learnt, indoctrinated and deeply mythologised way of seeing oneself in the world:

> Mikhail Gorbachev, former president of the Soviet Union. . . . The United States, he suggested, should get rid of this disease which I call the winner's complex.
> 'The victory complex is even worse than the inferiority complex,' Gorbachev explained. He does not specifically say it is the 'arrogance of power,' but I think that is what he means. US influence in the world can still flourish, Gorbachev said, but 'leadership should be done not by domination, not by becoming a policemen in the world, but by being a partner'.
> *(Greider, 2009, p. 33)*

Greider traces the complex or 'confident spirit' to post–World War II political buoyancy and the need to reclaim America as the world's success story. He writes that from his childhood, 'America Triumphant' has remained 'the bright, shining beacon of who are as a nation' (Greider, 2009, p. 25), and cites Madeline Albright, Secretary of State in the Clinton administration, as an enthusiastic advocate of this self-image: 'If we have to use force, it is because we are America. We are the indisputable nation. We stand tall. We see further into the future' (p. 25). It became clear to him though, that this entitlement to triumph is somewhat delusional, disproportionate and based on self-aggrandisement.

Consistent with Greider's argument, West sheds light on the Trumpian shadow; winning serves the privileged and influential, and 'American vulnerability, in any form, is soundly denied or devalued; it is consistently defended against' (2016, p. 243). Alluding to the more nefarious mythic/fairy tale characters driven by an insatiable need for self-glorification, often triggered by deep insecurity, she argues that the American ethos of winning *no matter what*, is a protective tactic against the reality that 'narcissistically claimed privilege and security in this world are not guaranteed' (West, 2106, p. 241). Francesco Duina (2011) approaches the victory complex in a more positive light. While maintaining America's obsession with winning and anxiety around the concept of losing, he argues that the dynamism of competition drives the fixation; victory alone takes second place to the ultimate gratification of having vied for the prize and won. Duina also argues though, that while the culture rewards the successful and the competitive, it largely ignores those who are unable to live up to these exacting expectations: 'our competitive mind-set has serious problems', he reasons, 'by pitting us against so much in the world, it generates enormous tension in our lives and is therefore utterly exhausting . . . despite all that it asks of us, it actually fails to satisfy us in a definitive manner' (p. 197).

Looked at from the perspective of analytical psychology, the concentration on, and entitlement to winning, and maintaining the role of victor to justify one's very participation in the culture, suggests ego inflation – not just of the individual, but the collective group (Jung, 1953/1966). In discussing the dominance of victory as a complex, and the complex itself as a set of involuntary physical, psychological and emotional behaviours driven by an unconscious thematic core, it is important to acknowledge the very concept of victory as archetypal. To attach one's self – persona and ego – to an archetypal motif, allowing it to govern one's identity, is classified as ego inflation: the individual who identifies as, for instance, a saviour, hero or champion to the exclusion of a deeper and more authentic sense of self. Anne Casement argues that failure to reconcile the personal and collective shadow limits the development of a robust, matured and emotionally fortified ego. This can potentially lead 'to the inflation of the ego with consequent delusions of omniscience and omnipotence – the ultimate road to madness' (2006, p. 100). It is not difficult to imagine how the winning culture could be exploited and pathologised as a crippling form of ego inflation that inhibits self-reflection. Historical trauma also plays a role in this kind of identification, as has been argued of the lost child complex. In his chapter, 'The Trump Complex, the John Wayne Archetype and States of National Possession', Steven Buser reinforces the idea that the 'wounds we sustain in life predispose us to developing complexes that can overtake us later in life. People can become so identified with a particular complex that it is as if they are possessed by it' (2016, p. 13).

Inflation can also be a consideration in the navigation of the lost child complex: that is, if identification with the archetypal child occurs to the determent of the individual's/the group's more genuine, multifaceted identity. However, the victory complex appears to be so culturally embedded – psychologically (in the collective sense), historically and mythically – more so than the lost child complex, that the potential for ego inflation on both a personal and social level is much more likely. From the arts to politics, education and the business sector, Australia does not tend to consciously and actively promote the lost child as a measure of Australian-ness – even in the light of Anzac Day celebrations – whereas winning, success and victory seem integral to an 'all-American' mindset, no matter how mythic or romantically disproportionate to lived experience.

The trauma of victories past

In developing a clearer perspective of the cinematic traditions of victory-driven narratives that expose the complex's positive and shadow aspects, it is useful to touch on the historic underpinnings at the root of the complex. This cannot be discussed in great depth here, but as with the lost child complex, it would seem that the multiracial American (excluding Native Americans) attachment to, and ego inflation of, victory began in trauma: as West writes, 'The archetypal wellspring of raw action that lies in the roots of Alpha dynamics has fueled the U.S. since its birth' (p. 241). North America's diverse communities, developed through exploration and colonisation from the sixteenth century, slavery, waves of European and Asian immigration, and the destabilising of indigenous peoples, were significantly influenced by internal and international wars. Unlike Australia, North America liberated itself from British rule through a war of independence fought on American soil (1775–1783). Less than a hundred years after victory, the northern and southern states plunged into civil war (1861–1865) over the abolition of slavery and slave trading.

Prior to conflicts of independence, settlers attempted to claim victory over the environment. The frontier myth was fuelled by the alpha dynamics of colonisers who invested in taming and owning the land, and consequently usurping Native American communities: 'our western "heroes" slaughtered . . . innumerable herds of buffalo that roamed the prairies' writes West, 'these undeniably destructive early expressions of Alpha dynamics lie deep within American Narcissism, driving us widely and wildly into ruthless domination over and over' (p. 242; see *The West*, dir. Ives, 1996). While the heroism, ingenuity and Manifest Destiny ideology of frontiersmen and women has been romanticised in the arts, particularly literature and classical western cinema (pre-1950s), exposing the darker shadow of this sense of entitlement and entrepreneurialism is a relatively recent mid-twentieth-century movement. *Deadwood* (2004–2006) is an example of this revisioning – a three season miniseries tackling the ruthless nature of colonisation, it debunked the traditional Western hero's journey by graphically depicting the brutal sexualisation and suppression of colonial women, racism and the underbelly of the victory/capitalist driven *Dream* (McGee, 2007; Waddell, 2010; Carter, 2014).

Singer, who popularised the notion of a cultural complex, talks of the more encouraging aspects of America's group spirit:

> We love and believe in our heroic potential, our freedom and independence, our worship of height and speed, youth, newness, technology, our optimism, and eternal innocence. We have enjoyed the profound resilience of the American spirit, which has shown itself repeatedly through very difficult historical trials, including our Civil War, World War I, the great Depression, Work War II, the Vietnam War, the 9/11 attacks, the Iraq War, the financial collapse in 2008, and other major crises.
>
> *(Singer, 2016, pp. 43–44)*

He balances this collective self-image with its shadow of 'inflation, arrogance, and grandiosity in our belief in our own exceptionalism and blindness to causing grave injury to other peoples at home and abroad' (p. 44). As well as early political and economic wins and their consequent traumas, Julie Levinson acknowledges that the 'etiology of the success myth is rooted in the social and religious doctrines of colonial America' (2012, p. 12). Along with victory, the notion of democracy that guides the ideology of the *Dream* is problematic; that is, if its intention, as Levision suggests, is to ensure that *everyone* has the opportunity to achieve and succeed.

The American dream

Defined by James Truslow Adams in 1931 as a vision of Americans advancing themselves, 'unhampered by the barrier which had slowly been erected in older civilizations, unrepressed by social orders which had developed for the benefit of classes rather than for the simple human being of any and every class', the *Dream* is a concept that has galvanised audiences and voters since the great depression and is arguably the core framework around which multicultural/multiracial USA attempts to shape a sense of futurity (Adams, 2017/1931, p. 405). This kind of engagement was most starkly demonstrated through the Trump campaign then presidency, and Oprah's rousing 2018 Golden Globes speech, characterised as presidential by the social and mainstream news media. More so than the dubious claims of democracy to be a system of majority rule, power and social decision making, the *Dream*, in all its undemocratic privileging of winners over losers, and its refining of winners into those with intellectual, emotional, socio-economic or racial advantage, is nevertheless an unfair cultural strategy and ideology that influences North American cinema (Hambly, 2018; Levinson, 2012; Winn, 2007; Hochschild, 1995). The desire to win and the expectation of success is accordingly a key component of the victory complex. On the flip-side, the complex's more shadowy potential would appear to be cultivated through loss and defeat – for failure, argues Jennifer Hochschild, 'challenges the blurring between anticipation and promise that is at the emotional heart of the American Dream' (1995, p. 30).

Since its inception, North American cinema has, according to Levinson, 'homed in on, and regularly renegotiated, the cultural schisms of the success myth' (2012, p. 18). While this negotiation involves criticism of, and direct challenge to, the success story, particularly in art house and independent cinema (see Ortner, 2013; Rindge, 2016) with dystopian or socially critical themes – *Fight Club* (dir. Fincher, 1999), *Blue Velvet* (dir. Lynch, 1986), *American Beauty* (Mendes, 1999) or *I Tonya* (dir. Gillespie, 2017) for example – it could be argued in a somewhat confident generalisation, that the majority of mainstream box-office successes and award-winning cinema, while reworking victory/self-improvement themes, nevertheless subscribe to Adams' principles of the *Dream*. Horchschild identifies four core tenets underpinning the *Dream*, that take victory as a given: 'everyone can participate equally and can always start over' (p. 26), each person has a 'reasonable anticipation of success' (p. 27), 'success results from actions and traits under one's own control' (p. 30) and success is associated 'with virtue' (p. 30). She then continues to detail the flaws of these beliefs. While the cultural reinforcement of each tenet shoring up the success narrative is intrinsic to its ongoing influence, Levinson also reasons that the *Dream's* hold extends beyond culture to the collective unconscious: the heartland of complexes.

In the edited compilation *A Clear and Present Danger: Narcissism in the Era of Donald Trump* (Cruz and Buser, 2016), Singer makes clear that the *Dream* and by association the victory complex can be variously interpreted; 'what I and others see as Trump's narcissism and his self-aggrandizing display of opulent wealth and brute power, others see as success and the ultimate achievement of the American dream' (Singer, 2016, p. 28). Winning is a slippery concept open to political exploitation. Although Oprah may position herself at the end of the success spectrum, where winning is not achieved at the expense of others, nor is it necessarily measured in material success (although many would argue that she equates happiness with consumerism), both she and Trump, in their polarity, have accrued mass appeal through a dependence on the resilience and unconscious veracity of the *Dream*. Both have personalised the *Dream* and Singer's sentiment concerning Trump's identification of his 'personal being with the Self of America' can also be applied to Oprah: 'He is encouraging Americans who have lost a foothold in the American dream to place their trust in him as a mirror of their own potential – a potential that he personally has already achieved' (Singer, 2016, p. 49). Singer further theorises the rise of Trump as symbolic of the national shadow of a narcissistic culture and victory in unpredictable times. He argues that Trump compensates for the collective psyche's self-image that is 'beginning to suffer severe self-doubt about our ability to navigate a highly uncertain future successfully and the nostalgic longing perfectly articulated in the phrase: "I want my country back"' (Singer, 2016, p. 44).

Writing in 1995, Hochschild's *Facing Up to the American Dream: Race, Class, and the Soul of the Nation* makes two claims of the *Dream*; it is 'a central ideology of Americans' and its most severe challenge is 'intricately entwined with race' (p. xi). The doubts about entitlement to and ability to achieve success raised by Singer have exploded into an America of 2018 struggling with itself – a division of class and (ever increasingly) gender and race, that Trump appears to exploit. Many white lower middle-class voters, struggling to accept the decline of once prosperous industries that ensured their livelihood, find validation in Trump's proclamation that the *Dream* 'is dead'. In talking about the paradoxes of the *Dream*, Hochschild recognises the division it creates. She argues that economic competition comes at the expense of winners and consequent losers, and yet the *Dream* with the idea of victory as its unshakeable cornerstone, 'obscures those structural facts under the cloak of individual agency, thus giving people unjustified hopes and unwarranted feelings of failure' (p. 259). Trump might want to revive the *Dream* and make America great again, but from what we have seen so far, his reach extends to some, at the expense of others. Among these others, ironically, are the 'DREAMers' (Development, Relief and Education for Alien Minors) – the grown children of undocumented immigrants, protected or seeking protection under former president Obama's DACA policy (Deferred Action for Childhood Arrivals). Trump, unsurprisingly, is seeking to repeal the scheme.

Despite overwhelming domestic and international media criticism, the buoyancy of the Trump administration (so far) can be attributed, in part, to the cultural insularity and shadow-ish turn of the *Dream*. Michael Wolff's appraisal of the 2017 presidency, *Fire and Fury: Inside the Trump White House* (2018) toping the New York Times best seller list (Macmillan Publishers, 2018), exposes Trump's version of the *Dream* at the expense of all else, including ethical and moral sensitivity. It needed an observer not beholden to the administration, as Wolff argues of his status to initially contextualise the breadth of White House dysfunction – presented until this point, in tweets, sound bites and media reportage. In the unfolding year, the ever more cynical investigative news media and a string of popular book publications – Bob Woodward's *Fear: Trump in the White House* (2018) and Omarosa Manigault Newman's *Unhinged: An Insider's Account of the Trump White House* (2018) for instance – further peeled back the chaos of this presidency and the insularity of an administration in damage control. In 2017 though, early into Trump's reign when he ventured to the German G20 summit, it took a non-American journalist to report candid impressions of Trump's impact and legacy without fear of reprisal for political bias. Australian ABC political editor, Chris Uhlmann's report for the political flagship programme *The Insiders*, went viral (James, 2017):

> [He] barks out bile in 140 characters, [and] wastes his precious days as President at war with the West's institutions like the judiciary, independent government agencies and the free press . . . Donald Trump is a man who craves power because it burnishes his celebrity. To be constantly talking and talked about is all that really matters. And there is no value placed on the meaning of words, so what is said one day can be discarded the next.
>
> *(Uhlmann, 2017)*

The victory complex can also be looked at as a collective phenomenon operating on a cultural and personal level simultaneously – most clearly exemplified in its shadow, Trump. His investment in the obsession to win exemplifies the way that the complex can dominate, dictate and define one's life. Beyond all other reported and satirised behavioural shortcomings – including racism, sexism, vulgarity, narcissism and a seeming lack of intellectual curiosity – Trump, as a figure seemingly overpowered by the complex, must seem, to a people for whom victory is a cultural anchor point, an object of both uncomfortable fascination and relevance, if only to bring awareness to the problematic nature of ego inflation and the potential pathologies the complex can trigger.

Cinema as the vehicle for *Dream* mythos

To detail the dominance and volume of *Dream* narratives, evolved and revised in the eras of Silent film (1911–1927), Classical Hollywood or the Golden Age (1927–1963), New Hollywood or New Wave (1960–1980) and Modern Hollywood cinema, with its various subcategories (1950s-present day), is beyond the scope of this brief chapter. Another way of grappling with the entrenched inevitability of *Dream* narratives is through American remakes of international films, with their conclusions often remodelled to incorporate the ethos of success against the odds:

> The American remake of a French/European film serves to reveal this difference [clean endings and good/bad duality of American film vs ambiguity of European film] primarily through film endings, with the former providing a comforting resolution altogether absent in their European

counterparts . . . American cinema deals in black-and-white oppositions with the neat elimination of all the grays. In this sense, the remake functions as the ideal point of cultural comparison between the two cinemas with one intended ostensibly for the supposedly naïve, childlike American, the other for the ironic, adult European.

(Forrest and Koos, 2002, p. 8)

Thomas Leitch argues that the remake doesn't just translate the language of its original but imposes a more palatable cultural sensibility. He highlights the 1993 remade heroic American ending of the Dutch psychopath film *The Vanishing* or *Spoorloos* (dir. Sluizer, 1988), where rather than the protagonist finally discovering the fate of his abducted lover by allowing her murderer to submit him to the same slow death, he is rescued by his current partner. For Leitch, Sluizer as director of both films, 'corrects the error that made the earlier film so bleak and unsettling by providing a happy ending for American audiences and Kiefer Sutherland, a star in whose welfare they could be expected to have residual investment' (2002, p. 57). A similar parallel can be seen in Australian cinema where more culturally driven motifs are rewritten into the original international material, not in terms of film adaptations, but the adaptation of plays to the screen. Shakespeare's *Macbeth*, for instance, under the direction of Australian Justin Kurzel (2015), is significantly structured around the lost child motif. Oliver Stone's *The Daughter* (2016), an adaptation of Ibsen's *The Wild Duck*, also invites us to consider the actions of the central characters as driven by a relentless inner lost child. And, as detailed in the previous chapter, the short story *All You Zombies* by North American author Robert A. Heinlein is reinvented for the screen as *Predestination*; a narrative of cyclic childhood loss and attempted redemption (Waddell, 2018).

Remakes can be interpreted as fairly obvious markers of how a culture most comfortably understands itself, but it is confronting to try and absorb the volume of material bolstering and, with independent film, challenging the foundation of the *Dream* as a nesting place for the victory complex, and then juxtaposing this volume of material with lost child narratives/themes in the less prolific Australian cinema. Looking beyond Australia's limited production output, with forty-one films produced in 2017 compared to North America's 913 (lagging only behind India and China), the lost child as only one of many complexes driving the culture, albeit one of longevity and consistency since the Australian film industry began, is not interwoven with the kind of ideologically led mythmaking across multiple arts, social and political platforms that reinforces the *Dream* (Screen Australia, 2017).

In a last word on the Trump/Oprah duality, it is important to raise the spectre of hero mythology. For this archetypal and stereotypical component of the *Dream*, exemplified by Oprah (persona and brand), is also bound to the concept of victory – succeeding against the odds while rescuing or helping others in the process – as the classic motif of North American cinema for both children and adults. 'Be your best self' is the abiding axiom of the (cross gender) hero that dominates not only the world of Disney as the biggest historically embedded US media institution with a focus on children and adolescents, but also the twenty-first-century superheroes of DC and Marvel comics, with Patty Jenkins' *Wonder Woman* (2017) ranked as the highest grossing superhero origin film until Coogler's *Black Panther* overtook box-office sales in 2018 (Box Office Mojo, 2018). Except for the superhero genre, with its pivotal Christ/saviour/divine child motif, the literal and symbolic child in North American cinema is not central to the victory complex, as it is of course for Australia's lost child complex. The *Dream* however, is personally and collectively fostered in childhood.

The popular story of company founder Walt Disney's rise from child newspaper delivery boy working early morning and evening rounds for his father while still in school, to an international business man, animator and entrepreneur, 'fit so well the American dream of individual success' (Wasko, 2001, p. 120). In the Disney brand's international multimedia, marketing and theme-park worlds, Janet Wasko identifies the company's role in reinforcing 'what America represents: business, progress, individual initiative' while also perpetuating values 'associated with such all-American traits such as conservatism, homophobia, Manifest Destiny, ethnocentricity, cultural insensitivity, superficiality, lack of culture, etc.' (2001, p. 224). She also acknowledges, along with other theorists, that 'the themes emphasized by Disney culture are reminiscent of a past America and may have less to do with the reality of America today' (p. 224). Hochschild also refers to the influence of Disney on the tenacity of the victory principle:

> The theme of most Walt Disney movies boils down to the lyric in Pinocchio: 'When you wish upon a star, makes no difference who you are, your dreams come true' . . . the global, amorphous vision of establishing a city upon a hill, killing the great white whale, striking a vein of gold, making the world safe for democracy – or simply living a life of decency and dignity – underlies all analyses of what success means or what practices will attain it.
>
> *(Hochschild, 1995, p. 24)*

Having purchased once competing Pixar, Marvel and Lucasfilm companies for over $17 billion, Disney's ever more global on-message themes of success though individual endeavour, exceptionalism and heroism, couched in more liberal and politically correct scripts, still tap into the resilience and manufacture of the *Dream* (McLauchlin, 2015).

The *Star Wars* collection, through original director George Lucas' much popularised relationship with myth scholar Joseph Campbell, has come to be associated with archetypally driven characters and narratives, particularly the hero monomyth. Vogler popularised a twelve-stage scriptwriting formula outlined in his successful *The Writer's Journey* (1998/2007), based on Campbell's *The Hero with a Thousand Faces* (1949). Vogler claims that such a psychologically informed narrative trajectory inevitably taps into the collective unconscious, and by doing so achieves a level of audience accessibility and engagement beyond, but entwined with, the cultural (Vogler, 1998/2007). As Hockley notes in his analysis of the impact of Vogler's model, in terms of the viewer's individual negotiation with cinema, 'films with inscribed psychological themes often do not work as psychological films, as the possibility of a personal psychological relationship with the film has been restricted and perhaps even closed down' (Hockley, 2014, p. 20). On the other hand, when playing with the more culturally and psychologically interwoven victory complex, dependent on a collective acceptance of the individual's inalienable right to achievement, self-improvement and self-driven destiny, formulaic *Dream* success narratives centred on a hero would be more likely to tap into a sense of collective audience aspiration. While not addressing aspects of cinema that can be processed by audiences on an intensely personal level, a function of film that drives Hockley's thesis, more contrived work can provide a mass point of archetypal identification – in this instance, the victory complex.

America the superhero – the world 'policeman' and divine rights

The Disney-Marvel branch and its competitor in the superhero arena, DC Entertainment, a subsidiary of Warner Bros., are intimately related to the kind of archetypally formulaic victory narratives produced by Lucusfilm-Disney. Based on the DC comic characters, Wonder Woman, Superman, Batman, Aquaman and Green Lantern for instance, these films of the American born and cultivated superhero reinforce the individual's almost 'divine' right to self-actualisation and victory over threatening opposing forces, and symbolise North America itself as superpower with the self-imposed right to lead the world. In 2017 this position met with tough opposition, prophetically noted by Greider: 'official America decided we really are indispensable. That's always a dangerous assertion for a country that styles itself on great power. In history, it has often been the reason for "powers" becoming no longer great' (2009, p. 27). This loss, based on an increasing sense of interiority, has been arguably cultivated by, as Uhlmann concluded in his report on the G20, its own presidency:

> We learned Mr Trump has pressed fast forward on the decline of the US as a global leader. He managed to isolate his nation, to confuse and alienate his allies, and to diminish America . . . some will cheer the decline of America, but I think we'll miss it when it's gone. And that's the biggest threat to the values of the West, which he claims to hold so dear.
>
> *(Uhlmann, 2017)*

Shortly after the release of Wolff's *Fire and Fury*, in another Trump-induced media storm, late-night comedian Jimmy Kimmel added to this sense of deterioration, by raising the spectre of Superman. In his opening monologue (January 15, 2018), after detailing Trump's reported naming of Haiti, El Salvador and African countries as 'shithole' in an immigration focused lawmaker's meeting (January 11, 2018), and then denying the language by claiming to journalists he was 'the least racist person you've ever interviewed' (Smith, 2018), Kimmel mused nostalgically on the now lost interconnectedness of each principle in Superman's mantra of *Truth, Justice and the American Way* (*Jimmy Kimmel Live!* 2018).

It is perhaps economic for the purposes of this chapter to focus on what Jeffrey Brown (2017) calls the nationalist superhero. Captain America and Superman fall into this category, but Superman remains the icon of most interest to not only the *Dream* and the victory complex, but also the Judeo-Christian inflected divine child. Brown is interested in how the nationalistic qualities of the 1938 DC *Superman* comics informed the superhero genre, an intrinsically North American invention with global reach that refined the mythology of the ancient gods into a figure ultimately 'synonymous with the American Dream' and designed to instil related ideologies including the inevitability of victory for the morally deserving (Brown, 2017, p. 84). Brown sums up the role of nationalist superheroes as figures who act as:

> fictional focus points for American values and consolidate a range of abstract ideas about what makes America unique. At the core of America's mythology, and its citzens' perception of the nation's superiority and uniqueness, is the cluster of beliefs typically grouped together under the notion of American Exceptionalism. Core American political and cultural principles, like individualism, democracy, capitalism, egalitarianism, Manifest Destiny, and freedom, that are rooted in the nation's revolutionary origins and remain bedrock ideologies today, contribute to the deep-seated belief that America is nobler than any other nation.
>
> *(Brown, 2017, p. 85)*

In an era of post-9/11 turbulent political leadership, internal conflict, economic hardship and slippage from the pedestal of world policeman, Brown argues that Superman, in print, but predominantly the live action hero of cinema, has become a symbol of unification and a source of nostalgic fantasy for intellectually comfortable good/evil dualities where 'the bad guys were always defeated' (p. 8). Originating from WWII and having seen a significant reinvigoration post-9/11, superheroes are also utilised to reinforce underlying victory related ideologies of US militarisation (Crowe, 2011).

In relation to how North America has been perceived internationally, and this would include an enmeshment of the concept of victory and military dominance, Brown makes an interesting point:

> During the promotional junket for *The Dark Knight Rises* (2012) Michael Caine, who played Bruce Wayne's assistant Alfred Pennyworth in the

Christopher Nolan directed trilogy, was widely cited for claiming: 'Superman is the way America sees itself. Batman is the way the rest of the world sees America.' The world may picture America as the corrupt and violent wasteland of Gotham City, and much of the American public may hold this view too, but as a nation there is still a desire to see itself as the shining light of nobility and defender of freedoms personified by Superman and Captain America.

(Brown, 2017, p. 101)

The illusion of righteousness can also be added to the superhero literary and cinema franchise framed around the victory complex. While culturally constructed, manicured and maintained, as are all cultural values, the superhero is bound in a psychology that *has us* beyond any sense of rational objectivity. Of interest in grappling with the lost child complex's difference from, and similarity to, the victory complex, is the former's special relationship to the child, which is predominantly of divine origin in the superhero cannon. It is unsurprising given North America's religiosity, that the divine child – whether exceptionally gifted, privileged or of supernatural birth – emerges as a saviour figure more literally connected to Christian mythology than its symbolic role in the non-sectarian Australian lost child context: it is a cultural undercurrent that as Levinson argues, is tied to the etiology of the American success myth. The 'American Exceptionalism' at the heart of this mythology, as Brown observes, when projected through vehicles like the superhero, binds the individual and the nation state to a sense of the divine: divine birth and therefore divine right to rule under the overarching Christian moral and ethical principles that have shaped its history, allowed for the concept of Manifest Destiny, and continue to influence its culture.

As we saw in Chapter 1, Jung understood the entwined mission of the divine child and the hero, as overcoming the forces of darkness (the unconscious), often projected in myth through the symbolic imagery of fantastic creatures or nefarious figures. Emerging into the light is equated with a breakthrough to consciousness – metaphorically the recognition of, and consequent confrontation with, shadows (monsters) of the psyche: 'Hence the "child" distinguishes itself by deeds which point to the conquest of the dark' (Jung, 1959/1968, p. 167). As in more stock black/white-good/evil fairy tale inflected narratives, Guillermo del Toro's *The Shape of Water* (2017) a recent example as I write, the superhero genre's good/evil-dark/light duality is informed by Judeo-Christian ethics of sacrifice and liberation. Given the importance of individual exceptionalism, it is possible to argue that ego gratification through victory is most aligned with images and allusions to 'the light'. Vogler focuses his model of the hero's journey as a path to ego gratification – questing, descent and eventual triumph. It is a *Dream*, victory complex focused trajectory that contradicts Campbell's original understanding of the global mythologies that position the hero as one able to, in her/his pursuit, rise above and so be divested of attachments by having 'died to his [sic] personal ego' (Campbell, 1949/1993, p. 243).

Destiny and divine right

Adam Barkman's (2013) work on Superman as a Christ-figure in both early comic and later cinematic incarnations references Nietzsche's Übermensch or superman/overman ideal of transcendence beyond social and religiously based moral and ethical codes. Barkman argues that the American, Judeo-Christian Superman of DC Comics was initially created to undermine the atheistically driven concept of the Übermensch, and develop the character into an actual Christ-inflected icon. The superman in the Nietzschian sense, writes Barkman,

> wouldn't worry about what others say is 'good' or 'bad' but would construct, with his own genius and creativity, his own norms in order to create a persona of his choosing. The superman would thus revile such 'weak' virtues as pity and mercy, since they would distract the superman from his own goals and self-actualization.
>
> *(Barkman, 2013, p. 112)*

I can't help but return to Trump's behaviour as symbolic of the shadow face of the victory complex. He emulates a warped version of the Übermensch in his public lack of regard to critical opposition and the concepts of 'pity and mercy' that through his twitter feed, he seems to construe as synonymous with weakness and 'losing'. When questions were raised about his mental stability in January 2018, he responded by referring to himself on twitter as 'a stable genius' (Trump, 2018). While his 'genius' and brilliance, a measure of the Nietzschian superman, are debatable, Trump is nevertheless characterised in the press as a man who, in both his election campaign and presidency, might be said to see himself as above the law, or at least the constitution. Like Nathan Leopold and Richard Lobe, the privileged sons of Chicago multimillionaires, who ascribed to the principals of the Übermensch and so murdered a child to prove their superiority (Baatz, 2008), Trump in his hubris (but without Leopold and Lobe's exceptional IQs or homicidal psychopathy), is also beholden to deeply entrenched ethical and moral codes that *earth* the self-imposed and distorted would-be superman: codes enforced by the judicial system, the media and public opinion. 'Superman's absolute devotion to the universal moral law and Judeo-Christian morality' claims Barkman, 'stands in stark contrast to Nietzsche's morality of power. Where Nietzsche sees sacrificial love as a weakness because it conforms to social standards, Superman sees sacrificial love as strength insofar as it conforms to the Highest Law' (p. 116). As Natasha Lennard writes in her review of Hugo Drochon's *Nietzche's Great Politics* (2016), Trump falls short of any defendable Übermensch parallels;

> Drochon has more recently commented that 'for Nietzsche, the celebration of a man like Trump was the inevitable result of a democratic culture built on the virtues of ignorance and self-fulfillment.' Trump is no Übermensch (overman) shattering the illusions of the herd. He is more like the 'last

man' of which Zarathustra speaks, the demagogue of anti-progress, seeking only comfort and personal security. Nietzsche's critique of modern democracy sits well with a narrative that understands Trump's ascent as paved by neoliberal stupor.

(Lennard, 2017, pp. 153–154)

Although Barkman never alludes to, or draws connections with, Trump's presidency – publishing in 2013 – the following comment is prescient: 'Love is only a weakness, however, if one thinks that true strength or happiness means as Nietzsche would have it, caring only about oneself' (p. 116).

Returning to the pop culture Superman, Judeo-Christian references to the character as the son of God are simply too prolific to include here, but briefly include: Barkman's finding that 'in Superman #1 (Summer, 1939), the Man of Steel's adoptive mother, Martha Kent, was originally named Mary, and his adoptive father, named in a later issue, is Jonathan Joseph Kent' (p. 114); the visual allusions to Salvador Dali's *Christ of St. John of the Cross* (1951) and *Corpus Hypercubus* (1954); Martha Kent's Michelangelo-*Pieta*-like cradling of the fallen Superman in *Superman Returns* (Singer, 2006); the angelic/god like ascensions of Zack Snyder's Superman, lit, in advertising posters, by heavenly light rays shining through blue/white clouds in *Man of Steel* (2013); the introductory speeches of Superman's father in *Man of Steel* and *Superman* (dir. Donner, 1978), before jettisoning his son to earth for a greater good; and the origins of Superman's original Hebrew sourced name Kal-El – 'If the Krytonian "El" means "child" and "Kal" means "star", then Kal-El is a "starchild" like Jesus, whose birth was heralded by the Star of Bethlehem' (Barkman, 2013, p. 114).

From an almost literal imitation of key aspects of the biblical Christ myth, to more general markers of divinity – sent to earth as a saviour figure, parented by mortals, threatened with near death and resurrected to defeat evil – the superhero catalogue has most recently found its feminist muscle in Jenkins' *Wonder Woman*, released in the year of the #metoo campaign. Still costumed in the American signature colours of red, white and blue, or rather red, blue, gold and white/silver, Gal Gadot as 'Diana of Themyscira, daughter of Hippolyta, queen of the Amazons', the child of Zeus and Hippolyta, is even more Christ-like than Superman. The product of a mortal and a god, like Christ, she is both demigod and hero, only reaching full saviour potential in adulthood after much personal testing. Related to interconnecting mythologies spun around miraculous children, Jung writes:

> Sometimes the 'child' looks more like a *child god*, sometimes more like a young *hero*. Common to both types is the miraculous birth and the adversities of early childhood-abandonment and danger through persecution. The god is by nature wholly supernatural; the hero's nature is human but raised to the limit of the supernatural – he is 'semi-divine'.
>
> *(Jung, 1959/1968: § 281, pp. 165–166)*

In broaching the spectre of the Übermensch, distorting the concept through Trump and comparing it to the domestically created and cinematically honed superhero, we can see that the victory complex framing these fantasy figures adopts a very specific form of the Judeo-Christian divine – as does the *American Dream*.

The lost child v. victory complex

In the first chapter I discussed the idea that the divine child, a motif in Jung's thinking that represented 'the strongest, the most ineluctable urge in every human being, namely the urge to realize itself' (Jung, 1959/1968: § 289), functions as a psychopomp able to steer the individuation process. The lost child complex seems to disrupt this function, so that the archetypal child becomes stuck between the desire for futurity and its inability to *become*; always experienced as a sense of latent possibility. It was also argued in the previous chapter, that the lost child can provide a liminal respite; a refuge to which we intermittently return, as in the practice of depth psychologies, to rediscover aspects of ourselves that have become unfocused, undervalued and lost to a critical adult sense of self that is less willing to explore and integrate unconscious material. For Jung the divine child is 'equipped with all the powers of nature and instinct, whereas the conscious mind is always getting caught up in its supposed ability to do otherwise' (Jung, 1959/1968: § 289). There are two approaches to understanding the implications of the lost child complex. In the first, the potential to move forward is inhibited, and in the second renewal is possible through a periodic return to the liminal spaces that the inner child inhabits.

This then suggests that Australia, when under the pull of the lost child complex, can have a conflicting relationship with America's victory complex and the cinema that amplifies its core attributes. On one hand, the *Dream* can be read as a proactive way to engage the potential of the inner divine child or urge to a more developed sense of agency – a quality that is impeded by the lost child complex. On the other hand, in the quest for victory and advancement, the more meditative and enriching aspects of returning to the child's hidden (lost) place – that the lost child complex can facilitate – are ignored. What seems clear to me living in Australia for most of my life, a country not dominated by any one organised religion, both working in and critically analysing our screen culture, is that as flooded and entertained as we are by American screen products there has always been an underlying ambivalence toward recycled hero monomyth narratives that consistently channel *Dream* thinking.

Australian director and scriptwriter Glenda Hambly, mentioned in Chapter 5's discussion of *Fran*, touches on this problematic relationship with North American screen content in her recent doctoral study (2018). She focuses on the constraint placed upon Australian screenwriters to adhere to a classically Hollywood-driven narrative style of script development to ensure their competitive edge for government funding, largely regulated by US-script-inspired policy frameworks. She argues that the traditional hero focused three-act tradition – key to what Australian screen writing agencies regard as *the* successful scriptwriting model – is formulated on misinterpretations of Aristotelian principles outlined in *Poetics* (300 BCE) and the templates of influential scriptwriting gurus like Vogler and Robert McKee (see, https://mckeestory.com) that favour the dynamic of the hero's journey and its predictable victory inflected finale:

> Screen agency executives advised me, for example, that a story should be driven by a goal-driven individual protagonist and not revolve around a group of disparate characters because that was what audiences preferred. Other 'principles of screenwriting' they promoted were a well-defined antagonist, a three-act structure and a climax in the third act.
>
> *(Hambly, 2018, p. 1)*

Hambly drew up a list of the twenty most successful Australian films at the Australian box-office over a period of over twenty years (1994–2013). She interviewed the twenty-two writers who wrote these films as a way of gauging their methodological approach to storytelling. Sixty-eight percent of the scriptwriters chose not to fall back on the Hollywood paradigm, contradicting the dominant rationale guiding the decisions of the agencies. Seven of the twenty-two scripts were written using some or all of the precepts of the Hollywood model. Many of the remaining thirteen demonstrated characteristics of a distinctly Australian narrative paradigm. While Hambly is not opposed to Australians choosing to adopt American structures, she argues that, 'If a lesson can be drawn, it is the importance of valuing this diversity and of acknowledging the Australian audiences' eclectic taste in storytelling modes' (Hambly, 2018, p. 170).

In this consideration of the bridging relationship between two very different cultural fixations, it seems appropriate to raise the intricate merging of lost child and victory complex in director Craig Gillespie's interpretation of skater Tonya Harding's struggle with the *American Dream*. *I Tonya* (2017) is an uncompromising and unsentimental film punctuated with black humour. It talks to the futile, but relentless, pursuit of winning. The twist in this film, above the controversial actual events it inspired, is that the protagonist, Harding, as the gifted and driven child of a dysfunctional and economically underprivileged family, would have under James Truslow Adams' estimation, been ideally suited to succeed in her pursuit of the *Dream*. Instead we are exposed to a somewhat divine child, systematically worn down by domestic violence, narcissistic parenting, poverty, her own sense of culturally driven entitlement to victory through perseverance and ultimately the realisation that she didn't physically or temperamentally fit the template of an American Olympic success story. What we see in the flashbacks of an adult Tonya (Margot Robbie) retelling the story of her career and its downfall, is the lost child beneath the surface repeatedly being held back from the *Dream* through a refusal to cower to its exacting and fickle expectations. We are also made starkly aware of the flaws inherent in the four tenets of *Dream* ideology raised by Hochschild: equal participation, expectation of success, success as the outcome of controlling one's destiny and success as synonymous with virtue.

'It is a striking paradox in all child myths that the "child" is on the one hand delivered helpless into the power of terrible enemies and in continual danger of extinction' wrote Jung, 'while on the other he [sic] possesses powers far exceeding those of ordinary humanity. This is closely related to the psychological fact that though the child may be "insignificant", unknown, "a mere child", he [sic] is also divine' (Jung, 1959/1968: § 289). We can see this symbolism in *I Tonya*, but like the lost child that 'has' Australian audiences, throughout the film Tonya carries a sense of the child as *perpetually becoming* – never to arrive. Unlike the aspect of the lost child that provides an opportunity for escape and reflection in Hillman's analysis of the orphan, Tonya appears too bound by the victory complex to see beyond it. When eventually striped of her ability to compete because of her involvement in the clubbing of fellow competitive skater Nancy Kerrigan, we see the shadow of the victory complex: an inflation, where one's identity is so dependent on the kind of winning that the complex demands, that in its focus on personal gain, it ultimately fails to serve the individual for whom loss is often processed as irreconcilable defeat. Tonya Harding, a self-proclaimed Trump supporter, and the character presented here, may just represent those who believe the *Dream is* dead. But while *I Tonya* takes a poke at *Dream* ideology, ironically the actual Harding found herself in the spotlight as Margot Robbie's plus-one at the 2018 Golden Globes – celebrated, thanked, but not quite redeemed as winning/*Dream* material.

I am not arguing that one complex is more palatable than another, or that individuals caught in those group obsessions are necessarily susceptible to the condition's more shadowy aspects. By looking at North American's deeply embedded emphasis on victory to reinforce the global nature of the complex and the way it can possess us, I also want to draw attention to the possibility of seeing one's self and one's culture *beyond* the complex and its dualities. Australia's pull toward lost child thinking and *affect* is so diametrically opposed to any automatic assumption of success as a cultural right, or shame as the consequence of failure, that our immersion in heavily *Dream*-dosed American popular culture is difficult to understand. Even more problematic, as Hambly argues, is the funding driven imperative to reshape *our* methods of screen storytelling to fit these more inauthentic frameworks.

CONCLUDING REMARKS

At the time of completing this manuscript, a number of synchronistic events happened. While I was focussed on writing about this particular Australian complex, the global media was preoccupied with images, reportage and archetypally inflected narratives of lost children. These accounts appeared in quick succession, and due to the days and weeks of their unfolding, there was also some overlap. Australia's refugee policies and problematic handling of children in detention, made even more public with the 2014 Triggs led report discussed in Chapter 4, seemed shameful and indicative of shadow/complex projection, but on a recent research trip with students to the United States in mid-2018 I saw a new kind of darkness. Donald Trump's move to repeal DACA, already a source of public debate, was exceeded by the implementation of his 'Zero Tolerance' policy for undocumented migrants that actioned the separation of children and toddlers from their parents at the Mexican border. Public outrage led to the order being repealed, but the damage had been done and families had been traumatised with an estimated 2,300 children removed from their parents (Miller, 2018; Solon, 2018).

While this story was unfolding, my students and I were absorbed in the dystopian *Handmaid's Tale*. This was touched on a little in Chapter 1 in reference to the 'divine' lost child's potential to effect change. The episodes screening at the time of the Mexican separations (produced months in advance), synchronistically focused more heavily and dramatically on the twisted, obsessional and nurturing aspects of motherhood and parental estrangement. The 'handmaids', forced into procreative sex by wealthy infertile couples, are callously obliged to relinquish at birth the newborns resulting from these rapes. Tensions reached their peak with the central handmaid character 'Offred' (Elisabeth Moss) giving birth in a painfully explicit scene and the baby removed from her care shortly after delivery. A recipient of eighteen industry awards to date, critical acclaim and significant enough global ratings to announce a third season, the programme seemed just *too relevant . . . too much* an amplification of cultural fixations and pathologies.

I didn't imagine these actual and fictional televised narratives in terms of a cultural complex, more as passionate reactions to a new kind of politics beyond the comprehension of those for whom the freedom to pursue success and victory was a cultural expectation. Both *The Handmaid's Tale* and the border crossing removal of children, seemed not so much about loss in the way that it's processed through the lost child complex, but the *elimination* of children from their parents' lives and the damaging ideologies of men in power.

At the same time, the briefest news came through the American media of a group of twelve missing Thai school boys, members of the 'Wild Boars' soccer team, who ventured too far with their coach into Thailand's treacherous Tham Luang Nang Non mountain cave. When I arrived back in Australia, with Thailand as our Asian-Pacific neighbour, the boys had been found but still remained trapped in an inner cavity of the cave system. The story was growing in momentum with the media following every move of the diving teams and the Thai government's efforts to rescue the boys before oncoming monsoon rains flooded their small chamber. As each boy was carried out of the cave, sedated by Australian anaesthetist and diver Richard Harris, the media covered every development. There was a sense of global community created through the interest, expectation and excitement of the rescue, coupled with an international contingent of experts. Medical, military, diving, family, community and news teams supported the effort without any of the expected 'media circus' demeaning the event. It was as if this particular story of childhood lostness, recovery and transnational effort had restored a lost sense of genuine and selfless unification.

There was also an underlying hint of the archetypal child about these boys who seemed to adopt the symbolism of futurity and peaceful coexistence, along with the mythology of the sacred mountain, its title translated by anthropologist Andrew Johnson as 'the cave of the reclining lady'. 'It is named after a princess who, as the legend goes, committed suicide after she was forbidden to be with her commoner love' he writes, 'Her body became the mountains, and her genitals, the cave. She is now the ruler – the "jao mae" – of both' (Johnson, 2018). As crudely literal as it might seem in the light of the mythic Jao Mae, reading the boys' emergence from the cave as a kind of symbolic birth with all its attendant *affect*, does have a Jung-like 'divine' ring to it.

The conflation of the captured migrant children and their ongoing trauma, the final episodes of *The Handmaid's Tale* thick with twisted motherhood and infant abduction, and the collective liberation of the Wild Boars soccer team over the June-July months of 2018, was capped off by another lost child – a baby blimp flying over London. On Trump's visit to the UK, Friday July 13, it was estimated that 'tens of thousands' turned out in protest (Booth et al., 2018). A giant four-metre balloon or blimp of a big Trump baby, bankrolled through crowd funding, loomed over Parliament square. Rotund, nappy clad and orange skinned with bright yellow hair, it clasped a mobile phone in its tiny hands and the small gaping mouth seemed to capture a mid-sentence rant. Here was the symbol of a man caught in toddler/adult liminality. In light of Chapters 2, 4 and 5, the association with double wounding and shadow projection seemed obvious. Considering Trump's *rendering* of child *others* as lost, the baby blimp signified not a culturally framed lost child complex, but a more personally twisted fusion of the infantile and the need to win. Jung is surprisingly helpful in trying to find a correlation between the obese baby balloon and the lost child complex: 'in every adult there lurks a child – an eternal child, something that is always becoming, is never completed, and calls for unceasing care, attention and education' (Jung, 1954/2014, pp. 169–170, § 286).

It is difficult to introduce the concept of an Australian complex and not appear nationalistic, oversimplified or generalised. Impossible as it is to speak for, and of, an overarching culture, given that all cultures are shaped by intricate overlapping cultural networks, some assumptions can be made about dominant *themes* repeatedly elevated to public attention. While the lost child as a motif doesn't galvanise the country with the tenacity of the *American Dream*, I have been arguing that in its many cinematic manifestations, the child displaced is a presence that is either overt, or lurks just below the surface of our storytelling. The arts allow us a window into the psyche. Cinema can powerfully talk to our lost child, and in its prolific reinvention of this image, encourage us to return again and again as a way of providing 'unceasing care, attention and education'. Television has the capacity to speed up this process in its immediacy, but the slower, more protracted nature of film-making is able to capture perhaps more intricate expressions of the lost child at work in us. Like psychotherapies and psychoanalysis, cinema can draw out the child, put it aside, return to it and renegotiate its significance.

I'd like to go back to the beach – to that rip I mentioned in the introduction that took me gently, silently and with a sense of determination. I often think back to that time because it is still so vivid. Did I imagine my calm and tenacity, or did I embellish the memory with a narrative – a three-act beginning, middle and climactic end? What seems most real was the certainty I'd get back. All these years later, whenever I get swept out over my head, I go to this kid inside who instinctively, if circuitously, seems to know what to do.

REFERENCES

Adams, J. T. (1931/2017) *The Epic of America*, London and New York: Routledge.
AEC – Australian Electoral Commission. (2018) 'Women and the Right to Vote in Australia', [online]. Available at: www.aec.gov.au/Elections/Australian_Electoral_History/wright.htm [accessed 2 July 2018].
AIATSIS – Australian Institute of Aboriginal and Torres Strait Islander Studies. (2018) [online]. Available at: http://aiatsis.gov.au [accessed 29 November 2018].
AIFS – Australian Institute of Family Studies, Australian Government. (2018) [online]. Available at: https://aifs.gov.au/cfca/publications/age-consent-laws [accessed 16 July 2018].
Appell, A. R. (2013) 'Accommodating Childhood', *Cardozo Journal of Law & Gender*, 19, pp. 715–779.
Assmann, J. and John Czaplicka, J. (1995) 'Collective Memory and Cultural Identity', *New German Critique*, 65, pp. 125–133.
AustLII – Australasian Legal Information Institute. (2003) *Native Title Act 1993*, [online]. Available at: www.austlii.edu.au/cgi-bin/viewdb/au/legis/cth/consol_act/nta1993147 [accessed 13 September 2017].
Australian Bureau of Statistics. (2015) 'Feature Article 3: Languages of Aboriginal and Torres Strait Islander Peoples: A Uniquely Australian Heritage', [online]. Available at: www.abs.gov.au/ausstats/abs@.nsf/Previousproducts/1301.0Feature%20Article42009%E2%80%9310?opendocument&tabname=Summary&prodno=1301.0&issue=2009%9610&num=&view= [accessed 2 July 2018].
Australian Government. (2017) *Migration Act 1953*, Compilation No. 135, Federal Register of Legislation, [online]. Available at: www.legislation.gov.au/Series/C1958A00062 [accessed 9 November 2017].
Australian Government: Department of Home Affairs. (2018) 'Abolition of the "White Australia" Policy', [online]. Available at: www.homeaffairs.gov.au/about/corporate/information/fact-sheets/08abolition [accessed 29 July 2018].
Australian Human Rights Commission. (2007) 'Social Justice Report 2007', [online]. Available at: www.humanrights.gov.au/publications/social-justice-report-2007-chapter-3-northern-territory-emergency-response-intervention [accessed 2 October 2017].

Australian War Memorial. (2018a) 'Boy Soldiers', [online]. Available at: www.awm.gov.au/articles/encyclopedia/boysoldiers [accessed 1 July 2018].

Australian War Memorial. (2018b) 'Conscription', [online]. Available at: www.awm.gov.au/articles/encyclopedia/conscription [accessed 1 July 2018].

Australian War Memorial. (2018c) 'Fatalities at Gallipoli', [online]. Available at: www.awm.gov.au/articles/encyclopedia/gallipoli/fatalities [accessed 1 July 2018].

Australian War Memorial. (2018d) 'First World War 1914–18', [online]. Available at: www.awm.gov.au/articles/atwar/first-world-war [accessed 1 July 2018].

Australian War Memorial. (2018e) 'Universal Service Scheme, 1911–29', [online]. Available at: www.awm.gov.au/articles/encyclopedia/conscription/universal_service [accessed 1 July 2018].

Baatz, S. (2008) *For the Thrill of It: Leoplold and Lobe, and the Murder That Shocked Chicago*, New York: HarperCollins.

Balym, T. (2013) 'Bombshell Finding Reveal "Toxic Culture" of Australian Swim Team at London Olympics', *Courier Mail*, 19 February.

Banakou, D., Groten, R., and Slater, M. (2013) 'Illusory Ownership of a Virtual Child Body Causes Overestimation of Object Sizes and Implicit Attitude Changes', *Proceedings of the National Academy of Science*, 110(31), pp. 12846–12851.

Barbican Centre, The. (2018) 'Picnic at Hanging Rock Malthouse/Black Swan Theatre Company', [online]. Available at: www.barbican.org.uk/whats-on/2018/event/picnic-at-hanging-rock [accessed 22 March 2018].

Barker, H. (1980) *For the Love of a Good Man*, London: J. Calder.

Barkman, A. (2013) 'Superman from Anti-Christ to Christ-Type', in M. D. White (ed.) *Superman and Philosophy: What Would the Man of Steel Do?*, West Sussex: Wiley-Blackwell, pp. 111–120.

Barrett, J. (1979) *Falling in: Australians and 'Boy Conscription' 1911–1915*, Sydney: Hale & Iremonger.

Bean, C. E. (1941–2) *Official History of Australia in the War of 1914–1918*, Series, Vols. 1–6, Australian War Memorial, [online]. Available at: www.awm.gov.au/collection/C1416844 [accessed 2 July 2018].

Bean, P. and Melville, J. (1989) *Lost Children of the Empire*, London: Unwin Hyman.

Bell, D. S. A. (2003) 'Mythscapes: Memory, Mythology, and National Identity', *British Journal of Sociology*, 54(1), pp. 63–81.

Biddington, M. (2013) 'Funding for the Royal Commission into Institutional Responses to Child Sexual Abuse', Parliament of Australia, [online]. Available at: www.aph.gov.au/About_Parliament/Parliamentary_Departments/Parliamentary_Library/pubs/rp/BudgetReview201314/FundingRoyalCom [accessed 26 May 2015].

Birch, D. (2009) *The Oxford Companion to English Literature*, 7th edn., Oxford: Oxford University Press.

Blackburn, K. (2016) *War, Sport and the Anzac Tradition*, London: Palgrave Macmillan.

Bliss, M. (2000) *Dreams Within a Dream: The Films of Peter Weir*, Carbondale and Edwardsville: Southern Illinois University Press.

Bloom, S. L. (1999) 'Trauma Theory Abbreviated', From the Final Action Plan: A Coordinated Community-Based Response to Family Violence, Attorney General of Pennsylvania's Family Violence Task Force, [online]. Available at: http://sanctuaryweb.com/Portals/0/Bloom%20Pubs/1999%20Bloom%20Trauma%20Theory%20Abbreviated.pdf [accessed 29 July 2018].

Booth, R., Topping, A., Gayle, D., and Brooks, L. (2018) 'Trump Protests: Tens of Thousands Take to Streets across UK', *The Guardian*, 14 July, [online]. Available at: www.theguardian.com/us-news/2018/jul/13/baby-blimp-cheers-takes-to-skies-protest [accessed 23 July 2018].

Box Office Mojo. (2018) 'Superhero-Origin', [online]. Available at: www.boxoffice mojo.com/genres/chart/?id=superheroorigin.htm [accessed 11 July 2018].
Briefel, A. (2017) 'Parenting through Horror: Reassurance in Jennifer Kent's *The Babadook*', *Camera Obscura*, 32(2 95), pp. 1–27.
Broszormenyi-Nagy, I. and Spark, G. M. (1973/1984) *Invisible Loyalties: Reciprocity in Intergenerational Family*, Oxfordshire and New York: Routledge.
Brown, J. A. (2017) *The Modern Superhero in Film and Television: Popular Genre and American Culture*, New York: Routledge.
Browning, D. (2017) 'Kinchela Boys' Home Survivors Tell of Removals Sexual Abuse and Redemption', *ABC News*, 2 May, [online]. Available at: www.abc.net.au/news/2017-05-02/kinchela-boys-home-survivors-tell-of-removals-and-sexual-abuse/8488976 [accessed 10 October 2018].
Buckingham-Jones, S. (2017) 'Hird: "I Reached Breaking Point"', *The Australian*, 17 March.
Buser, S. (2016) 'The Trump Complex, the John Wayne Archetype and States of National Possession', in L. Cruz and S. Buser (eds.) *A Clear and Present Danger: Narcissism in the Era of Donald Trump*, Ashville, NC: Chiron Publications, pp. 13–15.
Campbell, J. (1949/1993) *The Hero with a Thousand Faces*, London: HaperCollins.
Campbell, J. (1990) *Transformations of Myth through Time*, New York: Harper & Row.
Carter, M. (2014) *Myth of the Western: New Perspectives on Hollywood's Frontier Narrative*, Edinburgh: Edinburgh University Press.
Caruth, C. (1996) *Unclaimed Experience: Trauma, Narrative, and History*, Baltimore: Johns Hopkins University Press.
Casement, A. (2003) 'Encountering the Shadow in Rites of Passage: A Study in Activations', *Journal of Analytical Psychology*, 48, pp. 29–46.
Casement, A. (2006) 'The Shadow', in R. K. Papadopoulos (ed.) *The Handbook of Jungian Psychology*, Florence: Taylor and Francis, pp. 94–112.
Clarke, A. (2008) *History's Children: History Wars in the Classroom*, Sydney: UNSW Press.
Clarke, M. (1874/1897) *For the Term of His Natural Life*, London: Richard Bently and Son.
Clendinnen, I. (2003) *Dancing with Strangers*, Victoria: Text Publishing.
Collingwood Forever. (2018) 'Anzac Day Medal', [online]. Available at: http://forever.collingwoodfc.com.au/anzac-day-medal [accessed 2 July 2018].
Collingwood-Whittick, S. (ed.). (2007) *The Pain of Unbelonging: Alienation and Identity in Australian Literature*, Amsterdam: Rodopi.
Collins, F. (2013) 'Rachel Perkins: Creating Change through Blackfella Films', *Senses of Cinema*, 69, [online]. Available at: http://sensesofcinema.com/2013/contemporary-australian-filmmakers/rachel-perkins-creating-change-through-blackfella-films [accessed 21 July 2018].
Collins, F. and Davis, T. (2004) *Australian Cinema after Mabo*, Cambridge: Cambridge University Press.
Cooper, L. (2011) 'Cormac McCarthy's "The Road" as Apocalyptic Grail Narrative', *Studies in the Novel*, 43(2), pp. 218–236, [online]. Available at: www.jstor.org/stable/41228678 [accessed 26 February 2018].
Craps, S. (2013) *Postcolonial Witnessing*, New York: Palgrave Macmillan.
Creed, B. (1993) *The Monstrous Feminine: Film, Feminism, Psychoanalysis*, London and New York: Routledge.
Creed, B. (2001) 'Breeding Out the Black: *Jedda* and the Stolen Generations in Australia', in B. Creed and J. Hoorn (eds.) *Body Trade: Captivity, Cannibalism and Colonialism in the Pacific*, New York: Routledge, pp. 208–230.
Creed, B. (2005) *Phallic Panic: Film, Horror and the Primal Uncanny*, Melbourne: Melbourne University Press.

Crowe, L. A. (2011) 'Superheroes or Super-Soldiers? The Militarization of Our Modern-Day Heroes', in J. Marshall Beier (ed.) *The Militarization of Childhood*, New York: Palgrave Macmillan, pp. 111–132.

Cruz, L. and Buser, S. (eds.). (2016) *A Clear and Present Danger: Narcissism in the Era of Donald Trump*, Ashville, NC: Chiron Publications.

Currey, J. (ed.). (1793/2006) *The First Fleet Journal of John Hunter, October 1786–August 1788*, Malvern, Victoria: Colony Press.

Dermody, S. (1980) 'Action and Adventure', in S. Murray (ed.) *The New Australian Cinema*, Melbourne: Thomas Nelson Australia Pty Ltd., pp. 79–95.

Duina, F. (2011) *Winning: Reflections on an American Obsession*, Princeton, NJ: Princeton University Press.

Earley, L. and Cushway, D. (2002) 'The Parentified Child', *Clinical Child Psychology and Psychiatry*, 7(2), pp. 163–178.

Edwards, C. and Read, P. (eds.). (1989) *The Lost Children: Thirteen Australians Taken from Their Aboriginal Families Tell of the Struggle to Find Their Natural Parents*, Sydney: Doubleday.

Elliott, T. S. (1971) *Four Quartets*, Orlando: Harcourt.

Ely, R. (1984) 'Australian historians on 'Tall Poppies'. A survey', *Australian Cultural History*, 3, pp. 104–26.

Erll, A. (2008a) 'Cultural Memories Studies: An Introduction', in A. Erll and A. Nünning (eds.) *A Companion to Cultural Memory Studies: An International and Interdisciplinary Handbook*, Media and Cultural Memory 8, Berlin and New York: de Gruyter, pp. 1–15.

Erll, A. (2008b) 'Literature, Film, and the Mediality of Cultural Memory', in A. Erll and A. Nünning (eds.) *A Companion to Cultural Cultural Memory Studies: An International and Interdisciplinary Handbook*, Media and Cultural Memory 8, Berlin and New York: de Gruyter, pp. 389–398.

Feather, T. (1994) 'Attitudes Toward High Achievers and Reactions to their Fall: Theory and Research Concerning Tall Poppies', *Advances in Experimental Social Psychology*, 26, pp. 1–73.

Fidler, R. (2017) *Conversations with Richard Fidler*, ABC Radio National, Broadcast, 12 September, [online]. Available at: www.abc.net.au/radio/programs/conversations/conversations-nakkiah-lui/8876208 [accessed 13 September 2017].

Flanagan, R. (1997) *The Sound of One Hand Clapping*, Sydney: Palgrave Macmillan.

Flanagan, R. (2014) *The Narrow Road to the Deep North*, Melbourne: Penguin.

Flanagan, R. (2015) 'Triggs Was Attacked for Defending the Powerless- and One Day Another PM Will Apologise for It', *The Guardian*, 28 February, [online]. Available at: www.theguardian.com/commentisfree/2015/feb/26/triggs-was-attacked-for-defending-the-powerless-and-one-day-another-pm-will-apologise-for-it [accessed 3 July 2018].

Forrest, J. and Koos, L. R. (eds.). (2002) 'Reviewing Remakes: An Introduction', in J. Forrest and L. R. Koos (eds.) *Dead Ringers: The Remake in Theory and Practice*, Albany: State University of New York Press, pp. 1–36.

Fox, K. (2010) 'Rosalie Kunoth-Monks and the Making of *Jedda*', *Aboriginal History*, 33, pp. 77–95.

Fraiberg, S., Adelson, E., and Shapiro, V. (1975) 'Ghosts in the Nursery: A Psychoanalytic Approach to the Problems of Impaired Infant-Mother Relationships', *Journal of the American Academy of Child Psychiatry*, 14(3), pp. 387–421.

Freud, A. (1936/1966) *The Ego and the Mechanisms of Defense*, New York: International Universities Press.

Freud, S. (1899/1991) *The Interpretation of Dreams*, Harmondsworth: Penguin.
Freud, S. (1905/1953) *Complete Psychological Works of Sigmund Freud*, Vol. 7, *A Case of Hysteria, Three essays on Sexuality and Other Works*, 2nd edn., London: Hogarth Press.
Freud, S. (1917) *Standard Edition of the Complete Psychological Works of Sigmund Freud*, Vol. 14, *Mourning and Melancholia*, London: Hogarth Press.
Freud, S. (1919/1955) *The Complete Psychological Works of Sigmund Freud*, Vol. 17, 'The Uncanny', in *Infantile Neurosis and Other Works*, 2nd edn., London: Hogarth Press, pp. 217–256.
Freud, S. (1923–1925) *Complete Psychological Works of Sigmund Freud*, Vol. 9, *The Ego and the Id and Other Works*, London: Hogarth Press.
Froud, M. (2017) *The Lost Child in Literature and Culture*, London: Palgrave Macmillan.
Gammage, B. (1974/1980) *The Broken Years: Australian Soldiers in the Great War*, Melbourne: Penguin.
Garner, H. (2007) 'From Frogmore, Victoria: Understanding Raimond Gaita', *The Monthly*, May, pp. 40–45.
Gaunson, S. (2013) *The Ned Kelly Films: A Cultural History of Kelly History*, Bristol, Chicago: Intellect.
Gorbachev, M. (2016) *The New Russia*, Maldon, MA: Polity Press.
Grange, P. (2013) 'The Bluestone Review: A Review of Culture and Leadership on Australian Olympic Swimming', Abridged Report, Bluestone Edge, [online]. Available at: http://resources.news.com.au/files/2013/02/19/1226580/881151-swimming-australia-culture-review.pdf [accessed 2 July 2018].
Greider, W. (2009) *Come Home, America: The Rise and Fall (and Redeeming Promise) of Our Country*, Emmaus, PA: Rodale Press.
Gulliver, A., Griffiths, K. M., Mackinnon, A., Batterham, P. J., and Stanimirovic, R. (2014) 'The Mental Health of Australian Athletes', *Journal of Science and Medicine in Sport*, 18, pp. 255–261.
Gyngell, A. (2017) *Fear of Abandonment: Australia in the World since 1942*, Victoria: La Trobe University Press.
Haebich, A. (2011) 'A Potent Space: Australia's Stolen Generations and the Visual Arts', in K. Holmes and S. Ward (eds.) *Exhuming Passions: The Pressure of the Past in Ireland and Australia*, Western Australia: UWA Publishing, pp. 104–122.
Hall, B. (2016) 'A Huge Win for Doctors': Turnbull Government Backs Down on Gag Laws for Doctors on Naru and Manus', *The Sydney Morning Herald*, 20 October, [online]. Available at: www.smh.com.au/politics/federal/a-huge-win-for-doctors-turnbull-government-backs-down-on-gag-laws-for-doctors-on-nauru-and-manus-20161020-gs6ecs.html [accessed 3 July 2018].
Hambly, G. (2018) 'Myths and Misconceptions: Australian Screenwriting, 1994–2017', PhD thesis, Bundoora, Vic.: La Trobe University.
Hancock, J. (2017) 'Melbourne's Burke and Wills Statue Removed from Display to Make Way for Metro Rail', *ABC News*, 10 April, [online]. Available at: www.abc.net.au/news/2017-04-10/burke-and-wills-statue-in-melbourne-relocated-for-metro-tunnel/8428766 [accessed 15 July 2018].
Heinlein, R. A. (1959) 'All You Zombies', *The Magazine of Fantasy and Science Fiction*, 94, pp. 5–15.
Henderson, M. (2002) (composer) *Lindy* (opera), Opera Australia.
Hennessy, J. (2014) 'Statement in the Matter of WA Institutions Case Study: Statement of John Michael Patrick Hennessy', STAT.0236.001.0001_R, *The Royal Commission into Institutional Responses to Child Abuse*, Australia, pp. 1–23.

Hill, A. (2001) *Soldier Boy*, Victoria: Penguin.
Hill, D. (2008) *The Forgotten Children*, North Sydney: William Heinemann.
Hill, D. (2015) 'Submission to the Royal Commission into Institutional Responses to Child Sex Abuse-Response to Royal Commission Consultation Paper: Redress and Civil Litigation', January, [online]. Available at: http://childabuseroyalcommission.gov.au/getattachment/11837444-8178-4255-ab69-aeb29728da70/David-Hill [accessed 30 October 2017].
Hillman, J. (1975/1991) *Loose Ends: Primary Papers in Archetypal Psychology*, Dallas, TX: Spring Publications.
Hillman, J. (1989) *A Blue Fire: Selected Writings by James Hillman*, New York: Harper & Row.
Historical Child Abuse in Scotland. (2005–) [online]. Available at: www.childabuseinquiry.scot [accessed 5 January 2016].
Historical Institutional Abuse Inquiry. (2013–) [online]. Available at: www.hiainquiry.org/index.htm [accessed 5 January 2016].
Hochschild, J. L. (1995) *Facing Up to the American Dream: Race, Class, and the Soul of the Nation*, Princeton, NJ: Princeton University Press.
Hockley, L. (2014) *Somatic Cinema: The Relationship between Body and Screen: A Jungian Perspective*, London and New York: Routledge.
Howard, J. (1997) 'Transcript of the Prime Minister the Hon John Howard MP Opening Address to the Australian Reconciliation Convention: Melbourne', [online]. Available at: https://pmtranscripts.pmc.gov.au/release/transcript-10361 [accessed 13 September 2017].
Hughes, R. (1986) *The Fatal Shore*, London: Vintage.
Independent Inquiry into Child Sexual Abuse. (2015–) [online]. Available at: www.iicsa.org.uk [accessed 5 January 2016].
Irvine, N. (ed.). (1988) *The Sirius Letters: The Complete Letters of Newton Fowell, Midshipman & Lieutenant Aboard the Sirius Flagship of the First Fleet on Its Voyage to New South Wales*, Sydney: Fairfax Library.
Jacobi, J. (1959) *Complex, Archetype, Symbol in the Psychology of C. G. Jung*, New York: Princeton University Press.
Jacoby, M. (1990) *Individuation and Narcissism: The Psychology of Self in Jung and Kohut*, London: Routledge.
James, S. (2017) 'How Chris Uhlmann's Report on Donald Trump at the G20 Struck a Nerve Around the World', *ABC News*, 10 July.
Jenks, C. (1996) *Childhood*, London and New York: Routledge.
Johnson, A. (2018) 'Inside the Sacred Danger of Thailand's Caves', *The Conversation*, 10 July, [online]. Available at: http://theconversation.com/inside-the-sacred-danger-of-thailands-caves-99638 [accessed 23 July 2018].
Judah, T. (2017) 'Worlds Away: Geography and Belonging in Garth Davis' *Lion*', *Metro Magazine*, 192, pp. 6–13.
Jung, C. G. (1953/1966) *The Collected Works of C. G. Jung*, Vol. 7, *Two Essays on Analytical Psychology*, 2nd edn., Princeton, NJ: Princeton University Press.
Jung, C. G. (1954/2014) *The Collected Works of C. G. Jung*, Vol. 17, *The Development of Personality*, London and New York: Routledge.
Jung, C. G. (1956/1967) *The Collected Works of C. G. Jung*, Vol. 5, *Symbols of Transformation*, 2nd edn., Princeton, NJ: Princeton University Press.
Jung, C. G. (1959/1968) *The Collected Works of C. G. Jung*, Vol. 9i, *The Archetypes of the Collective Unconscious*, 2nd edn., Princeton, NJ: Princeton University Press.
Jung, C. G. (1959/1969) *The Collected Works of C. G. Jung*, Vol. 9ii, *Aion: Researches into the Phenomenology of the Self*, 2nd edn., Princeton, NJ: Princeton University Press.

Jung, C. G. (1960/1969) *The Collected Works of C. G. Jung*, Vol. 8, *The Structure and Dynamics of the Psyche*, 2nd edn., London and New York: Routledge.

Jung, C. G. (1963/1970) *The Collected Works of C. G. Jung*, Vol. 14, *Mysterium Coniunctionis: An Inquiry into the Separation and Synthesis of Psychic Opposites in Alchemy*, 2nd edn., London and New York: Routledge.

Jung, C. G. (1964/1970) *The Collected Works of C. G. Jung*, Vol. 10, *Civilization in Transition*, 2nd edn., Princeton, NJ: Princeton University Press.

Jung, E. and Von Franz, M. (1960/1998) *The Grail Legend*, 2nd edn., Princeton, NJ: Princeton University Press.

Jurkovic, G. J. (2014) *Lost Childhoods: The Plight of the Parentified Child*, London and New York: Routledge.

Kalsched, D. (1996) *The Inner World of Trauma: Archetypal Defences of the Personal Spirit*, London and New York: Routledge.

Kalsched, D. (2013) *Trauma and the Soul: A Psycho-Spiritual Approach to Human Development and Its Interruption*, London and New York: Routledge.

Kaplan, A. (2004) 'Traumatic Contact Zones and Embodied Translators: With Reference to Select Australian Texts', in A. Kaplan and B. Wang (eds.) *Trauma and Cinema: Cross Cultural Explorations*, Aberdeen: Hong Kong University Press, pp. 45–63.

Katz, J., Petracca, M., and Rabinowitz, J. (2009) 'A Retrospective Study of Daughters' Emotional Role Reversal with Parents, Attachment Anxiety, Excessive Reassurance-Seeking, and Depressive Symptoms', *The American Journal of Family Therapy*, 37(3), pp. 185–195. DOI: 10.1080/01926180802405596.

Kirchgaessner, S. (2018) 'Cardinal George Pell Trial a "Turning Point", Says Survivors' Tights Group', *The Guardian*, 2 May, [online]. Available at: www.theguardian.com/australia-news/2018/may/01/cardinal-george-pell-trial-ruling-catholic-church-abuse-welcomed-by-survivors-rights-group [accessed 3 July 2018].

Kremer, J. W. and Rothberg, D. (1999) 'Facing the Collective Shadow', *ReVison*, 22(1), pp. 2–4.

Kuipers, R. (2018) 'Curator's Notes: Manganinnie (1980)', *Australia Screen*, [online]. Available at: https://aso.gov.au/titles/features/manganinnie/notes [accessed 26 March 2018].

Lake, M., Reynolds, H., McKenna, M., and Damousi, J. (2010) *What's Wrong with Anzac: The Militarisation of Australian History*, Sydney: University of New South Wales Press Ltd.

The Law Society. (2016) 'Mandatory Sentencing', Briefing paper, Western Australia: The Law Society of Western Australia.

Leitch, T. (2002) 'Twice-Told Tales: Disavowal and the Rhetoric of the Remake', in J. Forrest and L. R. Koos (eds.) *Dead Ringers: The Remake in Theory and Practice*, Albany: State University of New York Press, pp. 37–62.

Lennard, N. (2017) 'The Philosopher with a Thousand Eyes', *Dissent*, 64(3), pp. 151–154.

Levinson, J. (2012) *The American Success Myth on Film*, London: Palgrave Macmillan.

Lindsay, J. (1967) *Picnic at Hanging Rock*, Melbourne, Canberra, and Sydney: F. W. Cheshire.

Loomis, R. S. (1963) *The Grail: From Celtic Myth to Christian Symbol*, New York: Columbia University Press.

Lupack, A. (2007) *Oxford Guide to Arthurian Literature and Legend*, New York: Oxford University Press.

MacFie, O. and Hargraves, N. (1999) 'The Empire's First Stolen Generation: The First Intake Point Puer 1834–39', *Tasmanian Historical Studies*, 6(2), pp. 129–154.

MacMillan Publishers. (2018) [online]. Available at: https://us.macmillan.com/books/9781250158079 [accessed 11 July 2018].

Main, S. (2008) *Childhood Re-Imagined*, London and New York: Routledge.
Manigault Newman, O. (2018) *Unhinged: An Insider's Account of the Trump White House*, New York: Simon & Schuster.
Marino, J. B. (2004) *The Grail Legend in Modern Literature*, Cambridge: Boydell & Brewer, D. S. Brewer. Stable. Available at: www.jstor.org/stable/10.7722/j.ctt81xc5.5.
Marr, D. (1991) *Patrick White: A Life*, Milson's Point: Random House.
Marr, D. (2008) *The Henson Case*, Melbourne: Text Publishing.
McCarthy, C. (2006) *The Road*, London: Picador.
McCormick. (1944) 'Advance Australia Fair', *Sunday Times*, 12 March, *Trove*, [online]. Available at: https://trove.nla.gov.au/newspaper/article/59184697 [accessed 2 July 2018].
McGee, P. (2007) *From Shame to Kill Bill: Rethinking the Western*, Malden, MA: Blackwell Publishing.
McLauchlin, J. (2015) 'Star Wars' $4 Billion Price Tage Was the Deal of the Century', *Wired*, 15 January.
Menadue, J. E. (1975) *The Three Lost Children 19867–1967*, Victoria: Daylesford and District Historical Society.
Mercer, J. A. (2003) 'The Idea of the Child in Freud and Jung: Psychological Sources for Divergent Spiritualities of Childhood', *International Journal of Children's Spirituality*, 8(2), pp. 115–132. DOI: 10.1080/13644360304625.
Miko, T. (2016) 'Film to Tell Story That Broke Silence on Child Sex Abuse', *The Chronicle*, 27 February.
Miller, E. (2018) 'How Children Are Still Suffering the Trauma of Trump's Family Separation Policy', *The Independent*, 22 July, [online]. Available at: www.independent.co.uk/news/long_reads/trump-children-separation-immigrant-families-trauma-us-border-a8455826.html [accessed 23 July 2018].
Miller, J. C. (2005) *The Transcendent Function: Jung's Model of Psychological Growth Through Dialogue with the Unconscious*, New York: State University of New York Press.
'Miranda Must Go Campaign'. (2018) [online]. Available at: www.mirandamustgo [accessed 2 March 2018].
Moran, A. (2005) 'White Australia, Settler Nationalism and Aboriginal Assimilation', *Australian Journal of Politics and History*, 51(2), pp. 168–193.
Nelson, K. and Fivush, R. (2004) 'The Emergence of Autobiographical Memory: A Social Cultural Developmental Theory', *Psychological Review*, 111(2), pp. 486–511.
Nettheim, M. (2017–2018) 'Sophie Lowe as Kate', [Photography Exhibition] *Starkstruck: Australian Movie Portraits*, Canberra: National Portrait Gallery and the National Film and Sound Archive. Available at: https://starstruck.gov.au/exhibition/239 [accessed 7 July 2018].
Newman, L. (2008) 'Trauma and Ghosts in the Nursery: Parenting and Borderline Personality Disorder', in A. S. Williams and V. Cowling (eds.) *Infants of Parents with Mental Illness Developmental, Clinical, Cultural, and Personal Perspectives*, Queensland: Australian Academic Press, pp. 212–227.
Oliver, J. H. (2014) *The Nether* [play] Directed by Jeremy Herrin, Royal Court Theater. London.
Ortner, S. (2013) *Not Hollywood: Independent Film at the Twilight of the American Dream*, Durham and London: Duke University Press.
Papapetrou, P. (2006) 'Haunted Country', [online]. Available at: www.polixenipapapetrou.net/work/haunted-country-2006 [accessed 30 June 2018].
Parliament of Australia. (2017) 'Boat Arrivals and Boat "Turnbacks" in Australia Sine 1976: A Quick Guide to the Statistics', [online]. Available at: www.aph.gov.au/

About_Parliament/Parliamentary_Departments/Parliamentary_Library/pubs/rp/rp1617/Quick_Guides/BoatTurnbacks [accessed 4 July 2018].

Peeters, B. (2004) 'Tall Poppies and Egalitarianism in Australian Discourse: From Key Word to Cultural Value', *English World-Wide*, 25(1), pp. 1–25.

Perry, J. W. (1970) 'Emotions and Object Relations', *Journal of Analytical Psychology*, 15(1), pp. 1–12.

Phillips, J., Park, M., and Lorimer, C. (2007) 'Firearms in Australia: A Guide to Electronic Resources', *Parliament of Australia*, [online]. Available at: www.aph.gov.au/About_Parliament/Parliamentary_Departments/Parliamentary_Library/pubs/BN/0708/FirearmsAustralia [accessed 8 July 2018].

Phillips, M. G. (1997) 'Sport, War and Gender Images: The Australian Sportsmen's Battalions and the First World War', *The International Journal of the History of Sport*, 14(1), pp. 78–96. DOI: 10.1080/09523369708713966.

Pierce, P. (1999) *The Country of Lost Children: An Australian Anxiety*, Cambridge, UK: Cambridge University Press.

Politifact. (2018) 'All False Statements Involving Donald Trump', [online]. Available at: www.politifact.com/personalities/donald-trump/statements/byruling/false/?page=2 [accessed 10 July 2018].

Poniewozik, J. (2018) 'What Politicians Could Learn from Oprah Winfrey', *The New York Times*, 8 January.

Puvanenthiran, B. (2017) 'Anzac Day 2017: Numbers Fall Away for Gallipoli Service', *The Sydney Morning Herald*, 24 April.

RCIRCSA – Royal Commission into Institutional Responses to Child Abuse. (2017) [online]. Available at: www.childabuseroyalcommission.gov.au [accessed 29 November 2017].

Reynaud, D. (1999) 'Convention and Contradiction: Representations of Women in Australian War Films, 1914–1918', *Australian Historical Studies*, 29(113), pp. 215–230. DOI: 10.1080/10314619908596099.

Reynaud, D. (2007) *Celluloid Heroes: The Great War through Australian Cinema*, Bowen Hills, QLD: Australian Scholarly Publishing.

Ricks, C. (1974) 'Gigantist', *New York Review of Books*, 21(5), [online]. Available at: www.nybooks.com.ez.library.latrobe.edu.au/articles/1974/04/04/gigantist [accessed 7 July 2018].

Rindge, M. (2016) *Profane Parables: Film and the American Dream*, Waco, TX: Baylor University Press.

Roche, S. (2011) *Don't Tell: Toowoomba Prep: The Case Which Broke the Silence on Child Sex Abuse in Australia*, Port Adelaide: Ginninderra Press.

Romeril, J. (1975) *The Floating World*, Sydney: Currency Press.

Rushing, J. H. and Frentz, T. (1995) *Projecting the Shadow: The Cyborg Hero in American Film*, Chicago and London: University of Chicago Press.

Schetzer, L. and Sandor, D. (2000) 'Mandatory Sentencing: Why It Is Unacceptable: The Impact of Mandatory Sentencing in the Northern Territory and Western Australia', discussion paper, Sydney: National Children's and Youth Law Centre.

Screen Australia. (2017) 'Film and Movie Industry: World Rankings: Number of Feature Films Produced and Key Cinema Data, 2008–2017', [online]. Available at: www.screenaustralia.gov.au/fact-finders/international-context/world-rankings/feature-films-and-cinemas [accessed 11 July 2018].

Screen Australia. (2018) 'Top 100 Australian Feature Films of All Time', [online]. Available at: www.screenaustralia.gov.au/fact-finders/cinema/australian-films/top-films-at-the-box-office [accessed 26 February 2018].

Seymour, A. (1962) *One Day of the Year*, Sydney: Angus and Robertson.
Shelburne, W. A. (1988) *Mythos and Logos in the Thought of Carl Jung*, New York: State University of New York Press.
Singer, T. (2016) 'Trump and the American Selfie: Archetypal Defenses of the Group Spirit', in L. Cruz and S. Buser (eds.) *A Clear and Present Danger: Narcissism in the Era of Donald Trump*, Ashville, NC: Chiron Publications, pp. 25–55.
Singer, T. and Kimbles, S. L. (2004) *The Cultural Complex Contemporary Jungian Perspectives on Psyche and Society*, London and New York: Routledge.
Slater, M. and Sanchez-Vives, M. (2014) 'Transcending the Self in Immersive Virtual Reality', *Computer*, 47(7), pp. 24–30.
Smith, D. (2018) 'Trump Insists "I Am the Least Racist Person" Amid Outrage over Remarks', *The Guardian*, 16 January, [online]. Available at: www.theguardian.com/us-news/2018/jan/15/i-am-not-a-racist-trump-says-after-backlash-over-shithole-nations-remark [accessed 11 July 2018].
Smith, P. A. (1978) *The ANZACS*, West Melbourne: Nelson.
Smith, P. A. (2007) 'Gorbachev: US "Victory Complex" Is Costly, Prevents More Peaceful World', *The Courier Journal* (Kentucky), 4 October.
Solon, O. (2018) 'Fate of 2,300 Separated Children Still Unclear Despite Trump's Executive Order', *The Guardian*, 21 June, [online]. Available at: www.theguardian.com/us-news/2018/jun/20/trump-family-separation-policy-reuniting-ngo-burden [accessed 23 July 2018].
Solzhenitsyn, A. (1974–1978) *The Gulag Archipelago 1918–1956: An Experiment in Literary Investigation: Parts 1–2*, Sydney: Collin & Harvill.
Staude, J. (1981) *The Adult Development of C. G. Jung*, London: Routledge.
Symonds, T. (2017) 'The Child Abuse Scandal of the British Children Sent Abroad', *BBC News*, 26 February, [online]. Available at: www.bbc.com/news/uk-39078652 [accessed 3 July 2018].
Tarrant, J. (1998) *The Light Inside the Dark: Zen, Soul, and the Spiritual*, New York: HarperCollins.
Taylor, L. and Medhora, S. (2015) 'Brandis Asked Gillian Triggs to Resign before Critical Child Detention Report', *The Guardian*, 13 February.
Tilley, E. (2012) *White Vanishing: Rethinking Australia's Lost-in-the-Bush Myth*, Amsterdam: Rodopi.
Torney, K. (2004) 'A City Child Lost in the Bush', *The La Trobe Journal*, 74, pp. 52–61.
Torney, K. (2005) *Babes in the Bush: The Making of an Australian Image*, Fremantle: Curtin University Books.
Triggs, G. (2014) *The Forgotten Children: National Inquiry into Children in Immigration Detention*, Sydney, NSW: Australian Human Rights Commission.
Trump, D. J. (2015) 'Transcript: Full Text: Donald Trump Announces a Presidential Bid', *The Washington Post*, 16 June, [online]. Available at: www.washingtonpost.com/news/post-politics/wp/2015/06/16/full-text-donald-trump-announces-a-presidential-bid/?utm_term=.53a77e8c9941 [accessed 10 July 2018].
Trump, D. J. (2018) '(RealDonaldTrump) . . . . to President of the United States (on My First Try): I Think That Would Qualify as Not Smart, But Genius . . . . and a Very Stable Genius at That!', 6 January, 10:30pm. Tweet.
Tsolkas, C. (2013) *Barracuda*, Crows Nest: Allen & Unwin.
Uhlmann, C. (2017) 'Political Editor, Chris Uhlmann at the G20, Hamburg', *The Insiders*, ABC, Australia, aired, 9 July.
Vogler, C. (1998/2007) *The Writer's Journey: Mythic Structure for Storytellers and Screenwriters*, 3rd edn., Studio City, CA: Michael Wiese Productions.

Waddell, T. (2006) *Mis/takes: Archetype Myth and Identity in Screen Fiction*, London and New York: Routledge.
Waddell, T. (2010) *Wild/lives: Trickster, Place and Liminality on Screen*, London and New York: Routledge.
Waddell, T. (2014) 'Australia's Lost Children at Play: The Films of Baz Luhrmann', *International Journal of Jungian Studies*, 6(2), pp. 96–107.
Waddell, T. (2018) 'The Australian Lost Child Complex in Adaptation: Kurzel's *Macbeth* and Stone's *The Daughter*', in L. Hockley (ed.) *The Routledge International Handbook of Jungian Film Studies*, London and New York: Routledge.
Waddell, T. and Jones, T. W. (2016) 'The Spoken and Unspoken Nature of Child Abuse in the Miniseries Devil's Playground: The Royal Commission into Institutional Responses to Child Sexual Abuse, the Catholic Church and Television Drama in Australia', *Media International Australia*, 159(1), pp. 83–93.
Wahlquist, C. (2017) 'Outgoing Human Rights Commissioner Gillian Triggs Wins Freedom of Speech Award', *The Guardian*, 3 May.
Wasko, J. (2001) *Understanding Disney: The Manufacture of Fantasy*, Cambridge, UK: Polity Press.
Webb, C. (2014) 'Story of Young Children's Survival in Wimmera Bush for Nine Days Endures 150 Years on', *The Age*, 19 January.
West, J. (2016) 'America in the Grip of Alpha Narcissism: The Predator within and Amongst Each and All of Us', in L. Cruz and S. Buser (eds.) *A Clear and Present Danger: Narcissism in the Era of Donald Trump*, Ashville, NC: Chiron Publications, pp. 237–250.
White, P. (1973) *The Eye of the Storm*, London: Vintage.
Wild, R. and Anderson, P. (2007) *The Report of the Northern Territory Board of Inquiry into the Protection of Aboriginal Children from Sexual Abuse*, Darwin: Northern Territory Government.
Winn, J. E. (2007) *The American Dream and Contemporary Hollywood Cinema*, New York: Continuum.
Winnicott, D. W. (1971) *Playing and Reality*, London: Routledge.
Wolff, M. (2018) *Fire and Fury: Inside the Trump White House*, London: Henry Holt and Company.
Wood, R. (1986/2002) 'The American Nightmare: Horror in the 70s', in M. Jancovich (ed.) *Horror: The Horror Film Reader*, London and New York: Routledge, pp. 25–32.
Woodward, B. (2018) *Fear: Trump in the White House*, New York: Simon & Schuster.
Zierold, M. (2008) 'Memory and Media Cultures', in A. Erll and A. Nünning (eds.) *A Companion to Cultural Memory Studies: An International and Interdisciplinary Handbook*, Media and Cultural Memory, Berlin and New York: de Gruyter, pp. 399–407.

SCREEN REFERENCES

4 Corners. (2016) [television current affairs] 'Australia's Shame', Australian Broadcasting Corporation, aired 25 July. Australia.
American Beauty. (1999) [film] Directed by Sam Mendes. USA.
Animal Kingdom. (2010) [film] Directed by David Michôd. Australia.
Anzac Girls. (2014) [television series] Directed by Ken Cameron and Ian Watson. Australia.
Australia. (2008) [film] Directed by Baz Luhrmann. Australia, UK, USA.
Babadook, The. (2013) [film] Directed by Jennifer Kent. Australia, Canada.
Babadook, The. (2014) [DVD 'Special Features'] Interview – Jennifer Kent and Essie Davis. Australia.
Babe. (1995) [film] Directed by Chris Noonan. Australia, USA.
Back of Beyond, The. (1954) [film] Directed by John Heyer. Australia.
Barracuda. (2016) [television miniseries] Directed by Robert Connolly. Australia.
Beautiful Kate. (2009) [film] Directed by Rachel Ward. Australia.
Bedevil. (1993) [film] Directed by Tracey Moffatt. Australia.
Beneath Clouds. (2002) [film] Directed by Ivan Sen. Australia.
Black Comedy. (2014–) [television comedy series] Executive Producers Kath Shelper and Mark O'Toole. Australia.
Black Panther. (2018) [film] Directed by Ryan Coogler. USA.
Blue Velvet. (1986) [film] Directed by David Lynch. USA.
Bran Nue Dae. (2010) [film] Directed by Rachel Perkins. Australia.
Breaker Morant. (1980) [film] Directed by Brice Beresford. Australia.
Careful He Might Hear You. (1983) [film] Directed by Carl Schultz. Australia.
Chant of Jimmy Blacksmith, The. (1978) [film] Directed by Fred Schepisi. Australia.
Charlie's Country. (2014) [film] Directed by Rolf de Heer. Australia.
Crocodile Dundee. (1986) [film] Directed by Peter Faiman. Australia.
Daughter, The. (2015) [film] Directed by Simon Stone. Australia.
Da Vinci Code, The. (2006) [film] Directed by Ron Howard. USA, Malta, France, UK.
Deadwood. (2004–6) [television series] Created by David Milch. USA.
Devil's Playground, The. (1976) [film] Directed by Fred Schepisi. Australia.
Devil's Playground. (2013) [television miniseries] Directed by Tony Krawitz and Rachel Ward. Australia.

Disappearance of Azaria Chamberlain. (1984) [telemovie] Directed by Michael Thornhill. Australia.
Don't Tell. (2017) [film] Directed by Tori Garrett. Australia.
Dressmaker, The. (2015) [film] Directed by Jocelyn Moorhouse. Australia.
Enemy Within, The. (1918) [film] Directed by Roland Stavely. Australia.
Erskinville Kings. (1999) [film] Directed by Alan White. Australia.
Evil Angels. (1988) [film] Directed by Fred Schepisi. Australia, USA.
Exorcist, The. (1973) [film] Directed by William Friedkin. USA.
Eye of the Storm, The. (2011) [film] Directed by Fred Schepisi. Australia.
Fight Club. (1999) [film] Directed by David Fincher. Germany, USA.
For Australia. (1915) [film] Directed by Monte Luke. Australia.
Forty Thousand Horsemen. (1940) [film] Directed by Charles Chauvel. Australia.
Fran. (1985) [film] Directed by Glenda Hambly. Australia.
Fran. (2010) [DVD 'Audio Commentary'] Commentary by Glenda Hamby, David Rapsey, Noni Hazelhurst and Alan Fletcher. Australia.
Gallipoli. (1981) [film] Directed by Peter Weir. Australia.
Girl of the Bush, A. (1921) [film] Directed by Franklyn Barrett. Australia.
Go Back to Where You Came From. (2011–15) [television reality series] Executive Producers Michael Cordell and Nick Murry. Australia.
Handmaid's Tale, The. (2017–) [television series] Created by Bruce Miller. USA.
Happy Feet. (2006) [film] Directed by George Miller. Australia, USA.
Head On. (1998) [film] Directed by Anna Kokkinos. Australia.
Here I Am. (2011) [film] Directed by Beck Cole. Australia.
Hero of the Dardanelles, The. (1915) [film] Directed by Alfred Rolfe. Australia.
High Tide. (1987) [film] Directed by Gilliam Armstrong. Australia.
Home Song Stories, The. (2007) [film] Directed by Tony Ayres. Australia.
Hounds of Love. (2016) [film] Directed by Ben Young. Australia.
Indiana Jones and the Last Crusade. (1989) [film] Directed by Steven Spielberg. USA.
Insiders, The. (2017) [television current affairs] Hosted by Barry Cassidy, aired 9 July. Australia.
Insight. (2017) 'Game Over' [television current affairs] Hosted by Jenny Brockie, aired 11 and 18 April. Australia.
Irresistible. (2006) [film] Directed by Ann Turner. Australia.
I Tonya. (2017) [film] Directed by Craig Gillespie. USA.
Jedda. (1955) [film] Directed by Charles Chauvel. Australia.
Jimmy Kimmel Live! (2018) [late night television] Hosted by Jimmy Kimmel, aired 15 January. USA.
Knightfall. (2017–) [television series] Created by Don Handfield and Richard Raynor. USA.
Know Thy Child. (1921) [film] Directed by Franklyn Barrett. Australia.
Leaving of Liverpool, The. (1992) [television miniseries] Directed by Michael Jenkins. Australia, UK.
Letters to Ali. (2004) [film] Directed by Clara Law. Australia.
Lighthorseman, The. (1987) [film] Directed by Simon Wincer. Australia.
Lion. (2016) [film] Directed by Garth Davis. Australia, USA, UK.
Looking for Grace. (2015) [film] Directed by Sue Brooks. Australia.
Lore. (2012) [film] Directed by Cate Shortland. Australia, Germany, UK.
Lost in the Bush. (1973) [film] Directed by Peter Dodds. Australia.
Lucky Miles. (2007) [film] Directed by Michael James Rowland. Australia.
Macbeth. (2015) [film] Directed by Justin Kurzel. UK, France, USA.

Maison Ensorcelée, La. (1908) [film] Directed by Segundo de Chomón. France.
Manganinnie. (1980) [film] Directed by John Honey. Australia.
Man of Flowers. (1983) [film] Directed by Paul Cox. Australia.
Man of Steel. (2013) [film] Directed by Zack Snyder. USA, UK.
Marking Time. (2003) [television miniseries] Directed by Cherie Nolan. Australia.
Martyrdom of Nurse Cavell, The. (2016) [film] Directed by Jack Gavin. Australia.
Memento. (2000) [film] Directed by Christopher Nolan. USA.
Molly and Mobarak. (2004) [film] Directed by Tom Zubrycki. Australia.
Monster, The. (2005) [short film] Directed by Jennifer Kent. Australia.
Monty Python and the Holy Grail. (1975) [film] Directed by Terry Gilliam and Terry Jones. UK.
Mulholland Drive. (2002) [film] Directed by David Lynch. USA.
Murphy of the Anzac. (1916) [film] Directed by J. E. Matthews. Australia.
Mystery Road. (2013) [film] Directed by Ivan Sen. Australia.
Ned Kelly. (2003) [film] Directed by Gregor Jordan. Australia, UK, USA, France.
Odd Angry Shot, The. (1979) [film] Directed by Tom Jeffrey. Australia.
One Night the Moon. (2001) [film] Directed by Rachel Perkins. Australia.
Oranges and Sunshine. (2010) [film] Directed by Jim Loach. Australia, UK.
Orphan of the Wilderness. (1936) [film] Directed by Ken G. Hall. Australia.
Others, The. (2001) [film] Directed by Alejandro Amenábar. USA, Spain, France, Italy.
Paradise Road. (1997) [film] Directed by Bruce Beresford. Australia, USA.
Picnic at Hanging Rock. (1975) [film] Directed by Peter Weir. Australia.
Picnic at Hanging Rock. (2018) [television series] Direcetd by Larysa Kondracki, Michael Rymer and Amanda Brotchie. Australia.
Polly and Me. (2010) [short film] Directed by Ian Darling. Australia.
Predestination. (2014) [film] Directed by Michael Spierig and Peter Spierig. Australia.
Rabbit Proof Fence. (2002) [film] Directed by Phillip Noyce. Australia.
Radiance. (1998) [film] Directed by Rachel Perkins. Australia.
Rats of Tobruk, The. (1944) [film] Directed by Charles Chauvel. Australia.
Repulsion. (1965) [film] Directed by Roman Polanski. UK.
Revanche, La. (1916) [film] Directed by W. J. Lincoln. Australia.
Road, The. (2009) [film] Directed by John Hillcoat. USA.
Road Home, The. (2003) [film] Directed by Kelrick Martin. Australia.
Romulus My Father. (2007) [film] Directed by Richard Roxburgh. Australia.
Safe Harbour. (2018) [television miniseries] Directed by Glendyn Ivin. Australia.
Samson and Delilah. (2009) [film] Directed by Warwick Thornton. Australia.
Satellite Boy. (2012) [film] Directed by Catriona McKenzie. Australia.
Saturday Night Live. (2017) [television sketch comedy] Created by Lorne Michaels, aired 4 February. USA.
Seven Little Australians, The. (1974) [television series] Directed by Ron Way. Australia.
Seven Types of Ambiguity. (2017) [television miniseries] Directed by Glendyn Ivin, Ana Kokkinos and Matthew Saville. Australia.
Shame. (1988) [film] Directed by Steve Jodrell. Australia.
Shape of Water, The. (2017) [film] Directed by Guillermo del Toro. USA.
Shinning, The. (1980) [film] Directed by Stanley Kubrick. USA.
Shiralee, The. (1957) [film] Directed by Leslie Norman. UK.
Silver City. (1984) [film] Directed by Sophia Turkiewicz. Australia.
Sisters of War. (2010) [telemovie] Directed by Brendon Maher. Australia.
Somersault. (2004) [film] Directed by Cate Shortland. Australia.
Sound of One Hand Clapping, The. (1997) [film] Directed by Richard Flanagan. Australia.
Spirit of Gallipoli, The. (1928) [film] Directed by Keith Gategood. Australia.

Spotlight. (2015) [film] Directed by Tom McCarthy. USA.
Story of the Kelly Gang, The. (1906) [film] Directed by Charles Tait. Australia.
Strangerland. (2015) [film] Directed by Kim Farrant. Australia, Ireland.
Strike me Lucky. (1934) [film] Directed by Ken G. Hall. Australia.
Sunshine. (2017) [television miniseries] Created by Matt Cameron and Elise McCredie. Australia.
Superman. (1978) [film] Directed by Richard Donner. USA.
Superman Returns. (2006) [film] Directed by Bryan Singer. USA.
Sweet Country. (2017) [film] Directed by Warwick Thornton. Australia.
Terror Nullius. (2018) [film] Directed by Soda Jerk. Australia.
Three Billboards Outside Ebbing Missouri. (2017) [film] Directed by Martin McDonagh. UK, USA.
Through My Eyes. (2004) [television miniseries] Created by Tony Cavanaugh and Simone North. Australia.
Toomelah. (2001) [film] Directed by Ivan Sen. Australia.
Top of the Lake: China Girl. (2017) [television miniseries] Directed by Jane Campion, Garth Davis and Ariel Kleiman. Australia.
Unbroken. (2014) [film] Directed by Angelina Jolie. USA.
Unfinshed Sky. (2007) [film] Directed by Peter Duncan. Australia.
Vanishing, The. (1988) [film] Directed by George Sluizer. Netherlands, France, West Germany.
Vanishing, The. (1993) [film] Directed by George Sluizer. USA.
Walkabout. (1971) [film] Directed by Nicholas Roeg. Australia, UK.
Water Diviner, The. (2014) [film] Directed by Russell Crowe. Australia, USA, Turkey.
West, The. (1996) [television documentary series] Directed by Stephen Ives. USA.
Will They Ever Come? (1915) [film] Directed by Alfred Rolfe. Australia.
Woman Suffers, The. (1918) [film] Directed by Raymond Longford. Australia.
Wonder Woman. (2017) [film] Directed by Patty Jenkins. USA.

INDEX

7:30 Report, The 64

abandonment 17, 91, 104–105, 114–115
Abbott, Tony 80
Adams, James Truslow 124–125, 136
Adam-Smith, Patsy 48
Adelson, Edna 85, 86, 92
Advance Australia Fair 46
affect 11, 65, 96, 115
Aion: Researches into the Phenomenology of the Self 66
Albright, Madeline 122
All You Zombies 103, 128
Alpha dynamics 123–124
American Beauty 125
American dream, the 6, 45, 119, 124–127; cinema as vehicle for mythos of 127–130; Donald Trump on 120
American Exceptionalism 132
American Narcissism 124
American victory complex 6, 26, 32, 53, 120; America as superhero, world police man, and divine rights 130–132; destiny and divine right in 133–135; ego inflation and 121–123; trauma of victories past and 123–124
amplification 68
analytical psychology 122–123
Animal Kingdom 115
anxiety: lost child as cultural 2, 19, 34; over losing 122; parentification and 88, 89; separation 47, 49
Anzac Day 44, 45, 48, 51, 57–59

Anzac Girls 57
Anzac hero, the *see* nationhood; war
Anzacs, The 48–49
Anzac Story, The 53
Appell, Annette 16
archetypes 2–3, 10, 13, 17–18; *trying* to disown 63
Assman, Jan 23
asylum-seekers 63, 79–83
Australia: Anzac Day celebrations 44, 45, 48, 51, 57–59; 'Apology to Australia's Indigenous Peoples' 74; as child of England 46; indigenous people of 19, 34–35, 69–74; as penal colony 18–19, 20; war and loss in nationhood building of 44
Australia (film) 28, 34, 35, 41, 72
Australian Academy of Cinema and Television Arts' (AACTA) 41, 85–86
Australian Cinema After Marbo 73
Australian Film Institute Awards 83
Australian Human Rights Commission 71–72
Australian Institute of Family Studies 16
autobiographical memory 106, 116
Ayres, Tony 85, 94, 96

Babadook, The 85, 87, 88–90, 92, 97
Babe 41
Babes in the Bush: The making of an Australian image 19, 21
Back of Beyond, The 27, 34
BAFTA (British Academy of Film and Television Arts) awards 41

Barker, Howard 51
Barkman, Adam 133
Barracuda 55–56
Batman 131–132
Beautiful Kate 103, 107, 109–110, 115
Bell, Duncan 22–23
Beneath Clouds 72
Berg, Amy 76
binding memories 22
birthing of personality 104
Blackburn, Kevin 50, 53, 54
Black Comedy 70
Black Panther 129
Bliss, Michael 37
Bluestone Edge Culture Review into Australian Olympic Swimming 55
Blue Velvet 125
Boron, Robert de 29
boy soldiers 46, 50–51, 54
Brandis, George 79, 80
Bran Nue Dae 72
Breaker Morant 49
Briefel, Aviva 92–93
Brierley, Saroo 39
Bringing Them Home Report: A Report into the Separation of Aboriginal and Torres Strait Islander Children from their families 71, 73
Broken Years, the 48, 50
Broszormenyi-Nagy, Ivan 87
Brown, Jeffrey 131–132
Bryson, John 38
Burke, Robert 9
Buser, Steven 123
bush mythology *see Lost in the bush*

Campbell, Joseph 34, 129–130, 132
Careful He Might Hear You 27, 28
Caruth, Cathy 11–12
Casement, Anne 66, 89–90, 123
Celan, Paul 68
Celluloid Anzacs: The Great War Through Australian Cinema 47
Chant of Jimmy Blacksmith, The 72
Charlie's Country 72, 103, 107, 110–111, 115
Chasing Asylum 82
child, lost *see* lost child
child convicts 20
child sexual abuse 63, 69–70; Royal Commission into institutional responses to 74–78
child soldiers 50–51
Chomón, Segundo de 88
Christian grail story 29–34
Christ of St. John of the Cross 134

Clarke, Anna 58
Clarke, Marcus 20
Clear and Present Danger: Narcissism in the Era of Donald Trump, A 125
collective belonging and memories 21–25
collective identity 18–19
Collins, Felicity 26, 29, 34, 35, 39, 73
colonisation: Australia's penal colony and 18–19; collective trauma and 43; lost aboriginal children and 69–74; lostness and 4, 12, 18; rhetoric of nationalism and 22
Come Home, America: The Rise and Fall (and Redeeming Promise) of Our Country 121
Commission to Inquire into Child Abuse 74
complexes 2, 9–13
Coogler 129
Cooper, Linda 31–34, 42, 98
'Cormac McCarthy's "The Road" as Apocalyptic Grail Narrative' 31
Corpus Hypercubus 134
Courier Mail 55
Craps, Stef 24
Craven, Wes 88
Creed, Barbara 72, 90
Crocodile Dundee 41
Crotty, Martin 54
Crow, Russell 49, 51
Cry in the Dark, A 38
cultural complex theory 2–3, 11, 13, 66, 124; cultural memory and 23–24
cultural memory 18–19, 23–24, 106
Cushway, Delia 97
Czaplicka, John 23

Dali, Salvador 134
Damousi, Joy 58
Daughter, The 28, 128
Da Vinci Code 30
Davis, Garth 26, 39
Davis, Therese 26, 29, 34, 35, 39, 73
Deliver from Evil 76
Del Toro, Guillermo 132
Dermody, Susan 26, 29, 35, 96
destiny and divine right 133–135
Devil's Playground, The 41, 75–76
Disappearance of Azaria Chamberlain, The 38
Disney company 129
divine, the child as 14–18
Don't Tell 75
double consciousness 66–67
double wounding 5, 83–84, 108, 111; of children seeking asylum 79–83; child sexual abuse as 63, 69–70, 74–78; film and television as filters for recognition

of 68–69; parentification and (*see* parentification); *see also* trauma
Doyle, John 83
Dream see American dream
Dressmaker, The 115
Drochon, Hugo 133
drowning 1
Duina, Francesco 122

Early, Louise 97
early reportage and storytelling of lost child mythologies 19–21
egalitarianism 48
ego 105, 114
Elliott, T. S. 112
Ely, Richard 45
'Empire' concept 48–49
Erll, Astrid 24
Erskinville Kings 28, 115
Eschenbach, Wolfram von 30
Evil Angels 28, 32, 38, 41
Exorcist, The 88, 89
Eye of the Storm, The 103, 109, 114

Facing Up to the American Dream: Race, Class, and the Soul of the Nation 126
Fidler, Richard 70–71
Fight Club 125
films, American 16–17, 119, 120–121; focus on success myth in 125; horror 88–90; as vehicle for *Dream* mythos 127–130; victory-driven 26, 32
films, Australian: adult-driven narratives and characters on 4; American horror films and 88; awards won by 41; bush mythology in 20–21; collective identities and belonging in 22; as filters for recognition of double wounding 68–69; the glorious dead in 47–52; haunting imagery in 27; hook of 25; large volume of lost child 41–42; lost child, the searchers, *and* the lost child as searcher in 34–36; lost child genre in 28–29; New Wave and Post New Wave 27, 44, 47, 49, 64; personal and collective return to childhood in 104–108; relationship with the complex expressed in 12–13; *see also* individual films
Fire and Fury: Inside the Trump White House 126, 130
Fisher King, The 30
Fisher King legend 30, 98
Fivush, Robyn 106
Flanagan, Richard 81, 103, 108

Floating World, The 44
For Australia 47
Forgotten Children, The 77, 80
Forgotten Children: National Inquiry into Children in Immigration Detention, The 79
Forrest, Jennifer 128
For the Love of a Good Man 51
For The Term Of His Natural Life 20
Forty Thousand Horsemen 47
4 Corners 64, 77
Four Quartets 112
Fraiberg, Selma 85, 86, 92
Fran 85, 87, 90–93, 98–99, 135–136
Frentz, Thomas 4, 68
Freud, Sigmund 2, 10, 11, 12, 13; on grief 89; on *unheimlich* and *heimisch* (strange and familiar) tension 90
Froud, Mark 27, 28, 36

Gaita, Raimond 93–94
Gallipoli 22, 48–50; sport-more analogy in 52–53
Gammage, Bill 48, 50
Garner, Helen 94
Garrett, Tori 75
generational remembering 18–19
ghosts, parentification and childhood 86–88
'Ghosts in the Nursery: A Psychoanalytic Approach to the Problems of Impaired Infant-Mother relationships' 86–87
Gillespie, Craig 136
Gilliam, Terry 30
Girl of the Bush, A 28
Go Back to Where You Came From 82
Gorbachev, Mikhail 119, 121–122
grail myth 29–34; parentification and 96–99
Grange, Pippa 55
Greer, Germaine 19
Greider, William 119, 121–122
grief and possession 88–93
Gulag Archipelago, The 67
Gulpili, David 104

Haebich, Anne 69, 74
Haleachs, Maurice 23
Haley, Jennifer 116–117
Hall, Ken 27
Hambly, Glenda 85, 92, 135–137
Handmaid's Tale, The 16, 138–139
Hany, Don 76
Happy Feet 41
Harding, Tonya 136–137
Hargraves, Nigel 20

Harris, Richard 139
haunting 27
Heer, Rolf de 104, 110–111
Heinlein, Robert A. 103, 128
Hennessy, John 77
Here I Am 28, 97
Here I Am, Toomelah 72
heroism: and of the glorious dead on screen 47–52; of superheroes 130–132; tall poppy syndrome and defeat as 44–47; trauma and 43
Hero of the Dardanelles 47, 53
Hero with a Thousand Faces, The 129–130
High Tide 28, 97
Hill, Anthony 50–51
Hillcoat, John 32
Hillman, James 2, 4, 6, 9; on archetypes 10, 39; on child remaining lost rather than repressed/disavowed 117, 118; as child to central to our character 29; on consequences of failing to recognise aspects of our heritage 81; on ego 114; on psychic condition in need 104–105; on repeated sourcing of the lost child 17
Hird, James 55
Historical Institutional Abuse Inquiry, The 74
Hochschild, Jennifer 125, 126, 129, 137
Hockley, Luke 25, 68, 130
Home Song Stories, The 28, 82, 85, 87, 90, 93–95, 108; autobiographical memory in 106
hook, projection as covert 25
horror films 88
Hounds of Love 34, 35, 41
Howard, John 109
Hussein, Saddam 121

illegitimacy 28
Independent Inquiry into Child Sexual Abuse 74
Indiana Jones and the Last Crusade 30
indigenous Australians 19, 34–35; *Stolen Generations* and 69–74
indigenous population of Australia 19; *Stolen Generations* and 69–74
inner child 103–104; organization of memories of 106–107; personal and collective return with childhood memories of 104–108; in *Predestination* 111–114; in *The Sound of One Hand Clapping, The Eye of the Storm, Beautiful Kate* and *Charlie's Country* 108–111; as *stuck* and *embodied* 114–118
Inquiry into Child Sexual Abuse, UK 76, 77
Insiders, The 127
Insight 55

instincts 2–3
Irrestible 28
I Tonya 125, 136–137

Jackson, Lauren 55
Jacobi 107
Jedda 27, 28, 72–73
Jenkins, Patty 129, 134
Jones, Timothy W. 75, 76
Joseph d'Arimathie 29
Judah, Tara 39
Jung, Carl 2, 3, 10, 11–12, 117, 132; concept of the outwardly projected shadow 2, 13, 63, 66–68; on the mythological child 14–15, 17, 23; on splinter psyches 11, 67
Jung, Emma 29; on the grail myth 30–31
Jurkovic, Gregory 87

Kalsched, Donald 11, 14–16, 25, 64–66, 89
Kaplan, Anne 12
Keating, Paul 71
Kelly, Ned 3, 9
Kent, Jennifer 85, 88, 92
Kimbles, Samuel 2–3, 11, 18, 22; on interpretation of child memories 24
Kimmel, Jimmy 130–131
Kinchela Aboriginal Boys' Training Home 69
King Arthur 30, 98
Kinnear, Rod 48
Klein, Melanie 15–16
Knightfall 30
Knights Templar 29–30
Know Thy Child 28
Kohut, Heinz 16
Koos, Leonard R. 128
Kremer, Jurhgen W. 67, 68
Kurzel, Justin 128

Lake, Marilyn 44, 46, 49, 57–58
La Maison Ensorcelée 88
Lanier, Jaron 116
La Revanche 57
La Trobe Reading Room 3
Lawson, Henry 21
Leaving of Liverpool, The 77
Ledger, Heath 4
Leitch, Thomas 128
Le Morte d'Arthur 30
Lennad, Natasha 133–134
Leopold, Nathan 133
Letters to Ali 82
Levinson, Julie 124, 125, 132
Lighthorseman, The 49

liminality 17, 110, 140
Lindsay, Joan 36
Lindy 38–39
Lion 22, 26, 28, 33, 99; lost/searcher synthesis in 39–41
Loach, Jim 76
Lobe, Richard 133
Locke, John 24
Longford, Raymond 27
Long Way Holdings 3
Long Way Home, A 39
Looking for Grace 34, 36, 39
Lore 28
Lost (painting) 21
lost child: abandonment of 17, 91, 104–105, 114–115; adult-driven narratives and characters in films on 4; collective belonging and memories of 21–25; the complex and the 9–13; complexes in approach to 2; as cultural anxiety 2; cultural complex theory of 2–3, 11, 13; as divine, the concept of soul, and lost 14–18; double wounding of (*see* double wounding); by drowning 1; early reportage and storytelling on 19–21; Enlightenment values and legal rights of 16; as film genre 28–29; indigenous 69–74; as inner element of the psyche 13; lost in the bush 1–2, 3, 20–21, 26, 27–28; and lostness as point of recognition 3–4; memories of (*see* inner child); migration of orphans and 76–77; as multiple elements of the grail myth 29–34; mythical/fantasy 3, 11; mythical/fantasy child as concept in 3; as parent and parent as (*see* parentification); refugees 63, 79–83; as searcher 34–36; searchers of 36–39; sexual abuse of 63, 69–70, 74–78; supernatural or ghostly imagery of 27; as traumatised 64–66; v. victory complex 135–136
Lost Child in Literature and Culture, The 27
Lost in the Bush (film) 21
Lost in the bush (trope) 1–2, 3, 20–21, 26; concept of illegitimacy or uncertain parentage and 27–28; parentification and 96–99; searchers and 34–39
lostness as point of recognition 3–4
Lucas, George 129–130
Lucky Miles 82
Luhrmann, Baz 35

Macfie, Peter 20
Mallory, Thomas 30
Mangannine 34–35, 38, 72

Manifest Destiny ideology 124, 131, 132
Man of Flowers 115
Man of Steel 134
Marking Time 83
Martin, James Charles 50
Martyrdom of Nurse Cavell, The 57
McCarthy, Cormac 31–33, 98
McCarthy, Tom 76
McCormick, Peter Dodds 46
McCubbin, Frederick 21
McKee, Robert 136
McKenna, Mark 49, 58
Media International 75
Méliès, George 88
Memento 112
memoir 93–96
memories, childhood *see* inner child
Mercer, Joyce 10, 14, 17
Miranda Must Go 37–38
Moffatt, Tracey 74
Molly & Mobarak 82
Monster, The 88
Montreuil, Gerbert de 30
Monty Python and the Holy Grail 30
Moses and Monotheism 12
Mourning and Melancholia 89
Mulholland Drive 112
Murphy of the Anzac 47
Mystery Road 32, 35, 72
mythical/fantasy child 3, 11
mythological child, Jung on 14–15
mythscape 22

Narrow Road to the Deep North, The 108
nationalism, rhetoric of 22
nationhood: mobilising the child in Anzac celebrations of 57–58; sport and 56–57; war and loss in building 44, 48–49
Ned Kelly 4
Nelson, Katherine 106
Nether, The 116–117
Newman, Omarosa Manigault 127
New Russia, The 121
New York Review of Books 109
New York Times 120
Nietzsche's Great Politics 133
Nietzsche, Friedrich 133
Nightmare on Elm Street 88
North American culture 44–45, 53
Nowlan, Cherrie 83

Obama, Barack 82, 126
Odd Angry Shot, The 48, 49
Oedipus complex 2, 10, 11, 13

Index **161**

One Day of the Year 44, 48
One Night the Moon 32, 38, 41
Operation Iraqi Freedom 121
Oranges and Sunshine 28, 33, 39, 41, 76–77, 115
Orphan of the Wilderness 27
orphans, migration of 76–77
Others, The 112

Papapetrou, Polixeni 27
Paradise Road 57
parentification 5, 85–86; childhood ghosts and 86–88; definition of 87–88; grail child and wastelands 96–99; grief and possession with 88–93; memoir and 93–96; pathological 87–88
Parsifal 30
Parzival 30
Patel, Dev 41
Patterson, Banjo 21
penal colony, Australia as 18–19; child convicts and 20
Perkins, Rachel 74
personal and collective return to childhood 104–108
Phillips, Arthur 18
Phillips, Murray G. 54
Picnic at Hanging Rock 22, 27, 32, 36–38, 41
Pierce, Peter 2, 17, 19, 35, 36–37, 39
playback 106
Poetics 136
Point Peur 20
Polly and Me 28
polymorphously perverse, child as 10
Poniewozik, J. 120
post-9/11 political environment 131
Predestination 26, 28, 32, 33, 39, 41, 103–104; inner child as *stuck* and *embodied* in 111–114; lost child embodiment in 117
projection 27, 29, 64, 71–73, 104, 121; archetypes and 10, 40–41, 47, 51, 72; of binding memories 22–23; of collective vulnerability 50; of the lost child complex 5, 19, 66–67, 71–73, 79–83; of inner child 12–13, 85–86, 90; of internal processes 4; outward child 95; parental 93; shadow 81, 138, 140; socially constructed by adults 16; unconscious outward 2, 64, 107
psychoanalysis 10, 86–87
psychotherapy 6

Rabbit Proof Fence 22, 26, 29, 34–35, 72–73
Rats of Tobruk, The 47

recombinant visionary mythologies 13
redemption 32–33, 128
refugee policies 63, 79–83
Report of the Northern Territory Board of Inquiry into the Protection of Aboriginal Children from Sexual Abuse, The 71
Repulsion 88
Reynaud, Daniel 47
Reynolds, Henry 44, 46, 57
Ricks, Christopher 109
Road, The 32–34, 42, 98
Road Home, The 69
Rogers, Mark 3
Rolling Stone 119
romanticism of the bush 3–4
Romulus My Father 22, 28, 85–87, 90, 93–95; autobiographical memory in 106
Rothberg, Donald 67, 68
Roxburgh, Richard 85, 93
Royal Commission into Institutional Responses to Child Sexual Abuse (RCIRCSA) 74–78, 81
Rushing, Janice Hocker 4, 68

Safe Harbour 82–83
Samson and Delilah 72, 73–74
Sanchez-Vives, Maria V. 116
Sandor, Danny 78
Satellite Boy 72
Schepisi, Fred 38, 109
Schetzer, Louis 78
searchers 36–39; lost child, searchers, *and* the lost child as 34–36; lost/searcher synthesis and 39–41
Self, the 14–15; myth of the grail and 30–31; as present self 24
self-aggrandisement 122
self-care system 14–15, 64–66
self-object status 109
Seven little Australians 21
Seven Types of Ambiguity 41
sexual abuse of children 63, 69–70; Royal Commission into institutional responses to 74–78
shadow 2, 13, 63, 66–68, 80, 119
Shame 97
Shape of Water, The 132
Shapiro, Vivian 85, 86, 92
Shiralee, The 28
Silver City 82
Singer, Thomas 2–3, 11, 18, 22; on cultural complexes 66, 124; on interpretation of child memories 24; on the shadow 119
Sinning, The 88

Sisters of War 57
Slater, Mel 116
Solzhenitsyn, Aleksandr 67
somatic nature of cinema 25
Somersault 28
soul, the child as a concept of 14–18
Sound of One Hand Clapping, The 28, 80, 97, 103, 107, 108–109, 115
Spark, Geraldine M. 87
Spierig, Peter and Michael 26, 103, 104
Spirit of Gallipoli, The 47
splinter psyches 11, 67
sport-war analogy 52–57
Spotlight 76
Star Wars 129
Stolen Generations 63, 69–74, 81
Stone, Oliver 128
Story of the Kelly Gang, The 3, 13, 22
Strangerland 32, 39
Strike Me Lucky 27
stuck and *embodied* inner child 114–118
Sumner, John 48
Sunshine 83
superheros 130–132
Superman Returns 134
Sweet Country 72

Tait, Charles 3
the tall poppy syndrome (TTPS) 44–47
Tarrant, John 90
television 88; as filter for recognition of double wounding 68–69
Terror Nullius 37
Thornburg, Newton 103, 109–110
Thornton, Warwick 73–74
Three Billboards Outside Ebbing Missouri 120–121
Through My Eyes 38
Tilley, Elspeth 19, 70
Tompson, Charles 70
Top of the Lake: China Girl 41
Torney, Kim 1, 19–20, 70; on Australia as child of England 46; on children lost in the bush 21; on defeated war dead 45
transcendent function 14, 104
trauma 11–12; affects of 11, 65, 96; government actions on 63–64; heroism and 43; of search in lost child genre 29; self-care system for 14–15, 64–66; sexual abuse 63, 69–70, 74–78; shadow of 2, 13, 63, 67–68; of uncertain parentage 28; *see also* double wounding
'Traumatic Contact Zones and Embodied Translators: with reference to select Australian texts' 12

Triggs, Gillian 79–81
Troyes, Chretien de 30, 32
Trump, Donald 44, 80, 82, 128–129, 138, 140; American dream and 125–126; Nietzsche's Übermensch and 133–135; popular books about 126–127, 130; victory complex and 120–121, 123, 133
Trump in the White House 127
Tsiolkas, Christos 55
Turnbull, Malcolm 82
Turner, Ethel 21

Übermensch 133–134
Uhlmann, Chris 127, 130
Unbroken 53
unconscious, the 2, 10; need to protect the soul's purity and 15–16
Unfinished Sky 82
Unhinged: An Insider's Account of the Trump White House 127
United States, the: American dream 6, 45, 119, 124–127; Manifest Destiny ideology 124, 131, 132; migrants to 44, 80, 82, 138; as superhero, world policeman, and divine rights 130–132; trauma of victories past and 123–124; victory complex 6, 26, 32, 53, 120, 121–123; War for Independence 123–124

Vanishing or Spoorloos, The 128
victory complex 6; American 26, 32, 53; cinema as vehicle for 127–130; destiny and divine right in 133–135; ego inflation and 121–123; lost child v. 135–136; trauma of victories past and 123–124
virtual body ownership 116–117
Vogler, Christopher 26, 29, 36, 129–130, 136
Von Franz, Marie-Louise 29, 31

Waddell, Terrie 76
Walkabout 27, 28, 32, 34
Walt Disney Company 129
war 43; boy soldiers in 50–51; and the glorious dead on screen 47–52; and mobilising the child in Anzac celebrations 57–58; nationhood built on loss and 44, 48–49; -sport analogy 52–57; tall poppy syndrome and defeat as heroism in 44–47
Warburg, Abby 23
Ward, Rachel 109–110
Wasko, Janet 129
wastelands of parentification 96–99

Water Diviner, The 49, 51–52
Weaving, Hugo 41
Weir, Peter 36, 48
West, Jacqueline 120
White, Patrick 103, 109
Wild Notes from the Lyre of a Native Minstrel 70
Wills, William 9
Will They Never Come? 47

Winfrey, Oprah 120, 125–126, 128–129
Winnicott, Donald W. 17
Wolff, Michael 126, 130
Woman Suffers, The 27, 28
Wonder Woman 129, 134
Wood, Robin 88
Woodward, Bob 127

Zierold, Martin 24–25

For Product Safety Concerns and Information please contact our EU
representative GPSR@taylorandfrancis.com
Taylor & Francis Verlag GmbH, Kaufingerstraße 24, 80331 München, Germany

www.ingramcontent.com/pod-product-compliance
Lightning Source LLC
Chambersburg PA
CBHW070617300426
44113CB00010B/1568